"Thanks to Paul Krassner for continuing to be the lobster claw in the tuna casserole of modern America."
—Tom Robbins

"The FBI was right; this man is dangerous—and funny, and necessary."
—George Carlin

"Krassner has the uncanny ability to alter your perceptions permanently."
—Los Angeles Times

"He is an expert at ferreting out hypocrisy and absurdism from the more solemn crannies of American culture."
—The New York Times

"I told Krassner one time that his writings made me hopeful. He found this an odd compliment to offer a satirist. I explained that he made supposedly serious matters seem ridiculous, and that this inspired many of his readers to decide for themselves what was ridiculous and what was not. Knowing that there were people doing that, better late than never, made me optimistic."
—Kurt Vonnegut

ONE HAND JERKING

Reports From An Investigative Satirist

Paul Krassner

Foreword by Harry Shearer
Introduction by Lewis Black

From one mad mind to another. Enjoy!
♡ *Vanessa*

Seven Stories Press

New York | London | Toronto | Melbourne

All the pieces in this book were originally published in *High Times,* the *New York Press* and *AVN Online*, except for the following: "Humor as a Spiritual Path" was published in *Wild Heart Journal*. "In Praise of Offensive Cartoons" was published in *The Education of a Comics Artist*. "Bite Your Tongue," "Nonpartisan Harassment," "Grammys, Shrammys" and "Media Mortuary" were published in the *L.A. Weekly*. "Bizarre Sexually Oriented Spam Subject Lines" was published in *Book of Lists*. "Marijuana vs. Cigarettes" was published in *Under the Influence*. "Harry Shearer Still Hears Voices" was published in *Funny Times*. "Occult Jeopardy," "Jews in the News" and "The Devil in the Desert" were published in the *Los Angeles Times*. "The Rise of Sirhan Sirhan in the Scientology Hierarchy" was published in *Abuse Your Illusions*. "Kerik's Nanny" and "Geezerstock" were published in *The Nation*.

Seven Stories Press
140 Watts Street
New York, NY 10013
www.sevenstories.com

IN CANADA
Publishers Group Canada, 250A Carlton Street, Toronto, ON M5A 2L1

IN THE UK
Turnaround Publisher Services Ltd., Unit 3, Olympia Trading Estate,
Coburg Road, Wood Green, London N22 6TZ

IN AUSTRALIA
Palgrave Macmillan, 627 Chapel Street, South Yarra, VIC 3141

College professors may order examination copies of Seven Stories Press titles for a free six-month trial period. To order, visit www.sevenstories.com/textbook/ or send a fax on school letterhead to 212.226.1411.

Book design by Jon Gilbert
Cover design by POLLEN, New York
Front cover image by Andrew Yeadon

Krassner, Paul.
   One hand jerking : reports from an investigative satirist / by Paul Krassner ; foreword by Harry Shearer ; introduction by Lewis Black.-- 1st ed.
     p. cm.
   ISBN-13: 978-1-58322-696-4 (pbk. : alk. paper)
   ISBN-10: 1-58322-696-6 (pbk. : alk. paper)
   I. Title.
PS3561.R286O54 2005
814'.54--dc22   2005022195

Printed in Canada

9   8   7   6   5   4   3   2   1

"It behooves every cow to be mad."
—Nancy Cain

———————————

THIS ONE IS FOR KEN KESEY, who once told me, "I wasn't trying to write a novel, I was trying to go all the way." Which is how he lived his life.

When Stewart Brand invited Kesey and me to co-edit *The Last Supplement to the Whole Earth Catalog*, I moved from New York to San Francisco. Near the end of production, Kesey asked me to review—in one sentence, because we were so short of space—a beautiful book of offbeat ink drawings, *Filipino Food* by Ed Badajos.

"It made me say 'far out' for the first time," I suggested.

"You Zen bastard," was his response.

When I began writing a column for the *New York Press*, I decided to call it "Zen Bastard." And my latest satirical CD is *The Zen Bastard Rides Again*.

Kesey was also instrumental in naming my column for *High Times*. I was originally planning to call it "Damage Control," but he said, "Why don't you call it 'Brain Damage Control'?" And that's what it became, immediately.

Kesey didn't help me with the title of my column for *AVN Online*, though. AVN stands for Adult Video News, and *AVN Online* is a print magazine for the Internet porn industry. The editor, Eric, former editor at the *Los Angeles Reader*, invited me to write a column for *AVN Online*. Eric was using a pseudonymous last name.

"Half the editors here don't use their own names," he said.

"Well, if I do a column, I would use my own name. And I'd want to call the column 'One Hand Jerking.'"

Eric liked it. So did Kesey. So does Seven Stories Press.

One Hand Jerking: Reports From an Investigative Satirist is a collection of my columns from those three periodicals over the last few years, plus several freelance articles for various publications.

And, of course, I've tried to go all the way.

Paul Krassner
April 2005

CONTENTS

Under the Counterculture

One Hand Jerking

Make Me Laugh

Gay Rights and Wrongs

9/11 and the Invasion of Iraq

THE WAR ON INDECENCY

BOOK RELATED ACTIVITIES

REBELS WITH CAUSES

BODY PARTS

FOREWORD

BY HARRY SHEARER

I've been a reader of Paul Krassner's since before the day, when I sat in the office of the humor magazine I edited at UCLA, and swore up and down to all who would listen that Paul's scabrous *Realist* essay, "The Parts Left Out of the Kennedy Book," was for real. It was a teaching moment: Paul had taught me that extreme stylistic accuracy could make even the most bizarre comedic concept credible.

In the years since then, Paul and I have become friends and colleagues. We even shared a stage at LA's Museum of Contemporary Art as part of a theatrical threesome, "Peter, Paul and Harry," also featuring Peter Bergman of the Firesign Theatre. Obviously, I was included for rhyming purposes. But Paul and I got to watch each other work for several nights, and I hope I taught him something, at least about good grooming.

Paul is a unique character on the American cultural landscape. A self-described "investigative satirist," he straddles the lines between politics, culture, pornography and drugs—in other words, the land where all of us, were we really honest with ourselves, would choose to dwell.

A serious crafter of jokes, Paul also lets his curiosity take him where more careful practitioners, such as myself, would not tread: conspiracy theories, spiritualist theories, working for porn kings, acid trips in federal court. He always returns from the journeys wiser if not sadder, his sense of humor intact if not inflamed.

On the trip of life, Paul Krassner has been a very good guide. Now, in this gumbo of a book, he offers insight on his background and outrage on the state of what only an optimist would call American culture. But, crucially, he never lets go of his sense of fun, and, in this book as in his life, that makes all the difference.

INTRODUCTION

BY LEWIS BLACK

I consider it to be quite a privilege and an absolute pleasure to be writing the introduction to Paul Krassner's wondrous book of essays. I have been a fan of his since I was a snot-nosed kid, and his words have been a driving force and influence on my life. I can remember how it happened. I was extremely lucky to have stumbled onto a copy of his magazine *The Realist* in my youth. There was neither glitz nor glamour to it. You actually had to read it for the articles. It was filled with words, and more than any drugs, words can alter perceptions, and mine were altered forever. He made me realize the importance of funny, but more than any writer I know, Paul always has a mission behind his wicked mirth.

He was the Swift of the Sixties. For a high school student like myself, his humor was a kind of comfort food, and it helped me realize that my angst and frustration with my sterile suburban lifestyle were legitimate. Most importantly, he made me laugh, and this book is no exception to that rule. The man knows funny. Unlike all the other great comic minds of that time, Krassner wasn't on vinyl, his words were on the page, which in a way made it more deeply affecting to me personally. He made me realize the importance of the profane, and if I have to explain that, we could be here for days. After reading the first few copies of *The Realist*, I was never the same, and I thank him for that.

If he wasn't pointing out that the emperor has no clothes, then he was making sure we understood that it's not the world that is off kilter, it's the people who run it. It doesn't really matter who is in charge, because Paul has always known and paid attention to the fact that power most definitely corrupts. Finding my own difficulty with authority figures, it was nice to know that I wasn't alone, and I was most definitely not crazy, because as crazy as Krassner may have appeared and still does to a portion of America, he is not. His insanity is stating the truth in no uncertain terms and doing it through humor without his object being financial gain. (If he were doing it for the money, then they wouldn't think he was so nuts.)

In many ways he was and still is the voice of the Sixties, but more important than that, he is the conscience we have tried to rid ourselves of. He was everywhere during the Sixties and knew everyone from Lenny Bruce to Andrew Weil. One could call him the Zelig of our time. Only he was for real. These essays alone will give you a taste of that, but hopefully they will lead you into more of Krassner's work. For make no mistake, it is important. He has pushed the boundaries of comedy as far as anyone in print or stand-up ever has, and for that we should be eternally grateful.

The prevailing culture should be thankful for such a figure, even though they feel the thorn that he is in their side. His outrageous comedy defuses the anger that so many of us feel. He is the keeper of the flame of the profane, and if we were living in the time of the Greeks, he would be considered as an absolutely essential member of the society, which would no doubt upset him, but it is his due.

If you have read his work before, you know the joys that you are in for. If you haven't, start reading, and consider this your lucky day. For Paul Krassner is an activist, a philosopher, a lunatic and a saint, but most of all he is funny. If words were my mother, then I am his bastard son.

Enjoy.

ZEN BASTARD

Humor As a Spiritual Path

I first woke up at the age of six.

It began with an itch in my leg. My left leg. But somehow I knew I wasn't supposed to scratch it. Although my eyes were closed, I was standing up. In fact, I was standing on a huge stage. And I was playing the violin. I was in the middle of playing the "Vivaldi Concerto in A Minor." I was wearing a Little Lord Fauntleroy suit—ruffled white silk shirt with puffy sleeves, black velvet short pants with ivory buttons and matching vest, white socks and black patent-leather shoes. My hair was platinum blond and wavy. On this particular Saturday evening—January 14, 1939—I was in the process of becoming the youngest concert artist in any field ever to perform at Carnegie Hall. But all I knew was that I was being taunted by an itch. An itch that had become my adversary.

I was tempted to stop playing the violin, just for a second, and scratch my leg with the bow, yet I was vaguely aware that this would not be appropriate. I had been well trained. I was a true professional. But that itch kept getting fiercer and fiercer. Then, suddenly, an impulse surfaced from my hidden laboratory of alternative possibilities, and I surrendered to it. Balancing on my left foot, I scratched my left leg with my right foot, without missing a note of the "Vivaldi Concerto."

Between the impulse and the surrender, there was a choice—I had *decided* to balance on one foot—and it was that simple act of choosing which triggered the precise moment of my awakening to the mystery of consciousness. *This is me!* The relief of scratching my leg was overshadowed by a surge of energy throughout my body. I was being engulfed by some kind of spiritual orgasm: by a wave of born-again ecstasy with no ideological context. No doctrine to explain the shock of my own existence. No dogma to function as a metaphor for the mystery.

Instead, I woke up to the sound of laughter.

I had heard that sound before, sweet and comforting, but never like this. Now I could hear a whole *symphony* of delight and reassurance, like clarinets and guitars harmonizing with saxophones and drums. It was the audience laughing. I opened my eyes. There were rows upon rows of people sitting out there in the dark, and they were all laughing together. They had understood my plight. It was easier for them to identify with the urge to scratch than with a little freak play-ing the violin. And I could identify with them identifying with me. I knew that laughter felt good, and I was pleased that it made the audience feel good. But I hadn't *intended* to make them laugh. I was merely trying to solve a personal dilemma. So the lesson I woke up to—this totally nonverbal, internal *buzz*—would serve as my lifetime filter for perceiving reality and its rules. If you could somehow translate that buzz into words, it would spell out: *One person's logic is another person's humor.*

There was, of course, an objective, scientific explanation for what had occurred. According to a textbook, *Physiological Psychology*, "It is now rather well accepted that 'itch' is a variant of the pain experience and employs the same sen-sory mechanisms." But for me, something beyond an ordinary itch had occurred that night. It was as though I had been zapped by the god of Absurdity. I didn't even know there was such a concept as absurdity. I simply experienced an over-powering awareness of *something* when the audience applauded me for doing what I had learned while I was asleep. But it was only when they laughed that we had really connected, and I imprinted on that sound. I wanted to hear it again. I was hooked. And the first laugh was free.

———————

It was as if I had been destined to become a stand-up comic and editor of *The Realist*. Although I was notorious for publishing outrageous social and political satire, I also published investigative journalism and conspiracy theory. I researched cults, from the Moonies to Scientology, and assassinations, from President Kennedy to Charles Manson. In the process, I underwent a paranoid freakout from information overload.

But I could still pass for sane in public. At the peak of my psychotic episode, I still managed to keep a dental appointment without revealing the utter tur-moil in my mind. However, I was on a bus from San Francisco to my home in Wat-sonville, and my thumb began to feel numb. It was obviously a direct result of the cavity in one of my molars having been filled. When the bus stopped in San Jose, I got off and called my dentist.

"I know who you work for," I said, "and I have two demands. I want every-body out of solitary confinement. And I want a cease-fire all over the world."

He hesitated a second. "Hold on, Paul, let me get your chart." He was stalling for time. When he got back on the phone, he asked, "Now, do you want my reaction?"

"No, that won't be necessary. I've gotta go. Goodbye."

I hung up the phone and got back on the bus. The man sitting in front of me, an operative for the CIA, adjusted the ring on his finger in order to let his partner outside know that I was on the bus again. I had to let the man in front of me know that I was onto his game. So I took out my ballpoint pen. Clicking the top over and over like a telegraph key—this was before cell phones—I kept repeating, "Paul Krassner calling Abbie Hoffman"—just loud enough for the man sitting in front of me to hear—"Paul Krassner calling Abbie Hoffman." The CIA operative fidgeted nervously. He knew I was onto him now.

My mind had finally snapped. Allen Ginsberg's poem *Howl* began, "I saw the best minds of my generation destroyed by madness, starving hysterical naked," and I had always identified with the "best minds" part but never with the "madness" part. Eventually I told fellow Yippie founder Abbie Hoffman, who was now on the lam as a fugitive, how I had tried to convince the CIA operative sitting in front of me on the bus that I was calling Abbie by using my ballpoint pen as a telegraph key.

"Oh, yeah," Abbie said. "I got your call, only it was collect, so I couldn't accept it."

The turning point in my insanity came inadvertently one day while hiding out with my friend Lee Quarnstrom and his wife Guadalupe. I was sitting in the back seat of his car at a gas station. While Lee was out of the car, I noticed two guys staring at me. Just as I was convincing myself that now *they* were out to get me, I flashed back five years to the West Side Highway in New York. My secretary Sheila was driving her motor scooter, with me sitting behind her, my arms circling her waist. She was wearing a miniskirt. Truck drivers were making animal sounds and whistling. "They *recognize* me," I joked to Sheila. And now, the moment I realized that these two guys in the gas station were staring, not at me in the back seat, but at Guadalupe in the front seat, my perspective began to return. I would be okay again.

Losing my sense of humor had been the direction of my insanity. I had violated the 11th Commandment by taking myself as seriously as my causes. I developed an investment in my craziness, and I needed to perpetuate it. Only in retrospect would I realize that, in response to my megalomaniacal demands, what my dentist had said—"Hold on, Paul, let me get your chart"—was unintentionally, screamingly funny. By publishing controversial articles, I had been on a mission from the God I didn't believe in. I had bought into a *celestial* conspiracy. I had gone over the edge, from a universe that didn't know I existed, to one that did. From false humility to false pride.

In 1987 I went to a chiropractor, who referred me to a podiatrist, who referred me to a physiatrist, who wanted me to get an MRI to rule out the possibility of cervical stenosis. But the MRI ruled it *in*. The X-rays indicated that my spinal cord was being squeezed by spurring on the inside of several discs in my neck. The physiatrist told me that I needed surgery. I panicked. I had always taken my good health for granted. I went into heavy denial, confident that I could completely cure my problem by walking barefoot on the beach every day for three weeks. "You're a walking time bomb," the podiatarist warned me. He said that if I were in a rearend collision, or just out strolling and I tripped, my spinal cord could be severed, and I would be paralyzed from the chin down. I began to be conscious of every move I made. I was living, not one day at a time, not one hour at a time, not one minute at a time—I was living one *second* at a time.

A walking time bomb! I was still in a state of shock, but since I perceived the world through a filter of absurdity, now I would have to apply that perception to my own situation. The breakthrough came when I learned that my neurosurgeon moonlighted as a clown at the circus. "All right, I surrender, I surrender." *Paralyzed from the chin down!* I tried dialing—that is pressing—Nancy's phone number with my nose. I fantasized about using a voice-activated word processor to write a novel called *The Head*, in which the protagonist finally dies of suffocation while performing cunnilingus because he can't use his hands to separate the thighs of the woman who is sitting on his face.

I met my doctor the night before the operation. He sat on my bed wearing a trenchcoat and called me Mr. Krassner. I thought that if he was going to cut me open and file through five discs in my upper spinal column, he could certainly be informal enough to call me Paul. He was busy filling out a chart.

"What do you do for a living, Mr. Krassner?"

"I'm a writer and a comedian."

"How do you spell comedian?"

Rationally I knew that you don't have to be a good speller to be a fine surgeon, but his question made me uneasy. At least his *hands* weren't shaking while he wrote. Then he told me about how simple the operation was, and he mentioned almost in passing that there was always the possibility I could end up staying in the hospital for the rest of my life. *Huh*? There was a time when physicians practiced positive thinking to help their patients, but now it was a requirement of malpractice prevention to provide the worst-case scenario in advance.

Early the next morning, under the influence of Valium and Demerol, I could see that my neurosurgeon had just come from the circus, because he was wearing a clown costume, with a round red plastic nose above his surgical mask. He could hardly reach the operating table because his outlandish, pointed shoes were so long, and when he had to cleanse my wound he asked the nurse to please pass the seltzer bottle. . . .

"Wake up, Paul," the anesthesiologist said. "Surgery's over. Wiggle your toes." Nancy was waiting in the hall, and I was so glad to see her smile. That evening, at a benefit in Berkeley, Ken Kesey told the audience, "I spoke with Krassner today, and the operation was successful, but he says he's not taking any painkillers because he never does any legal drugs." Then Kesey led the crowd in a chant: "Get well, Paul! Get well, Paul!" And it worked. The following month I was performing again, wearing a neck brace at a theater in Seattle.

———

In 1976, I attended a symposium held in Sun Valley, Idaho, "The American Hero: Myths and Media," where I delivered a keynote address. I met Tom Laughlin, of *Billy Jack* movie fame, at the conference, and a couple of years later he invited me to a dinner party. He was a Thomas Jefferson enthusiast. In his home, there was Thomas Jefferson's furniture, Thomas Jefferson's silverware, Thomas Jefferson's recipes—we started with peanut soup—and even Thomas Jefferson's violin. I mentioned playing the violin as a child, and Laughlin invited me to play this one. I hadn't held a violin for 25 years—not since I had used it as a prop when I started doing stand-up comedy—and four decades had passed since that concert in Carnegie Hall. It felt like a previous incarnation. But now Billy Jack himself was handing me Thomas Jefferson's violin.

"I'd like to dedicate this to Thomas Jefferson's slaves," I said.

And then I played the only thing I felt competent enough to perform—"Twinkle, Twinkle, Little Star." While I was playing, I stood unobtrusively balancing on my left foot, and scratched my left leg with my right foot.

It was a private joke between me and the god of Absurdity.

IRREVERENCE IS OUR ONLY SACRED COW

Late one extremely hot night in the spring of 1958, alone and naked, I was sitting at my desk in Lyle Stuart's office, preparing final copy for the first issue of *The Realist.* I had served my journalistic apprenticeship at Stuart's anti-censorship paper, *The Independent*, where I had become managing editor, and now I was launching my own satirical magazine. The '60s counterculture was in its embryonic stage, almost ready to burst out of the blandness, repression and piety of the Eisenhower-Nixon administration, Reverend Norman Vincent Peale's positive thinking and Snooky Lanson singing "It's a Marshmallow World" on TV's *Lucky Strike Hit Parade.*

I was supposed to have everything ready for the printer next morning. I felt exhausted, but there were two final pieces to write. My bare buttocks stuck to the leather chair as I created an imaginary dialogue about clean and dirty bombs. Then I borrowed a form from *Mad* and composed "A Child's Primer on Telethons." Our office was on the same floor as *Mad* in what became known as the *Mad* building, at 225 Lafayette Street.

Mad's art director, John Francis Putnam, designed *The Realist* logo and also became my first columnist. Although *Mad* staffers weren't allowed to have any outside projects, Putnam was willing to risk his job to write for *The Realist.* Gaines appreciated that and made an exception for him. Putnam's column was titled "Modest Proposals."

My second columnist was Robert Anton Wilson. I had already published his first article, "The Semantics of God," in which he wrote, "The Believer had better face himself and ask squarely: Do I literally believe 'God' has a penis? If the answer is no, then it seems only logical to drop the ridiculous practice of referring to 'God' as 'He.'" Wilson's column was titled "Negative Thinking."

This was before *National Lampoon* or *Spy* magazine, before *Doonesbury* or

Saturday Night Live. I had no role models, and no competition, just an open field mined with taboos waiting to be exploded.

In New York, the son of the owner of a newsstand in front of Carnegie Hall became my distributor. In Chicago, *The Realist* was distributed by the manager of an ice-cream company. Steve Allen became the first subscriber, he gave several gift subscriptions, including one for Lenny Bruce, who in turn gave gift subs to several others, as well as becoming an occasional contributor.

I never knew where I would find new contributors.

One time I woke up at 3 o'clock in the morning. My radio was still on, and a man was talking about how you would try to expain the function of an amusement park to visitors from Venus. It was Jean Shepherd. He was on WOR from midnight to 5:30 every night, mixing childhood reminiscence with contemporary critiques, peppered with such characters as the man who could taste an ice cube and tell you the brand name of the refrigerator it came from and the year of manufacture. Shepherd would orchestrate his colorful tales with music ranging from "The Stars and Stripes Forever" to Bessie Smith singing "Empty Bed Blues." He edited several of his stream-of-conscoiusness ramblings into article for *The Realist* under the title "Radio Free America."

At first the entire office staff consisted of me. I took no salary, but I had to figure out how to continue publishing without accepting ads, so naturally I got involved with a couple of guys who had a system for betting on the horses. Although I lost all my savings, there was one blessing in disguise. At the racetrack, I bought a handicap newsletter, *The Armstrong Daily*, which included a clever column by Marvin Kitman.

I invited him to write for *The Realist*, and he became our consumer advocate with "An Independent Research Laboratory." His first report, "I tried the Rapid-Shave Sandpaper Test," called the bluff of a particular advertising campaign when he described his personal attempt to shave sandpaper with shaving cream. He also wrote sardonic pieces such as "How I Fortified My Family Fallout Shelter," on the morality of arming yourself against neighbors who *didn't* have a fallout shelter.

Meanwhile, I was becoming bad company. Campus bookstores were banning *The Realist*, and students whose parents had burned their issues often wrote in for replacement copies. But I was publishing material that was bound to offend. For example, Madalyn Murray was a militant atheist who had challenged the constitutionality of compulsory Bible reading in public schools, and she concluded her first article, "I feel that Jesus Christ is at most a myth—and if he wasn't, the least he was, was a bastard—and that the Virgin Mary obviously played around as much as I did, and certainly I feel she would be capable of orgasm."

I seemed to be following a pattern of participatory journalism.

In 1962, when abortion was still illegal, I published an anonymous interview with Dr. Robert Spencer, a humane abortionist who was known as "The Saint." Patients came to his office in Ashland, Pennsylvania, from around the country. He had been performing abortions for 40 years, started out charging $5, and never charged more than $100. Ashland was a small town, and Dr. Spencer's work was not merely tolerated; the community *depended* on it—the hotel, the restaurant, the dress shop—all thrived on the extra business that came from his out-of-town patients. He built facilities at his clinic for Negro patients who weren't allowed to obtain overnight lodgings elsewhere in Ashland.

After the interview was published, I began to get phone calls from scared female voices, from teenagers to matrons. They were all in desperate search of a safe abortionist. Even a nurse couldn't find one. It was preposterous that they should have to seek out the editor of a satirical magazine, but their quest so far had been futile, and they simply didn't know where to turn. With Dr. Spencer's permission, I referred them to him. I had never intended to become an underground abortion referral service, but it wasn't going to stop just because in the next issue of *The Realist* there would be an interview with someone else.

A few years later, state police raided Dr. Spencer's clinic and arrested him. He remained out of jail only by the grace of political pressure from those he'd helped. He was finally forced to retire from his practice, but I continued mine, referring callers to other physicians he had recommended. Eventually, I was subpoenaed by district attorneys in two cities to appear before grand juries investigating criminal charges against abortionists. On both occasions, I refused to testify, and each time the D.A. tried to frighten me into cooperating with the threat of arrest.

Bronx D.A. (now Judge) Burton Roberts told me that his staff had found an abortionist's financial records, which showed all the money that I had received, but he would grant me immunity from prosecution if I cooperated with the grand jury. He extended his hand as a gesture of trust. "That's not true," I said, refusing to shake hands. If I *had* ever accepted any money, I'd have no way of knowing that he was bluffing.

At this point, attorney Gerald Lefcourt filed a suit on my behalf, challenging the constitutionality of the abortion law. He pointed out that the D.A. had no power to investigate the violation of an unconstitutional law, and therefore he could not force me to testify. In 1970, I became the only plaintiff in the first lawsuit to declare the abortion laws unconstitutional in New York State. Later, various women's groups joined the suit, and ultimately the N.Y. legislature repealed the criminal sanctions against abortion, prior to the Supreme Court decision in Roe vs. Wade.

In 1964, I assigned Robert Anton Wilson to write a feature article, which he called "Timothy Leary and His Psychological H-Bomb." A few months later, Leary invited me to his research headquarters in Millbrook, and I took my first acid trip. When I told my mother about LSD, she was quite concerned. "It could lead to marijuana," she said. My mother was right.

While covering the anti-Vietnam-war movement, I ended up co-founding the Yippies (Youth International Party) with Abbie Hoffman and Jerry Rubin. After what was officially described as "a police riot" at the 1968 Democratic convention in Chicago, I became an unindicted co-conspirator. I testified at the trial after ingesting 300 micrograms of acid. This was during my psychedelic macho stage. I even tripped when I was a guest on the *Tonight* show, and also while riding the subway during rush hour.

I had been supporting myself by writing film criticism for *Cavalier* magazine, and with college speaking engagements. *Cavalier* declined to publish a particular column—my review of *M*A*S*H* as though it were a Busby Berkeley musical called *Gook Killers of 1970*—ostensibly on the grounds of bad taste, but I learned that three wholesalers had told the publisher they were pressured by the FBI and would refuse to distribute *Cavalier* if my column appeared in it.

And my name was on a list of 65 "radical" campus speakers, compiled by the House Internal Security Committee. Their blacklist was published in the *New York Times* and picked up by newspapers across the country. My college bookings suddenly stopped. Just a coincidence.

When I got married in 1964, John Francis Putnam had an idea for a poster that would be our housewarming gift. He designed the word FUCK in red-white-and-blue lettering emblazoned with stars and stripes. Now he needed a second word, a noun that would serve as an appropriate object of that verb. He suggested AMERICA, but that didn't seem right to me. It certainly wasn't an accurate representation of my feelings. I was well aware that I probably couldn't publish *The Realist* in any other country. Besides, FUCK AMERICA lacked a sense of irony.

This was at the time that a severe anti-Communist hysteria was burgeoning throughout the nation. The attorney general of Arizona rejected the Communist Party's request for a place on the ballot because state law "prohibits official representation" for Communists and, in addition, "The subversive nature of your organization is even more clearly designated by the fact that you do not even include your Zip code." Alvin Dark, manager of the Giants, announced that "Any pitcher who throws at a batter and deliberately tries to hit him is a Communist." And singer Pat Boone declared at the Greater New York Anti-Communism Rally in Madison Square Garden, "I would rather see my four daughters shot before my eyes than have them grow up in a Communist United States. I would rather see those kids blown into Heaven than taught into Hell by the Communists."

I suggested COMMUNISM as the second word, since the usual correlation between conservatism and prudishness would provide the incongruity that was missing. Putnam designed the word COMMUNISM in red lettering emblazoned with hammers and sickles, then presented me with a patriotic poster which proudly proclaimed, FUCK COMMUNISM!—suitable for framing. I wanted to share this sentiment with *Realist* readers, but our photo engraver refused to make a plate, explaining, "We got strict orders from Washington not to do stuff like this." I approached another engraver, who said no because he had been visited by the FBI after making a plate of a woman with pubic hair. I finally found an engraver who agreed to do it. I published a miniature black-and-white version of the poster in *The Realist* and offered full-size color copies by mail. And if the Post Office interfered, I would have to accuse them of being soft on Communism.

At a midwestern college, one graduating student held up a FUCK COMMUNISM! poster as his class was posing for the yearbook photo. Campus officials found out and insisted that the word FUCK be air-brushed out. But then the poster would read COMMUNISM! So that was air-brushed out too, and the yearbook ended up publishing a class photo that showed this particular student holding up a blank poster. Very dada.

And then there was Robert Scheer. He had been researching a booklet, *How the United States Got Involved in Vietnam*, to be published by the Fund for the Republic. He was frustrated because he wanted to witness first-hand what was happening in Southeast Asia, but they wouldn't send him. Since *The Realist* had already sold a couple of thousand FUCK COMMUNISM! posters at a dollar each, I was able to give him a check for $1900, the price of a round-trip airline ticket. He traveled to Vietnam and Cambodia, then wrote his seminal report.

————————

Four months after the assassination of John Kennedy, William Manchester was authorized by the family to write a book, *The Death of a President*. Jackie Kennedy submitted to ten hours of intimacy with his tape recorder. Two years later, she insisted on cutting material that was too personal for publication. Bobby Kennedy sent a telegram to Evan Thomas, editor-in-chief at Harper & Row, suggesting that the book "should neither be published nor serialized." Thomas wrote to Kennedy advisers, asking for help in revising the manuscript, which he felt was "gratuitously and tastelessly insulting" to Lyndon Johnson.

Bennett Cerf of Random House read an unedited manuscript and said it contained "unbelievable things that happened after the assassination." Jackie filed a lawsuit, and in 1967 the case was settled out of court. Harper & Row made the requested deletions. So did *Look* magazine, which had purchased serialization rights for $665,000. I tried unsuccessfully to obtain a copy of the original manuscript, so I was forced to write "The Parts Left Out of the Kennedy Book" myself, imitating Manchester's style.

It began with a true news item. During the Democratic primaries, LBJ attacked his opponent on the grounds that his father, Joseph Kennedy, was a Nazi sympathizer when he was U.S. ambassador to England, from 1938-1940. Then I segued into stories—such as JFK's affair with Marilyn Monroe and LBJ's incredibly crude behavior—that media folks knew about, but not the general public. Next came made-up anecdotes that reeked of verisimilitude, all leading up to a few paragraphs that plunged *The Realist* into the depths of its notoriety:

"During that tense flight from Dallas to Washington after the assassination, Jackie inadvertently walked in on Johnson as he was standing over the casket of his predecessor and chuckling. . . .

"Of course, President Johnson is often given to inappropriate response—witness the puzzled timing of his smiles when he speaks of grave matters—but we must also assume that Mrs. Kennedy had been traumatized that day and her perception was likely to have been colored by the tragedy. This state of shock must have underlain an incident on Air Force One which this writer conceives to be delirium, but which Mrs. Kennedy insists she actually saw.

"'I'm telling you this for the historical record,' she said, 'so that people a hundred years from now will know what I had to go through. . . . That man was crouching over the corpse, no longer chuckling but breathing hard and moving his body rhythmically. At first I thought he must be performing some mysterious symbolic rite he'd learned from Mexicans or Indians as a boy. And then I realized—there is only one way to say this—he was literally fucking my husband in the throat. In the bullet wound in the front of his throat. He reached a climax and dismounted. I froze. The next thing I remember, he was being sworn in as the new president.'

"[Handwritten marginal notes: *1. Check with [Warren Commission head] Rankin—did secret autosy show semen in throat wound? 2. Is this simply necrophilia, or was LBJ trying to change entry wound from grassy knoll into exit wound from Book Depository by enlarging it?*]"

My printer refused to print that issue of *The Realist*, and I spent a couple of months trying to find a new printer. I never labeled an article as satire, in order not to deprive readers of the pleasure of discerning for themselves whether something was the truth or a satirical extension of the truth. The most significant thing about "The Parts Left Out of the Kennedy Book" was its widespread acceptance as truth—if only for a fleeting moment—by intelligent, literate people, from an ACLU official to a Peabody Award-winning journalist to members of the intelligence community.

Daniel Ellsberg said, "Maybe it was because I *wanted* to believe it so badly."

My favorite response came from Merriman Smith, the UPI correspondent who always ended White House press conferences with the traditional "Thank you, Mr. President." He wrote that I had published "filth attributed to someone of national stature supposedly describing something Johnson allegedly did. The incident, of course, never took place. . . ."

That issue reached a circulation of 100,000, with an estimated pass-on readership of a few million. In 1974, however, I ran out of money and had to suspend publication of *The Realist*, only to reincarnate it in 1985 as a newsletter. "The taboos may have changed," I wrote, "but irreverence is still our only sacred cow."

When I originally started publishing, I was truly a lone voice, but now irreverence has become an industry. *The Realist* served its purpose, though—to communicate without compromise—and today other voices, in print, on cable TV and especially on the Internet, are following in that same tradition.

The last words in my final issue, published in 2001, came from Kurt Vonnegut: "Your planet's immune system is trying to get rid of you." My own swan-song editorial concluded: "And so this little publication comes to an end, neither with a bang nor with a wimper. Just a deep sigh of satisfaction. *The Realist* has been a way of life for me, but, of course, old editors never die, they just run out of space."

In Praise of Offensive Cartoons

In the late 1950s, I read an article in *Esquire* by Malcolm Muggeridge, former editor of *Punch*, the British humor magazine. "The area of life in which ridicule is permissible is steadily shrinking," he wrote, "and a dangerous tendency is becoming manifest to take ourselves with undue seriousness. The enemy of humor is fear and this, alas, is an age of fear. As I see it, the only pleasure of living is that every joke should be made, every thought expressed, every line of investigation, irrespective of its direction, pursued to the uttermost limit that human ingenuity, courage and understanding can take it. . . . By its nature, humor is anarchistic, and it may well be that those who seek to supress or limit laughter are more dangerous than all the subversive conspiracies which the FBI ever has or ever will uncover. Laughter, in fact, is the most effective of all subversive conspiracies, and it operates on *our* side."

The article was called "America Needs a *Punch*," and I took the implications of that title as my personal marching orders. After I launched *The Realist* in 1958, it developed a reputation as a haven for material which could be published nowhere else.

Our first cartoon, unsolicited, by Drury Marsh, was a reaction to the National Association of Broadcasters amending its TV code to ban the use of actors in "white-coat commercials." The revised ruling read: "Dramatized advertising involving statements or purported statements by physicians, dentists or nurses must be presented by accredited members of such professions." The cartoon showed a man dressed like a doctor doing a cigarette commercial, then changing to his civilian clothes in a dressing room, going back to his office, getting dressed like a doctor again, and finally telling a patient, "You're going to have to give up smoking."

Another unsolicited cartoon arrived from syndicated editorial cartoonist Frank Interlandi. It showed a man walking along, spotting a poster of a mushroom cloud with the question, "If a BOMB Falls, What Would You Do?" He continues walking—thinking, thinking—and finally says out loud to himself, "I'd shit!" Interlandi told me that he simply could not conceive of a more appropriate reaction, and he had refused to compromise.

When the Cuban missile crisis occurred, Richard Guindon created his most popular cartoon for *The Realist*, which I put on the cover. It depicted a reclining nude woman, leaning on her elbow with her back to us—her buttocks a globe with latiduinal and longitudinal lines—as she faced a couple of faceless men, both naked except that one was wearing boxer shorts with stars and stripes while the other had a hammer and sickle tattooed on his chubby arm. The Kennedy-like American was gesturing toward the Khrushchev-like Russian and speaking to the Earth-woman: "It's his turn and then me again." That cartoon captured a feeling of powerlessness that permeated the country. Two Broadway stars—Orson Bean in *Subways Are for Sleeping* and Anthony Newley in *Stop the World, I Want to Get Off*—had it framed on their dressing-room walls, even while several bookstores and newsstands were displaying that issue face down.

When abortion was illegal, I published a cartoon by Mort Gerberg, depicting a Mother Goose character—the old lady who lived in a shoe and had so many children she didn't know what to do—speaking on the phone: "Dr. Burnhill?— uh—you don't know me, but—uh—I've been told that you could—uh—perform a certain operation—" It turned out there was an actual Dr. Burnhill, an obstetrician-gynecologist, who called me in distress after patients started bringing that issue of *The Realist* to his office.

Every succeeding cartoon by Gerberg had a character named Burnhill, except for his double-page spreads, "The Poverty Pavilion," "The Junkie Battalion" and "The Fag Battalion."

New Yorker regulars sent me their cartoons that were rejected for controversial subject matter, poor taste and taboo violation. Ed Koren had a centaur on the Unemployment line, being asked by the clerk, "Are you sure you looked for work this week?" Another Koren centaur at a cocktail party was saying to a woman, "I find it very difficult to be an intellectual in the United States." Ed Fisher depicted a Native American ceremony with a few hippies sitting cross-legged among a large group of Indians, with the chief saying to an associate, "Yes, ever since drug-trances were ruled a legitimate practice of our religion, they've been drifting in . . ." Fisher was so prolific that "Ed Fisher's Page" became a regular feature in *The Realist*.

Another *New Yorker* cartoonist who preferred to omit a byline presented a TV talk-show guest saying, "Frankly I didn't give a *damn* about it!" Then we see a family at home watching him say, "Frankly I didn't give a *bleep* about it!" Thought balloons show the mother thinking "Fuck?"; the father thinking "Piss?"; the grandmother thinking "Shit?"; and the little kid thinking "Crap?" That cartoon graced many kitchen refrigerators and office bulletin boards, especially at TV channels.

And Lee Lorenz sent a cartoon—bypassing the *New Yorker* because he *knew* it would be rejected—where, in the corridor of an office building, a man with an attache case is about to enter the office of the Anti-Defamation League, while right directly across from him a man with a briefcase is opening the door to the office of the Italian Anti-Defamation League. The caption: "Wop!" "Kike!"

William M. Gaines was the head of Entertaining Comics, which published a line of crime and horror comic books—plus *Mad*. Here was a comic book that poked creative fun at society in general and comic books in particular. What a kick it was to see "Clark Bent" undressing in a phone booth to change into his "Superduperman" outfit, only to find that it was already occupied by a woman. *Mad*'s gang of artists and writers were slicing through American piety with irreverence and imagination.

When *Mad* became a magazine, I started writing free-lance articles for them. My first article was based on the premise, "What if comic strip characters answered those little ads in the back of magazines?" I wrote the script and Wally Wood did the artwork. Orphan Annie sent for Maybelline for her hollow eyes. Dick Tracy sought a nose job. Alley Oop got rid of his superfluous hair, only to reveal that he had no ears. But Popeye's flat-chested girlfriend, Olive Oyl, wasn't permitted to send away for falsies.

Gaines explained, "My mother would object to that."

"Yeah," I complained, "but she's not a typical subscriber."

"No," he replied, "but she's a typical mother."

Other ideas of mine were rejected because the subject matter was considered "too adult." Since *Mad's* circulation had already gone over the million mark, Gaines intended to keep aiming it at teenagers.

"I guess you don't want to change horses in mid-stream," I said.

"Not when the horse has a rocket up its ass," Gaines responded.

John Francis Putnam, *Mad's* art director, wrote a piece about the apocryphal publication of an collection, *Tillie and Mac: Those Little Comic Books That Men Like*, resulting in an obscenity charge. Accompanying this was *Mad's* Sergio Aragones' hysterical full-page parody of the genre, labeled as "Exhibit A," with "excerpts" ranging from Blondie in bed with her husband's boss—"Now Dagwood, stop complaining! You're disturbing Mister Dithers!"—to Orphan Annie copulating with Sandy, her hollow-eyed canine. "Gee," Annie says, "a girl's best friend *is* a dog!" And Sandy, wagging his tail, barks back, "Arf! Arf! (Pant, pant) *Aaaarrrf!*"

Recently, Simon & Schuster published an *actual* such anthology, *Tijuana Bibles: Art and Wit in America's Forbidden Funnies, 1930s–1950s*. It was a case of satirical prophecy. The introduction is by Pulitzer Prize-winner Art Spiegelman, whose cartoon showing two soldiers smooching on a bench in front of a sign—"Make Love, Not War!"—appeared in *The Realist*. As the Vietnam war escalated, and monks began immolating themselves as the ultimate form of protest, Don Addis depicted a gas station attendant asking a Buddhist holding a gas-can, "Regular?" During the burgeoning days of underground comics, I published Disney adversary Dan O'Neill, S. Clay Wilson, Skip Williamson and Jay Lynch, who contributed a psychedelicized logo.

The Realist was the first to publish Sam Gross, a mild-mannered accountant who visited my office with his samples one day and eventually replaced Charles Addams as the king of macabre cartoonists. Take, for example, his drawing of a man with a hammer *nailing* a sandwich-board, reading "Christ Died For Our Sins," onto the back of a religious zealot. Or his Cyclops-inspired gynecologist with one large eye centered on his forehead. Or a Gross full-page spread, "Humor of the Handicapped," offensive to many, though lauded by disabled readers.

Ed Sorel's first published illustration, "A War for Civilization"—with a parade led by Cardinal Spellman, followed by a biker gang and other assorted stalwarts—appeared on a *Realist* cover, bleeding through to the back cover. Robert Grossman contributed a series of movie posters, starting with the musical, "Ethel and Bob Kennedy in *I Got Rhythm*, produced by 18th Century Fox." Charles Rodrigues did a sardonic full-page spread, "Up With Violence," and B. Kliban gave me a cartoon with a door marked "Sperm Bank," with a nearby slot for "Night Deposits."

Proceeds from a poster—a cartoon first published in *The Realist*, depicting an anthropomorphic deity sodomizing Uncle Sam, with the legend, "One Nation Under God"—were used to bail the artist, Frank Cieciorka, out of jail after he was arrested for voter registration work in Mississippi.

When Walt Disney died, I somehow expected Mickey Mouse and Donald Duck and all the rest of the gang to attend the funeral, with Goofy delivering the eulogy and the Seven Dwarfs serving as pallbearers. Disney's death occurred a few years after *Time* magazine's famous "God Is Dead" cover, and it occurred to me that Disney had indeed acted as the Intelligent Designer of that whole stable of imaginary characters who were now mourning in a state of suspended animation. Disney was *their* Creator and he had repressed all their baser instincts, but now that he had departed, they could finally shed their cumulative inhibitions and participate together in an unspeakable Roman binge, to signify the crumbling of an empire. I contacted *Mad's* Wally Wood and, without mentioning any specific details, I told him my general notion of a memorial orgy at Disneyland. He accepted the assignment and presented me with a magnificently degenerate montage:

Pluto is pissing on a portrait of Mickey Mouse, while the real, bedraggled Mickey is shooting up heroin. His nephews are jerking off as they watch Goofy fucking Minnie Mouse on a combination bed and cash register. The beams shining out from the Magic Castle are actually dollar signs.. Dumbo is simultaneously flying and shitting on an infuriated Donald Duck. Huey, Dewey and Louie are peeking at Daisy Duck's asshole as she watches the Seven Dwarfs groping Snow White. The prince is snatching a peek of Cinderella's snatch while trying a glass slipper on her foot. The Three Little Pigs are humping each other in a daisy chain. Jiminy Cricket leers as Tinker Bell does a striptease and Pinocchio's nose gets longer.

This centerspread became so popular that I decided to publish it as a poster in 1967. (A digitally colored edition of the original poster is now available via my

Web site, paulkrassner.com.) The Disney corporation considered a lawsuit but realized that *The Realist* was published on a proverbial shoestring, and besides, why bother causing themselves further public embarrassment? In Baltimore, a news agency distributed that issue with the Disneyland Memorial Orgy removed; I was able to secure the missing pages, and offered them free to any reader who had bought a partial magazine. In Oakland, an anonymous group published a flyer reprinting a few sections of the centerspread, and distributed it in churches and around town.

The police would have moved in for an arrest had it not been for my west coast distributor, Lou Swift, who asked them not to act until they got a *complete* issue of *The Realist*. In Chicago, however, a judge found the whole issue to be obscene—for the cover story was "Parts Left Out of the Kennedy Book"—but the ACLU sought a federal injunction restraining authorities from interfering in any way with local distribution. I tried to imagine a prosecutor telling a jury how they might get horny because "look what Goofy and Minnie Mouse are doing," but even if the memorial orgy *did* arouse prurient interest, the rest of *The Realist* was not *utterly* without redeeming social value.

In 1971, Ken Kesey and I co-edited *The Last Supplement to the Whole Earth Catalog*, which would also serve as an issue of *The Realist*. Kesey had been reading a book of African Yoruba stories. The moral of one parable was, "He who shits in the road will meet flies on his return." With that as a theme, we assigned R. Crumb to draw his version of the Last Supper. He came through with a cover so delightfully irreverent that it could zap Mel Gibson with severe apoplexy. In response to Mr. Natural reciting the moral of that parable, Jesus says, "Tsk! Please, I'm eating!"

Many years later, when Woody Allen was accused of sexually molesting his own child, I wrote a full-page comic strip, "Honey, I Fucked the Kids," illustrated by Kalynn Campbell. Stewart Brand wanted to reprint it in the *Whole Earth Review* but their printer refused, so they blacked out that entire page and found a new printer for the next issue.

In 2001, I was awaiting inspiration for a cover of the last *Realist*. Norman Rockwell's paintings on the covers of the *Saturday Evening Post* had always been synonymous with saccharine wholesomeness, but now on C-Span I saw his son, Peter, speaking at the National Press Club, and he mentioned that his father's long-standing ambition was to visit an opium den. Ultimately, he was dissuaded from taking that trip by advertisers in the magazine, but I immediately assigned Kalynn Campbell to capture the venerated artist's secret vision in Rockwell's familiar style. And, indeed, this under-the-surface image of American culture served as an appropriate metaphor for the final issue of *The Realist*.

THE PARTS LEFT OUT OF THE REAGAN MOVIE

The way CBS chickened out of telecasting their miniseries, *The Reagans*, you would've thought that the screenplay had referred to the claim, in a biography of Peter Lawford by his widow, that Nancy Reagan "was known for giving the best head in Hollywood." You would've figured that it must have revealed the details of her affair with Frank Sinatra—he did it *her* way—or maybe, who knows, her apocryphal fling with Los Angeles Police Chief Darryl Gates. You would've been certain there was footage from that gay orgy in which, according to Larry Flynt, Ronald Reagan had participated before he was president.

When I was eight years old, I saw the movie, *Knute Rockne—All American* (the Notre Dame football coach), starring Ronald Reagan as "The Gipper." Reagan immediately became my first role model—he was handsome and dynamic, with a twinkle in his eye—and I even started combing my hair just like his, using water to maintain a fancy pompadour.

Eventually, I got disillusioned, and when I grew up to be a stand-up comic, Reagan became a favorite target. I didn't have to make stuff up, just report it. For example, he promised, "If I am elected, I will end the inheritance tax, for rich and poor alike." My career as a TV writer was bracketed by the Reagan family.

In 1980, I was hired as head writer for an HBO special, satirizing the election campaign. The show, titled *A Funny Thing Happened On the Way to the White House*, took place in a modern newsroom, with Steve Allen as anchor. This was the first time in American history that three major presidential candidates—Ronald Reagan, Jimmy Carter and John Anderson—had all publicly declared themselves to be born-again Christians. So the election was no longer a choice between the lesser of two evils; it had become a matter of choosing between the least of three sinners.

Near the end of March 1981, I delivered a keynote address at the Youth International Party convention in New York. (These were latterday Yippies, originally launched as Zippies during the 1972 Republican convention.) I asked the audience a rhetorical question, "How would *you* like to be a Secret Service agent guarding Ronald Reagan, knowing that his vice president, George Bush, is the former head of the CIA?" On March 30, the new president was shot by John Hinckley in order to make a favorable impression on actress Jodie Foster. And if *that* seemed crazy, Hinckley later came out for gun control, and Reagan came out against it.

Although it took more than a decade after the assassinations of John and Robert Kennedy for there to be a band called The Dead Kennedys, it took only a few months after the attempted assassination of Ronald Reagan for there to be a group called Jodie Foster's Army. (Other bands were named Sharon Tate's Baby, Jim Jones and the Suicides, and Lennonburger.)

"In the '60s we knew that the CIA was smuggling heroin from Southeast Asia," I'd say at a campus gig. "In the '80s we know that they're smuggling cocaine from Central America. The same planes that fly weapons for the *contras* to airports in Panama, Honduras and Costa Rica come back to Florida, Louisiana and Arkansas with their cargos filled to the brim with cocaine, even though the Administration is carrying on its antidrug campaign. The pilots only have to be careful to evade the radar screen. So while Nancy Reagan is saying, 'Just say no,' the CIA is saying, 'Just fly low.'"

When I met the Reagans' daughter, Patti Davis, in 1981, I told her, "I really respected your decision to appear at that antinuke rally while your dad is the president."

"I was doing that *before* my father was president," she said. "I *have* to do it. I'm serious about that. It's the *planet*." (This was a logical extension of the time musician Graham Nash told Patti that she had a cute ass for a president's daughter, and she said, "I had a cute ass *before* I was the president's daughter.") Patti's Secret Service guards had been at that antinuke rally. "I wanted to take a stand," she told me, "by having all female Secret Service guards, but there's very few of them."

I met Patti's brother Ron in 1991, when I was hired as a writer on *The Ron Reagan Show*. It was an ironic association in view of the kind of material I had written and performed about his father. But young Ron was a fellow cultural mutation, and he understood that I had treated his parents as political symbols. One time I noticed a bumper sticker that said "Subvert the Dominant Paradigm," which I mentioned to Ron, and he adopted it as the syndicated talk show's unspoken credo.

We decided to defuse the fact that he was the son of the former president in a promo which included a recent clip of Ron as host of *Evening At the Improv*, saying, "I am the love child of Frank Sinatra"—immediately followed by an old black-and-white film clip of Ronald Reagan saying, "Can you imagine what the Commies will do with this!" But Fox head Barry Diller happened to be watching TV at home. He felt that the promo was exploitative and yanked it off the air.

In the original CBS script of *The Reagans*, when Ron told his parents he was getting married, the reaction was, "Thank God he's not gay." In real life, Ron had been falsely outed by militant gays in New York. We knew this issue was likely to enter the dialogue on an upcoming program about gay rights, so he was prepared. In fact, gay activist Michelangelo Signorile was one of the guests, and he mentioned those rumors on the show.

"I was a ballet dancer," Ron responded, "and any straight ballet dancer gets a rather thick skin about this sort of thing. But it occurred to me that it's insulting to my wife of eleven years, because it says she's living a lie, and I don't like that."

Ron had a charming sense of irreverence. In the conference room, we were watching a clip from the film *The Rapture*, which was to be included on a program about religion. "I met a guy," Mimi Rogers is telling her husband. "You should meet him. You could love him too."

"You fell for some rich homosexual," the husband says, laughing.

"He's the Lord Jesus Christ."

"And," Ron added, "he's hung like a stallion."

A producer, another writer and I were the pot-smokers on this show. We would smoke a joint while walking around the block. The producer bought his stash from an actress on a popular series, and one time we drove to her house to make a purchase. Ron came along for the ride. He told us how, when he had been a toker as a youth, his dad once found a marijuana-filled baggie in his bureau and confiscated it.

Another time, the four of us went for lunch at a nearby restaurant, and the hostess shook hands with Ron, saying, "I thought it was really cool for your sister to talk about masturbating in *Vanity Fair*." However, that particular scene was not included in *The Reagans* when it appeared on Showtime.

WHY I'M OPTIMISTIC ABOUT THE FUTURE

Recently, on a beautiful, serene afternoon, I was strolling along the crowded Venice, California boardwalk, playing my part in God's ant farm. A common spirit seemed to transcend age, gender, appearance, vocation, ethnicity, language, religion. It was like a mobile oasis; as if a truce had been declared, where inhumanity was replaced by empathy. Despite my awareness of unspeakable anguish occurring around the world, a feeling of hope surged through my body. That kind of epiphany had occurred many times before.

The first time it happened, I was seven years old. A fellow student had stood in front of the class, unzipped his fly, and exposed his penis. He was sent to reform school. Without having the vocabulary to express it, I thought that the punishment didn't fit the crime. The next morning, I walked to school with a mission. I stood in front of the class, unzipped my fly, and exposed a portrait of my penis that I had drawn the previous evening. While carrying out that self-assigned art homework, I had become engulfed by a blast of pure optimism—I was totally confident that I would not get in trouble for what I planned to do. My parents were called to school and advised to take me to a psychiatrist, but they knew better. In retrospect, though, I still have to wonder, "What the fuck ever made me do that!" If it were to happen now, I would undoubtedly be force-fed Ritalin through a Pez dispenser.

I never knew when I would experience these flashes of optimism. In December 1960, when I traveled to Cuba, the State Department was financing counterrevolutionary broadcasts from a radio station on Swan Island in Honduras. Program content ranged from telling Cubans that their children would be taken away, to warning them that a Russian drug was being added to their food and milk which would automatically turn them into Communists.

In the Sierra Maestra, where battles once raged, there were now under construction schools and dormitories for 20,000 children—to match the 20,000 Cubans who lost their lives, many after torture, under the U.S.-supported Batista regime. At one of these educational communities, some young students removed the string that been set up by a landscaping crew to mark off a cement foundation. Next morning, the school director lectured them about such immorality. "Even a little thing like that," he explained, "does harm to the revolution." The children of Cuba were being programmed for cooperation rather than competition, and it made me quiver with hopefulness.

A recent study concluded that human beings are "mentally wired to cooperate," and I witnessed that concept in action at the shadow conventions in Philadelphia and Los Angeles during the 2000 presidential campaign. Once, at a benefit, I met songwriter/troubadour Harry Chapin backstage, and I'll never forget his words: "If you don't act like there's hope, there is no hope." Placebos do work, after all. And yet, in retrospect, I realize that I often acted as if there were no hope.

During the '60s, when abortion was illegal, I ran an underground abortion referral service, but I never dreamed that it would become legal in my lifetime. I didn't like to eat in restaurants or fly in planes because of cigarette smoking, but I never thought it would become illegal in my lifetime. I joined protest demonstrations against the Vietnam War and for civil rights, against circumcision and for an end to nuclear testing, never speculating as to how effective we were, but always knowing that the other option was to do nothing.

I became obsessed with investigating a government plot to neutralize the countercultural threat to control-freaks and economic-forecasters—the FBI had a special "Hippie Squad" where they were taught how to roll joints, the better to infiltrate—and I eventually freaked out from information overload. A turning point in this psychotic episode came late one night while talking with an old friend, Julius Karpen. As we spoke, we were rolling billiard balls back and forth across a pool table in the living room, pushing and catching them with our hands rather than hitting them with a cue-stick and waking up our hosts.

"How long is it gonna go on?" I asked.

"How long is *what* gonna go on?"

"You know, the battle between good and evil, when is it gonna *end*?"

"Maybe never."

Suddenly I felt a wave of relief. So it *wasn't* all my responsibility. Such a heavy burden had been lifted from my soul. I understood that I could participate in the process of change without becoming attached to it. That I could maintain sanity in the midst of insanity by developing the ability to be a passionate activist and an objective observer simultaneously. That I needn't take myself as seriously as my causes.

I asked my friend and former *High Times* editor Steve Hager, who is deep into conspiracy research, how he remains optimistic. He replied, "My rule is: Forget about tearing down the establishment (it'll never happen, the Octopus is too powerful). Instead, concentrate on building an alternative culture and passing it down to anyone who cares. Real ceremonies create positive energy, but when you focus solely on exposing Nazis, you are living in their twisted world."

This renewed my sense of optimism, but of course that may merely be a result of my damaged chromosomes from taking too many acid trips.

Got Porn?

Showing Pink

As *Penthouse* magazine was on its way to bankruptcy, publisher Bob Guccione said, "The future has definitely migrated to electronic media." And *Hustler* publisher Larry Flynt—who eagerly joined that migration—has complained, "If you ever cruise the Net and see everything that's available, it's glutted with sleaze. It's a nightmare out there. This has to be affecting the revenues of people like myself."

But both have played pivotal roles in the evolution of popular pornography. Men's magazines had started out showing breasts but not nipples, buttocks but not anuses—and never, *never* a vagina. Nor did pubic hair used to be all over the place, only to eventually get Bikini-waxed out of existence except for occasional exclamation points. Even nudist magazines had once air-brushed men and women into department-store manikins without genitalia playing volleyball.

The great pubic breakthrough occurred in *Penthouse* in 1971. A triangular patch of dark curly hair eventually opened Pandora's Box wider and wider until *Hustler* began "showing pink" in 1974. Even Flynt's own wife Althea showed pink. One issue featured a Scatch-'n'-Sniff centerspread. When you scratched the spread-eagled model in her designated area, a scent of lilac bath oil emanated from her vulva.

In November 1977, Larry Flynt was flying with Ruth Carter Stapleton, the evangelist sister of President Jimmy Carter, in Flynt's pink-painted private jet, which when it belonged to Elvis Presley had been painted red, white, and blue. Up in the air, Flynt had a vision of Jesus Christ. Flynt's entire body was tingling, and he fell to his knees, clasping his hands in prayer. Thus was he converted to born-again Christianity.

The next month, at *Hustler's* Christmas party, Flynt announced that I was going to be the new publisher. This was the first that *I* heard the news. Before, I had been wondering how the magazine would change, and now it turned out that I was the answer to my own question. For Flynt to bring *me* in as redeeming social value was an offer too absurd to refuse.

Now that Flynt has evolved from a con artist into an authentic First Amendment hero—in July 2000, he spoke at the Commonwealth Club in San Francisco—I recall what a pariah he was in 1977. In Los Angeles, at the building in Century City which housed his office, *Hustler* was not allowed to be listed in the lobby.

At the time, I was writing a syndicated column for alternative weeklies. Specifically, I was working on my "Predictions for 1978," leading off with this: "Since Larry Flynt has been converted to born-again Christianity, the new *Hustler* will feature a special Scratch-'n'-Sniff Virgin Mary."

"Hey, that's a great idea," said Flynt on New Year's Day at Nassau Beach in the Bahamas. "We'll have a portrait of the Virgin Mary, and when you scratch her crotch, it'll smell like tomato juice."

He was rubbing suntan lotion on my back.

"I'll bet Hugh Hefner never did this for you," he said.

Flynt wanted to know who would be an appropriate person to write an article for *Hustler* that would expose the Pope as gay. I suggested Gore Vidal, who had already stated in an interview that Cardinal Spellman was gay. So much for our first editorial conference.

There was an unwritten agreement among men's magazines that human female nipples would not be clearly visible on a cover. I was also learning to accept certain arbitrary rules then governing the inside pages. An erect penis must not be shown. Semen must not be shown. Penetration must not be shown. Oral-genital contact must not be shown.

A few months later in Georgia, Flynt was shot during a lunch break in his obscenity trial. I flew to Atlanta and went directly to the hospital. Althea brought me to Larry's room. It was extremely unsettling to see such a powerful personality so helpless, kept alive by medical technology, with one tube feeding him and another breathing for him. He appeared bug-eyed with painkiller. Althea lifted the sheet and showed me his gaping wounds, a truly awesome sight.

"Oh, God, Althea," I said, "he's showing pink."

"I'm arranging for a photographer to come in here," she said. "We're gonna publish Larry's wounds in *Hustler*. I want people to see what they did to him."

I sat down in a chair by Larry's bed. I didn't know what to say, We simply clasped hands for a while. Finally I broke the silence. "Larry, tomorrow is Good Friday," I said. "So, uh, you don't have to go to work."

I glanced toward Althea to reassure myself that I had't indulged in irreverence that was *too* inapppropiate, but she said, "Oh, Paul, *look*," gesturing toward Larry—"he wants to show you something." Above the oxygen mask, Larry was blinking his eyes over and over again in rapid succession.

"He's *laughing*," Althea explained.

It was a moment of unspeakable intimacy.

Althea had transformed the Coca-Cola Suite of Emory University Hospital into her office, where she was studying the slides of a "Jesus and the Adulteress" photo spread, including a semi-life-sized poster in the form of a centerfold pull-out. There was a generic barbershop-calendar Jesus, looking reverently toward the sky as he stands above the prone Mary Magdalene—almost naked, her head bleeding from the stones that have been cast upon her—and, just as the Bible says, he is covering her, *but not quite*, and she is, inadvertently, still showing pink. Sweet, shocking, vulnerable pink. This was a startling visual image, unintentionally satirizing the change from the old *Hustler* to the new *Hustler*. The marketing people were aghast at the possibility that wholesalers, especially in the Bible Belt, would refuse to distribute the magazine with such a blatantly blasphemous feature.

Faced with a crucial decision, Althea made her choice on the basis of pure whimsicality. She noticed a pair of pigeons on the window ledge. One was waddling toward the other. "All right," she said, "if that dove walks over and pecks the *other* dove, then we *will* publish this." The pigeon continued strutting along the window ledge, but stopped short and didn't peck the other pigeon, so publication of "Jesus and the Adulteress" was postponed indefinitely. And the poster would instead remain on my wall as a memento of my six-month stint at *Hustler*. Maybe I should try to auction it off on eBay.

As for Larry Flynt's born-again conversion, he now attributes it to "a chemical imbalance in his brain."

PEE-WEE HERMAN MEETS PETE TOWNSHEND

Name two famous people who were both born on August 27. And the answer is: Pee-wee Herman and Mother Teresa. Okay, now, what was the reference to Pee-wee Herman that was censored out of the 1991 Emmy Awards? And the answer: Comedian Gilbert Gottfried's observation that, "If masturbation is against the law, then I should be on Death Row." This was, of course, a reference to the arrest of Pee-wee for playing with his wee-wee as he watched *Nancy Nurse* in the darkened privacy of a porn movie theater.

The bust for that victimless crime took place later in the lobby. Yes, the cops caught him coming and going. Inquiring minds wanted to know, did they force him to wash his hands before they fingerprinted him? It all seemed to be straight out of an old Lenny Bruce bit, where just such a hardened criminal must ultimately be rehabilitated by going "cold jerky."

The arrest of Pee-wee Herman might not have occurred today because, although he would indoubtedly be performing that same dastardly act of masturbation, this time it would most likely happen while he was watching porn on the computer screen in his own home. That is to say the arrest would not occur if he were watching an *adult* video.

But now he has been charged with possession of *kiddie* porn. How did this come about? A teenager had registered a complaint about Pee-wee and a friend, actor Jeffrey Jones. The complaint was dismissed, but detectives had already searched both of their homes. As a result, Jones was accused of taking pornographic photos of a juvenile, which is a felony, whereas Pee-wee faced the lesser charge of possession. If convicted of the misdemeanor, he could have been sentenced to a year in prison.

Then came the legal troubles of Pete Townshend, famed British rock guitarist and co-founder of The Who, who has admitted to downloading child pornography from the Internet for the purpose of researching the autobiography that he's writing. What follows is the transcript of a conversation between Pee-wee and Pete, based on the actual facts of their respective cases.

Pete: It's so ironic. Not only am I not a pedophile, but I have been a high profile campaigner *against* child pornography on the Web. I mean my own grandmother sexually abused me when I was six years old. I even offered to have the hard drive of my computer analyzed by police so they could ascertain for themselves that if I did anything which is technically illegal, it was purely for research.

Pee-wee: That's your smoking gun, silly. See, I didn't download anything, because then your credit card number becomes a matter of record. Me, I'm just a collector of vintage erotica, like those classic physique magazines that were published in the 1940s. I have 100,000 items in my archives, but none of them are from the Internet. The detectives spent a whole year studying every single one of those images, and the district attorney finally said there was no case. But then—only one day before the statute of limitations would have expired—the Los Angeles city attorney issued a warrant for my arrest.

Pete: Why? What did they find?

Pee-wee: At first they were going to charge me with possessing a tape of the actor Rob Lowe doing an underage girl, but since *he* was never charged with child porn, they changed their minds about charging me with *watching* it.

Pete: And you don't have any child pornography among your collection?

Pee-wee: Oh, there are a few minutes of grainy footage of teenage boys masturbating or performing oral sex. But I wasn't even aware of that.

Pete: Well, in England, if you possess images of children engaged in sexual activity, it's against the law, and even if you view those images *accidentally*, without really possessing them, it's still illegal.

Pee-wee: It's the same thing in the United States. If someone anonymously e-mailed child porn to me, I could be arrested for possession. Even if I immediately deleted it, that would not be acceptable as a defense.

Pete: One would think that if you happen to be an *anti*-porn investigator, you will be considered immune to prosecution, but unfortuntely I was not working as a *government* pervert.

Pee-wee: Hey, maybe you could prove in court that you didn't *enjoy* looking at those photos. That you *hated* the images, but you felt it was a necessary evil.

Pete: Look, the bottom line is that I am simply an innocent victim of the puritanical urge to punish.

Pee-wee: I know *you* are, but what am *I*?

SATIRICAL PROPHECY

In my capacity as a stand-up comic, several years ago I did a line on stage about a Fundamentalist Christian who had tattooed on his penis, "What would Jesus do?" Recently, that metaphorical concept which I had made up in the recesses of my warped mind came literally true. A Sunday School teacher in St. Paul, Minnesota advised one of his students to write on his penis, "What would Jesus do?" I must be careful not to let this power fall into the wrong hands.

It was a case of satirical prophecy.

In March 1991, I published in *The Realist* a satirical article by Lenny Lipton, titled "Computerized Kiddie Porn." Lipton described his meeting with a character he called Harvey, who had created—and now sells for big bucks—special computer generated images, such as "a pretty little girl engaged in an unspeakably bestial act with an adult male who looked very much like Harvey."

Lipton wrote, "I was particularly startled by an image of a homosexual act performed on a male baby."

He asked Harvey how, in the face of a Supreme Court decision that made child pornography illegal, he nevertheless gets away with running a one-man child pornography cottage industry that brings in a six-figure income.

"It was the Supreme Court that *put* me in business," Harvey explained. "Justice Byron White, who wrote the majority opinion—it was 6-3, upholding an Ohio law—said that it's illegal to possess nude photographs of children, even if they are used privately in the home. A ban on private possession is justified, according to White, because owning such photos helps perpetuate commercial demand and thus the exploitation of helpless children. If you accept the Court's logic, then the government could intrude into the home any time a seemingly private activity is thought to perpetuate a commercial market for actions that might exploit others. This is a whole new theory of censorship, and therein lies my golden opportunity.

"You see," he continued, "no one is being exploited by my creations. These dirty pictures come out of my mind via a computer. No child is exploited. These images are perfectly legal, if I am to believe the Court is being up front with regard to the basis for its decision. As far as I am able to tell, you have nothing to worry about if you take one of my loathsome pictures home and hang it on your wall."

Back in real life, in April 2002, the Supreme Court struck down part of the federal child pornography law that makes it a crime to own or sell images of computer created children engaged in sex. Since no actual children were portrayed in the photos and films at issue, Justice Anthony Kennedy said that the government could not make it a crime to show sexual images that only "appear to be" children.

The ruling reversed a section of the Child Pornography Act of 1996—backed by then-Senator John Ashcroft—which broadened the definition of child pornography to include any "visual depiction that is, or appears to be, a minor engaging in sexually explicit conduct," specifically mentioning a "computer generated image or picture."

The Court's decision served to provide immunity from the law for a whole new generation of virtual child pornographers who rely entirely on computer generated images. As long as no real children were portrayed, or morphed into a sex scene, then the photographer or filmmaker could not be prosecuted.

How had this all come about?

In 1992, a man in Texas downloaded digital files from a bulletin board system in Denmark. He was indicted for "receiving child pornography." His attorney argued that the government could not prove that the images had been made using actual children. He put on the witness stand a graphic artist, who showed how even someone with only basic computer knowledge could use a software program such as Photoshop to alter a photograph. Nonetheless, the defendant was found guilty.

Eventually, the Free Speech Coalition, a California trade association for the adult entertainment industry, went to federal court in San Francisco to challenge the law on the grounds that real children were not being exploited. That claim was rejected, but a 2-1 vote by the 9th Circuit Court of Appeals agreed that it should not be illegal to show "images of fictitious children engaged in imaginary sex acts," and the Supreme Court upheld that ruling.

Eleven years earlier, Lenny Lipton had written about his imaginary acquaintance: "Harvey lifted a print off the pile, placed it in a large manila envelope and handed it to me. I put the envelope in my briefcase and after some pleasantries I bid him *adieu*. On my drive home I thought about Harvey, the Supreme Court and the world I lived in. As I drove toward the Golden Gate Bridge, computer generated child pornography on the seat beside me, I felt blessed to be living in a world where technology could put an end to the exploitation of children."

It was another case of satirical prophecy.

However, in February 2003, with the backing of the Bush administration, the Senate unanimously approved a revised version of the law, which would create a new definition of a minor identifiable in pornographic images as one "virtually indistinguishable" from an actual child. Moreover, defendants in criminal pornography cases would be required to provide evidence that they did not use real children to produce the images.

I guess the time has come for somebody to write a satire about the new judicial process, where an accused person is considered guilty until proven innocent. Oops, too late, that's already come true.

THE MARRIAGE OF HIP-HOP AND PORNOGRAPHY

Entertainment reporter Geoff Boucher wrote in the *Los Angeles Times*: "You might be able to imagine Garth Brooks without his cowboy hat or Britney Spears without the bare midriff . . . but Snoop Dogg without a joint in his hand? It may be a pipe dream, but the chronic king of hip-hop has announced that he is abstaining from marijuana as well as alcohol.

"This is shocking news considering that Snoop was named the 2002 Stoner of the Year by *High Times* magazine and has made a habit of openly toking before, during and after his concerts and interviews. He has been, arguably, the most public pothead performer since Bob Marley."

The rapper explained in an interview on BET: "I'm 30 years old now. Three kids. A wife. A mom. Brothers. Artists. Family. Friends. They all need me. They depend on me. I've been leading [homeboys] off the cliff for five, six years. So now I'm going slow."

However, *High Times* editor Steve Bloom considers the possibility that Snoop's surprise declaration is not necessarily a true change of heart, since he had been fined and placed on probation for a pot offense in Ohio the previous year.

"He was the biggest, baddest pot smoker out there," says Bloom, "and maybe he's just stepping back because it got too hot. Maybe he really has decided he wants to take a break or not smoke anymore. But all this could be a smoke-screen."

Sort of like when Timothy Leary and Ken Kesey, both of whom, after they were busted for dope, advised young people to stop taking LSD (*wink, wink*).

Indeed, *Rollingstone.com* has reported: "In a closed-door session at the Department of Justice, Snoop Dogg engaged the attorney general in a spirited debate about medical marijuana. 'The Doggfather and I have our differences,' an unusually expansive John Ashcroft told reporters afterward, 'but we are both committed to relieving chronic pain.' 'Or at a mutherfuckin' minimum,' rejoined Dogg, 'relievin' with the Chronic.'"

In any case, on the Internet, Snoop's fans reacted to his announcement with both dismay and skepticism. The news also inspired commentary in Aaron McGruder's controversial comic strip, *The Boondocks*. Huey Freeman, the radical African-American kid, says, referring to Snoop's announcement, "It's the potential impact on the global economy that I'm worried about," and his little neighbor Jazmine responds, "Think he'll do a benefit song for his dealer?"

Dogg seems to have a double standard, though, when it comes to victimless "crimes." Whereas his flamboyant image once graced a cover of *High Times*, he now appears instead, seated on a throne, in full pimp regalia, on the cover of the September 2002 issue of *Adult Video News* a slick trade journal for the $20-billion pornography industry. Their accompanying article states:

"While Snoop Dogg wasn't the first rapper to make porn—DJ Yella of N.W.A. has been producing it since the mid-1990s—*Doggystyle*, more than any other porn/hip-hop synthesis, awakened the adult industry to the immense commercial possibilities of the genre. The tape, Snoop's first collaboration with Hustler Video, in which he introduces the sex scenes but doesn't have sex on camera, has sold more than 150,000 units world-wide, garnering *AVN's* Top Selling Tape of 2001 Award. . . . Largely due to the success of *Doggystyle*, more and more rappers are appearing in porn videos with no fear of alienating fans."

Snoop believes that the hip-hop/porn connection benefits both industries.

"The adult video world is so much what rap music is all about," he says in *Adult Video News*, "about expressing ourselves and having fun, and a lot of times radio and TV don't understand that so they censor us. So I feel like we're doing each other justice by being hand-in-hand and working with each other. I mean, a lot of people be in the closet about it, but they all listen to rap music or watch adult videos one way or another.

"I always wanted to do it because I felt like I had a lot of records that would never get no airplay or never get no visuals, and I just wanted to make some type of video where I could do these songs and have naked ladies in them and doing that type of shit. And then when I figured out that I could make a whole movie, I got with the right director and then put my ideas down and made it happen."

Speaking of his follow-up to *Doggystyle*, titled *HUSTLAZ, Diary of a Pimp*, he expounds, "It's just basically the day in the life of a pimp, everything he's got going on with all the ladies in different rooms in the house and different situations that occur. And videos. So it's just like a live, put-together movie. It's a diary. It's like a documentary in movie fashion. We made three new records ['Break These Hoes for Snoop,' 'Doin' It Too' and 'Pussy Like This'] that were just specifically for this, where we could make records that was hot and we knew they were X-rated and they would fit the movie, fit the theme. This shit is hot. When it's all side-by-side, the videos and the acting and the music all comes together."

Apparently, Snoop Dogg's family—those three kids, his wife and his mother—are all completely supportive of his current activity. And so he maintains a hard-on all the way to the bank. Snoop's new public agenda can be summed up in four little words: "Porn, *sí*. Pot, *no*."

PORN AND THE MANSON MURDERS

The recent TV movie, *Helter Skelter*, perpetuated the myth of Charles Manson. In 1969, when the news broke about the massacre of pregnant actress Sharon Tate and her house guests, there was a sudden epidemic of paranoia in certain Hollywood circles. Actor Steve McQueen fled to England, for example, and I wondered why. After the trial of Manson and his brainwashed followers, I began my own private investigation, if only to satisfy my sense of curiosity about the case.

I corresponded with Manson, visited Charlie's Devils in prison, including Susan Atkins, and—in a classic example of participatory journalism—I took an acid trip with a few family members, including Squeaky Fromme, who is now behind bars for the attempted assassination of then-President Gerald Ford.

Ed Sanders' book, *The Family*, had mentioned that Los Angeles police had discovered porn flicks in a loft at the crime scene, the home Tate shared with her director husband, Roman Polanski (who was in London at the time of the murders). And yet, the prosecutor in Manson's trial, Vincent Bugliosi, denied in his book, *Helter Skelter*, that any porn flicks had been found. It was possible that the police had indeed uncovered them but lied to Bugliosi.

I learned why when I consulted the renowned San Francisco private investigator, Hal Lipset, whose career had been the basis for an excellent film, *The Conversation*, starring Gene Hackman. Lipset informed me that not only did Los Angeles police seize porn movies and videotapes, but also that individual officers were *selling* them. He had talked with one police source who told him exactly which porn flicks were available—a total of seven hours' worth for a quarter-million dollars.

Lipset began reciting a litany of those porn videos. The most notorious was Greg Bautzer, an attorney for financier Howard Hughes, together with Jane

Wyman, the former wife of then-Governor Ronald Reagan. There was Sharon Tate with Dean Martin. There was Sharon with Steve McQueen. (That was a silent *Aha!* moment for me.) There was Sharon with two black bisexual men.

"The cops were not too happy about *that* one," Lipset recalled.

There was a video of Cass Elliot from the Mamas and the Papas in an orgy with Yul Brynner, Peter Sellers and Warren Beatty. Coincidentally, Brynner and Sellers, together with John Phillips of the Mamas and the Papas, had offered a $25,000 reward for the capture of the killers.

I always felt the executioners had a prior connection with their victims. I finally tracked down a reporter who had hung around with police and seen a porn video of Susan Atkins with one of the victims, Voytek Frykowski. When I asked Manson about that, he responded: "You are ill advised and mis-led. [Victim Jay] Sebring done Susan's hair and I think he sucked one or two of her dicks. I'm not sure who she was walking out from her stars and cages, that girl *loves* dick, you know what I mean, hon. Yul Brynner, Peter Sellers . . ."

Meanwhile, Charlie has become a cultural symbol. In surfer jargon, a "manson" means a crazy, reckless surfer. For comedians, Manson has become a generic joke reference. I asked him how he felt about that. He wrote back: "I don't know what a generic is, Joke. I think I know what that means. That means you talk bad about Reagan or Bush. I've always ran poker games and whores and crime. I'm a crook. You make the reality in court and press. I just ride and play the cards that were pushed on me to play. Mass killer, it's a job, what can I say."

But Manson has apparently been moonlighting, because his new CD, *All the Way Alive*, was recently released. He was discussing with the producer of his album the notion that people's public images can be vastly different from the way they behave in their private lives. As an example, Charlie mentioned "the sex movies Steve McQueen and Peter Sellers were doing with Sharon Tate."

EATING SHIT FOR FUN AND PROFIT

I am in complete awe of the democracy of the Internet, which presents an infinite menu for individual tastes and ideologies, and in this context, specifically to viewers of online porn. From golden showers to farm animals, the World Wide Web caters to virtually every imaginable desire. With the privacy provided by a computer screen, you can worship at the fetish of your choice. But, in the process of surfing porn sites—for research purposes only, of course—I realized that I had never come across a site specializing in coprophagia. It means eating shit. Literally.

There's an old saying among nutritionists: "You are what you eat." However, comedian Darryl Henriques, playing the role of a New Age swami, says, "You are what you don't shit."

One of the nastiest things you can say to someone is, "Eat shit." A non-fiction book, *The Pit*, reveals a strange cult in San Francisco where a group of successful businessmen were forced, along with other acts of humiliation, to eat their own shit. Ultimately, they were represented in a lawsuit by flamboyant attorney Melvin Belli. But that was involuntary shit eating, and what we're talking about here is the voluntary kind.

For many years I heard stories that comic actor Danny Thomas, the star of *Make Room For Daddy*, was a coprophagiac. I assumed it was just another urban legend until I bumped into an old friend who was now working as a prostitute in Hollywood. Over lunch, she mentioned the names of some of her celebrity clients, including Danny Thomas. She told me how he had hired her to save her solid waste in her panties so that he could rub the panties on his face and gobble up her shit as though it were cotton candy.

When he finished, he would wash himself thoroughly, then pay her, and, as if coming out of a trance, he'd say, "Where was I?" He was trying to distance himself from what he had just done. Instant denial. Since then, I have believed that Danny Thomas's fundraising for Saint Jude's Hospital was really for the purpose of having secret access to their bedpans.

Anyway, I googled "Eating Shit." Topping the list was "Shit Eating Grins: In Defense of Adam Sandler, *South Park* and the Proud Tradition of Poop Humor"—an article in *Salon.com*. But sure enough, I was soon led to hard-core shit-eating sites, which I found totally disgusting yet absolutely riveting. You may not want to read any further, but we both know you will.

There are photos of beautiful women shitting; if you click for a close-up you can spot a yellow kernel of corn in one big brown chunk o' shit. Women are spreading shit all over their naked bodies and inside their vaginas. A pair of lovely lesbians are eating handfuls of shit, then tongue kissing each other. Two women are eating the same lengthy turd, starting from opposite ends. A woman, fully dressed, wearing a mini-skirt, is shitting as she walks along the sidewalk. One woman is shitting into another woman's mouth. Mmmm, good to the last dingleberry.

Among the shit-eating sites, there are Asian movies. Here's a couple of descriptions: "A bunch of kinky Japanese guys find some truly hot looking girls and take them down below the streets of Tokyo into a real sewer full of shit." And, "Cute Kyoko's diarrhea suddenly acts up again. Her piano teacher becomes a willing student of hot scat games. Lots of shit pours out of her hot ass into his waiting mouth. Then she asks if he would rub it all over her. Sure, why not, he says."

If there is one particular image that remains in my mind's eye, it is an innocent looking, attractive teenager—she's over 18, of course—and she is cheerfully drinking a shit shake through a straw in an old-fashioned malted milk glass.

I thought about her father discovering that photo in cyberspace, yet he is unable to confront his daughter about it because he would then have to admit what *he* was doing at that site. I mean, this isn't exactly the type of thing that would be mass e-mailed by one of those selfless spammers. And even if the father did confess to his daughter, he would undoubtedly hesitate to ask if he could eat *her* shit, because that could be considered a form of incest, and you have to draw the line somewhere, right?

There must be an especially strong bond among coprophagiacs, though, because they have experienced in common a form of liberation from a taboo that can be traced all the way back to infancy, when a parent would cringe and say, "Stop! Don't eat that! I said *no!*"

Who knows, some day coprophagia might even become a religion?

Holy shit!

LISTS FOR THE LISTLESS

PREDICTIONS FOR 2004

The annual frenzy of psychic prophesizing in the supermarket tabloids is now in full swing. Help yourself to some free samples of predictions from the weekly *Sun*:

☞ In an effort to boost the sagging tourism industry, Florida will provide free airfare to anyone wanting to vacation in the Sunshine State.

☞ A plot to assassinate President Bush will be uncovered in the nick of time by CBS newsman Dan Rather.

☞ A nationwide anti-smallpox inoculation program will have the astonishing side effect of increasing the average life span by eleven years.

☞ A chorus of 1,000 angels will appear over the Pentagon.

☞ Pope John Paul II will be miraculously cured of Parkinson's disease while conducting a special memorial mass at the World Trade Center.

☞ An attempt to clone terrorist kingpin Osama bin Laden from one of his beard hairs will be thwarted by U.S. troops in Afghanistan.

☞ Scientists working on an antidote for anthrax infections will stumble upon a cure for Alzheimer's disease.

☞ The three major television networks will announce that they will stop airing shows that glorify violence.

☞ It will be revealed that the Taliban has been kidnapping American children and selling them on the white slave market.

☞ The weather this winter will be unseasonably warm, reducing our dependence on oil from the Middle East.

But tabloid prognostication has its academic counterpart at the University of Alabama. This is the 23rd year of their traditional making of forecasts, "Educated Guesses." Spokesperson Chris Bryant told the *Birmingham Post-Herald*, "We ask the faculty to speculate within their areas of expertise, to go out on a limb and make predictions of what will happen in the next 12 months."

For example, last January, Donald Snow, professor of political science and an expert in military and political affairs, predicted that George W. Bush would lose his bid for re-election if the United States were to go to war against Iraq in

2003. He placed the likelihood at two to one in favor of a military strike. "If we go to war with Iraq," he said, "it will cost George W. Bush the election in 2004. Even if the war itself goes well, the post-war will not, and that's what's going to do him in. Post-War Iraq is going to be an extraordinarily messy place that we are going to have to occupy for a long time. We will become the recruiting poster for al Qaeda and other terrorist organizations."

The previous January, Snow predicted that Osama bin Laden would be captured "in the next few months, but possibly not in Afghanistan. I think he's left the country, but eventually we will catch him. Somebody will rat on him. Someone will see him going through a village and will have dreams of sugar plums in that $25 million reward and turn him in. Islamic brotherhood is one thing, but $25 million in cold cash is another."

That same year, Nick Stinnet, professor of marriage and family studies, predicted that there would be a mini-baby boom in June or July 2002, directly correlated with the attacks of September 11, 2001. "In times of stress and crises," he explained, "people often draw closer to one another for comfort and consolation as an antidote to uncertainty and loneliness. And in couple relationships, that drawing closer may involve sexual activity and consequently the possibility of pregnancy. Some people regard sex as a good stress reliever."

Robert Robicheaux, professor of retailing and director of the Hess Institute for Retailing Development, predicted the demise of the computer companies: "A midwestern United States-based entrepreneur will announce the introduction of a technology that completely makes obsolete traditional integrated computer chips. The product will enable easy and inexpensive remote Internet service via satellite transmission technology."

And so here am I, caught somewhere between the tabloids and the academics, with a selection of my own humble predictions:

☞ The first legally sanctioned marriage of two metrosexuals will take place in Massachusetts.

☞ Michael Jackson and Kobe Bryant will be cellmates.

☞ Charles Manson will be released on parole and announce that he's looking forward to spending more time with his family.

☞ Arnold Schwarzenegger will introduce a bill that would legalize the sale and use of steroids.

☞ Fidel Castro will come out for term limits.

☞ Counterfeit euros will flood the international market.

☞ Wal-Mart will move its corporate headquarters to China.

☞ The draft will be reinstated and will not exclude women, gays, lesbians, bisexuals, sado-masochists, transvestites or the transgendered.

☞ The weather will remain unpredictable.

☞ John Ashcroft will be diagnosed with multiple sclerosis and consequently change his mind about medical marijuana.

☞ Rush Limbaugh will get arrested for purchasing his painkilling pharmaceuticals in Canada.

☞ Laura Bush will overdose on Botox.

☞ Saddam Hussein will be sentenced to a lifetime of community service.

☞ Jessica Lynch will become a director.

☞ The stunt doubles for Ben Affleck and Jennifer Lopez will get married.

☞ The world's tallest building, to be built at the site of the World Trade Center, will be sponsored by the Target chain, whose corporate logo of a bull's-eye a few floors below the spire will be visible for miles.

☞ It will be discovered that Libya has been selling off its weapons of mass destruction to North Korea.

☞ The Patriot Act will be expanded to include thought crimes.

☞ The ACLU and PETA will combine forces to fight for the civil liberties of all animals.

☞ The use of cell phones with cameras for the instant communication of personal porn will bring about pandemic performance anxiety among masturbators.

☞ The reappearance of pubic hair will become so fashionable that bikini waxes will be outlawed.

☞ A combination penis-enlarger and erection-stimulator patch will be invented.

☞ A pill taken daily by men will transform their semen into a contraceptive device.

☞ Strom Thurmond will be tried posthumously for statutory rape.

☞ Jesse Jackson and Johnnie Cochran will compete against each other in a national poetry slam.

☞ Bottled water will be imported from Mars.

☞ There will be an epidemic of genetically engineered crops being inundated with genetically engineered crop circles.

☞ Particles of food will be embedded into dental floss for those who are too busy to eat between flossings.

☞Dick Cheney's pacemaker will fail when he tries out the microwave oven he was given for Christmas by Rudy Giuliani.

☞The Bill O'Reilly action figure dolls will all be recalled because they have a tendency to self-destruct.

☞Monica Lewinsky and Paris Hilton will enter a convent and become nuns for a reality TV series.

☞Senator Joe Lieberman will convert to Islam.

☞God will at last be given credit for creating evolution.

☞The Second Coming will occur, and Jesus will reveal himself as the antichrist.

☞And finally, you will definitely not die this year.

BIZARRE SEXUALLY ORIENTED SPAM SUBJECT LINES

Every one of the spam senders in this informal survey is trying—in the hope that you won't immediately press the delete key—to entice you into checking out their messages and purchasing their products. In that process, they will sometimes deliberately (but not always delliberately) misspell words in the subject lines of their spams in order to bypass any electronic filters you happen to set up.

A friend writes to me, "I just upgraded to AOL 9 which has a feature that takes out spam before it gets to you. Theoretically you submit and save a list of words you don't want in your subject line—in my case some are Viagra, Xanax, cheerleaders and mortgages—then *voila*! But, as always, the spammers are one step ahead. Now I'm getting spam for Viagara, Xannax, cheer leaders and mort.gages. I don't know why they think I'd do business with anyone whose spelling skills were so faulty, but I guess their target audience may not care."

And from another friend: "Has anyone had a problem with blocked e-mail? I have had fully one-third of my mail blocked by my ISP that is running Norton's 'Barracuda Spam Firewall.' *Phooey*! It blocks e-mail from friends and newsletters but lets the porn, Viagra and 'grow your penis pills' through. I am ticked! Anyone else all of a sudden not hearing from friends?"

Meanwhile, federal agents have arrested a man for repeatedly making death threats against employees of an Internet advertising firm. He faces a maximum penalty of five years in prison and a $250,000 fine if convicted. He had mistakenly believed that the company was the source of unsolicited e-mail ads he received about penis enlargement. Well, everybody has their breaking point.

Carol Liefer observed on Comedy Central that apparently there are a lot of people who want *her* to have a bigger penis. And, on the all-female morning TV talk show, *The View*, this rhetorical question was posed: "Which is worse, a tiny little penis or a lot of violence?" As if in response, a dwarf detective on a Comedy Central promo for their movie, *Knee-High P.I.*, observed, "Sometimes the best dick is a small dick," though you'll never see *that* in a subject line.

Anyway, here's a quaint selection of penis-enlarger subject lines:

There's the impress-a-female approach—"Women have always said: Size Matters!" . . . "No girl will give U a damn if U have little pe-nis" . . . "Hey My Girl Bought Me the Patch" . . . "She likes my new weenie" . . . "I am lookin for a big man like U! C*U*M* to me!" . . . "Wanna be big enough to shock people?" . . . "You will leave her speechless" . . . "Make her scream OHHH YEAAA!"

But men also like to impress *other* men, as in "Feal proud when your in the locker room" and "Your friends will envy you"—(guaranteed up to 4 rock hard inches).

Plus some more choices for the road: "gipzyxdtcbidvd + yeilopcecsu" . . . "Keep praying eyes away!" . . . "Monster Cocks at Discount Price" . . . "impede her ybpajh" . . . "dont worry about ur stupid little penis, ha ha" . . . "do u think u still can fuck like those who has macho dick?" . . . "Every man wishes he had a larger penis" . . . "Be a man and add a third leg" . . . "Enlarge your Manhood" . . . "Increase your penis size in one day" . . . "my hole was bored out by the reaper" . . . "Be happy when you make love!" . . . "With these pills you can shoot cum like a porn star!" . . . "Penus Enlarged in 2 Hours!"

The misleading subject line is a popular method of tricking you. "Tickets arrived" led to this message: "there is no other way to enlarge your penis." This vague subject line—"Hey, shit happens"—and this non sequitur subject line—"Do you like oranges?"—both led to the same message: "Use this patch and it will grow i SWEAR. . ."

All right, so now the good news is that every man has a larger penis. However, the bad news is that none of them can get it *up*.

"I remember a spam," writes a friend, "about free Viagra after a Penis Enlargement operation that would take place someplace in Nigeria just before the search for my share of several hundred million dollars that my new friend is cutting me in on. Seems his dad stashed bullion in foreign accounts to which they'd have no access until I brought several thousand dollars first. Could have gotten way rich while erect for days while I fucked myself."

Another friend quotes a spam—"Massive rock-solid Erections, new natural product bmrgwhmsmnmb"—and adds, "I like how it turns into nonsense at the end. I kind of picture like it's a mild mannered guy at the beginning who takes the 'natural' Viagra somewhere in the middle and then by the end he's like the incredible Hulk with a hard-on so powerful he can't even make coherent sounds. Also: 'From Keith Moon: Re: Generic Viagra'—At least they have a sense of humor. Maybe they'll start coming from 'Rush Limbaugh' next."

And now for your reading pleasure, here's an erection selection:

"Stick it on you then stick it to her" (Viagra-like patch) . . . "Beef up the size of your willy" . . . "Bob Dole loves Viagra, so should you!" . . . "terrifying terpsichorean" . . . "The Assay Test" . . . "Men let the pillz do the talking" . . . "Is it time to upgrade your system?" . . . "You will be a sex machine"—(erectile dysfunction) . . . "condolence maverick expedition" . . . "Goodbye to Soft Equipment" . . . "Are you hard at work?"

"You blocked my ICQ" . . . "ur di.cky is so smalllll" . . . "Enh..anc,e_yo*ur RO . . . D" . . . "G*et a ,*B-UL^;K,Y 'PO*L;E" . . . "Incr*eas^e :D'IC^-K :LENGTH' easil'y" . . . "B^oost y-our c'onf'ide;nc,e" . . . ",T:h_e na_tio*na:l i;nfrast*ru:ctu re i:s fal:li^ng."

"Stay hard for 72 hours"—*Editor's note*: Viagra ads in magazines state, "You should call a doctor immediately if you ever have an erection that lasts more than 4 hours. If not treated right away, permanent damage to your penis could occur."

This vague subject line—"Hi"—led to this message: "Sometimes people call it 'Magic Lubricant.' Sometimes 'Power Bottle.' Why? An amazing erection WITHIN SEVERAL SECONDS is guaranteed to you! Double-strengthed orgasm and full satisfaction."

Both "Can I Make It Up to You?" and "One Last Question" are spam subject lines for this message: "Did you know you could discreetly order Viagra over the Internet? You don't have to go through all the problems of getting it in a local pharmacy store or explaining your problems to the doctor." And then there was this charming misleader: "Enlarge your Bank Account 2-3 inches in days."

Okay, so now all these horny men have gigantic penises and also the medical means to help them defy gravity and become oh so erect, but there's simply nobody around with whom to share these huge hard-ons. That's where Internet porn—a $10 billion industry—comes to the rescue.

"Amateur Girls Never Before Seen" . . . "Fresh hot assets" . . . "Drunk party babes" . . . "Wow—Screwing Machines" . . . "Bondage at Mistress Shaved's Nasty Fetish Club" . . . "Pussies Getting Slammed" . . . "Pregnant Girls Getting Laid!" . . . "Look inside a pussy with our dildo-cam" . . . "watch this girl get her poousy lips get parted with a tongue" . . . "Big Clits—Monster Clits" . . . "enter this place and you willl see hard nipples and pink beavers" . . . "I have a multi-colored bush for you to see" . . . "The Executive's Dream"—(your secretary is a dirty little thing, and wants your Man Meat!)

"Hey, *psst*, you wanna see some nice breasts? Try these for size: "All we have are Breasts!" . . . "Do You Like Tits"—(100,000+ pics of big titty girls) . . . "Big Huge Breasts" . . . "Melon size boobies" . . . "Jumbo Juggy Jugs" . . . "Big juicy titties" . . . "Petite Little Boobs . . ."

How about interracial? "Choked white whores used as black cum recepticals" . . . "White Ladies and Dark Meat Look of Pain!" Or what about international? "Nasty Asian sex" . . . "Viet Yummy" . . . "Latin girls getting fucked" . . . "Re: travel plans"—(We've got girls from countries all over Asia spreading their pink pussies) . . . "I put the stalian back in Italian. . . ."

Do you prefer four-legged friends? "Watch me fuck a poodle" . . . "Oh my God, I had S-E-X With My Dog!" . . . "Meet Harvey the pussy eating wonder dog!" . . . "Teen takes a horse dong deep inside her flower" . . . "She takes the 20 inch horse pole" . . . "The real farm movie they tried to ban"—(guess Ramo's [the horse's] cock size and win a free ticket to the show) . . . "Dacy Does Donkeys" . . . "S*X WITH PETS"—(Taken to the Xtreme) . . . "This is sicker than Michael Jackson's daycare"—(girls with farm animals) . . . "Hot women do everything in my car"—(You ever wanted to see a live donkey show?) *Editor's note*: Gosh, that must be a very large car.

You dig first-timers? "Angel's First Facial" . . . "Erika's First five finger Experience" . . . "First Time Lesbians!"

Know how to make (or take) a fist? "Miss Fist-a-Lot!" . . . "Porn Queens Fistfucked for Real" . . . "Get Your Fisting Party Started!"

Got oral sex? "Cum Squad Squat!" . . . "Free pics of teen Sluts Sucking Almighty Cocks!" . . . "Teens covered in cum!" . . . "Young Pussy Lickers" . . .

"Girls love to tasty cum" . . . "Shooting Incident"—(Max Cumshot) . . . "See them spurt!"—(Cumshakes, Thousands of Hot Cum Covered Girls) . . . "I blew my load all over her"—(Facial Fiasco) . . . "She swallowed it all, Cum splattered all over her face" . . . "Jizz drizzled all over my face help me!" . . . "Sarah sucking balls" . . . "Bite that cock!"

Or maybe anal? "Doing Her Ass" . . . "My Girl Likes Anal Sex" . . . "Nasty Girls Doing Backdoor" . . . "I've applied to 4 Universities, but this one has the best programs"—(We're going to send you to Anal University).

Golden shower, anyone? "She's a Pee Fanatic!" . . . "She peed on me!"

Age is no barrier: "Virgin Schoolgirls" . . . "Cranky debutantes" . . . "Teen sluts gone wild" . . . "Tight Teen Cunts" . . . "watch me spread this teens Pucey lips" . . . "Ordinary Girls with Spread Legs—naughty girls fresh out of high school" . . . "Cute girls in college spreading their legs" . . . "Aged woman spreads legs" . . . "Loving for grannies" . . . "Hot Nude Granny"—(The Premier Mature Lady Site).

Neither is gender a barrier. "Crazy Gay Action only the BIGGEST Gay Cocks Inside" . . . "New reality site with young boys" . . . "Gay closet movies" . . . "sex crazed lesbians" . . .

Nor marriage vows. "I'm ready to cheat on my husand" . . . "With the kids asleep, mom gets wild and kinky" . . . "Sit back, relax and get a blow job from a woman at EZ Cheatng tonight" . . . "watch these ladies get nailed while the kids are in bed" . . . "in here is over 5 hundred thousand pictures of hot moms naked" . . . "Look at a hot mom taking a shower and shaving her vagina" . . . "The State Survey"—(How many children do you claim? Real yummy mummys) . . . "Don't Be Shy" and "Please don't tell anyone"—(both lead to "a revolutionary new service connecting cheating wives with single men.")

Celebrities in home-made sex videos are of course a special treat on the World Wide Web, from Pamela Anderson to Paris Hilton. From "Paris Hilton just drinks love juice" and "Paris Hilton is on a see men diet" to "J. Lo's Nipples" and "J. Lo caught eating a booger"—whatever turns you on.

Here, have a subject-line montage: "Bob said you'd want this" . . . "Naked Girls Next Door"—(Enter here to fuck these hot girls) . . . "(no subject)"—(Do you ever find yourself thinking about what it would be like to see naked girls all day?) . . . "lusty transvestites take picture for you" . . . "Upskirt panty peaks" . . . "Her cherrry gets popped!" . . . "Watch these young teens get exploited—severely!" . . . "100% hot bitches" . . . "As vulg@r as it getz" . . . "The sickest place on earth"—(midgets, animals, trannies, fisting, pregnant, enemas) . . . "Unreal Penetrations" . . . "Security Guards F_ucking Hot Girls" . . . "Take care"—(Insane orgies) . . . "3 Girls gangbanged" . . . "These Guys Don't have a Chance!"—(Hot Young locals Seduce Unknowing Tourist!) . . . "Stop wasting money on women!"

These are spam subject lines that have a certain sexual aura, but lead you to non-sexual messages: "Do you know I love you"—(money lender) . . . "See my newest movie"—(Wholesale prescription medicines) . . . "As good as it gets"— (online poker) . . . "It is hard"—(Banned CD, Government don't want me to sell it. Your own FBI file, driving record, criminal databases) . . . "We Got the Spread"—(Nude, but click here to bet now! NFL odds) . . . "Beach Girls"—(Forget Aging and Dieting forever) . . . "First Time"—(for both "Wholesale prescription medications at bargain prices" and "Term-life coverage at reduced rates is now available") . . . "I can come" and "Corrupted existentially" both lead to weight-loss messages.

Or, a subject line can appear to be political, such as "How Saddam Survived," which turned out to be a pitch for a growth hormone releaser from the American Society For the Treatment of Aging.

And finally, here's my own personal favorite spam, which came from Dark-Profits.com. The subject line reads: "Your credit card has been charged for $234.65"—which leads to the following message, headlined *Important Notice*:

"We have just charged your credit card for money laundry service in amount of $234.65 (because you are either child pornography webmaster or deal with dirty money, which require us to laundry them and then send to your checking account). If you feel this transaction was made by our mistake, please press 'No.' If you confirm this transaction, please press 'Yes' and fill in the form below. Enter your credit card number here. Enter your credit card expiration date."

In the immortal words of Bart Simpson, "I didn't think it was physically possible, but this both sucks and blows."

Postscript: Had to share this one: Spam subject line: "Ethan is the paper ready yet?" The message: "Make her scream with joy! Become the 9 incher today!" Also, 40 days before the 2004 presidential election, I spotted a new—though temporary—trend. Here are a few subject lines, courtesy of Viagra: "Kerry Isn't Feeling Well"; "George Bush Is a Liar"; and "Breaking News: Osama Bin Laden Captured."

TV SHOWS OF THE NEAR FUTURE

Although reality has been nipping at the heels of satire for many years, reality has increasingly been overtaking satire. I thought of a TV show called *Feng Shui Vigilantes*, only to find out there are *already* similar series, such as *While You Were Out*. So here I am, trying to extrapolate on industry trends in order to forecast programs of the future, while simultaneously hoping that none of them will be on the air by the time you read this.

The News Dude—Recent polls indicate that less and less young people watch the network news. In order to entice that demographic, a 19-year-old will deliver the evening news accompanied by appropriate music. For example, when reporting the latest corporate crime, this one involving the Carlyle Group, he will be backed by a tape of Jimmy Cliff singing "The Harder They Come, the Harder They Fall."

Snitch—At last viewers will be like flies on the wall, free to observe, in the comfort of their living rooms, paid informants divulge information to their control officers. A split screen will reveal the informee reacting to a monitor in the greenroom. Security will be very tight. The show will be hosted by Bill Maher who, at the NORML convention, outed Ted Turner and Harrison Ford as pot smokers; that pair will perform a hilarious parody of the good cop/bad cop syndrome in the pilot. (Maher has since outed himself as a toker.)

Tips for Terrorists—This is a spin-off of those segments on the news, originally intended to inform American citizens about the plethora of vulnerabilities in our infrastructure. However, intelligence agents learned that international terrorists were busy taking notes, ever vigilant for weaknesses in this, their target country. When the first episode is aired—disclosing the lack of security at the nine dams scattered around Los Angeles—it will be attacked as stretching the First Amendment too far, but defended as the risk of democracy.

The Gay Mafia—This series, *The Sopranos* meets *Will and Grace*, has an all-gay cast. The doubly-stereotypical gang extorts interior decorators and runs gay bathhouses. Softcore-porn scenes with bumping buttocks occur each episode. Limp wrists are in, stiff dicks are out. Dialogue ("Who moved my soap opera?") and T-shirts ("It's OK to Be Hetero") serve as cute condiments.

Pot Party—An ongoing reality show for those who find themselves smoking marijuana alone, but feel more gregarious to at least see fellow stoners on the screen passing joints around the room, talking, laughing, listening to music and munching the hours away.

Voices From Hell—This show will be the result of an FCC equal-time requirement in response to such mediums as James Van Praagh and John Edward, who hear only from departed souls that are in Heaven.

The D Files—D, of course, is for disinformation. Ever since the Bush administration announced that there would be an Office of Disinformation—and then, as its first official act, the Office of Disinformation announced that there would not be an Office of Disinformation after all—folks have been wondering what they're clandestinely up to. This game show provides the answers, as contestants attempt to distinguish between facts and propaganda.

Libel—Each week a panel of experts in public relations will take a completely unknown person and, like alchemists transforming underground buzz into mainstream awareness, they will turn the subject into an instant commodity with total name recognition. When that project is successfully completed, then the panel will carry out a vigorous campaign to libel those same individuals, who cannot sue because they are now public figures.

The Nielsen Family—Sponsors used to depend on the number of eyeballs that a TV show could deliver. But, since a study indicated that scenes of sex and violence tend to distract from the viewer's attention to commercials, this new series is actually *intended* to be dull, thus aiming for quality—that is, brand-name consciousness—rather than quantity. And, indeed, the ratings should soar to the top, perhaps because it will feature a different Nielsen family each week, and all the other Nielsen families will watch it regularly.

Celebrity Enemas—Executives at the Fox network will readily admit that it was a real challenge to develop this particular series. "It was important," according to one spokesperson, "that this program be presented in a tasteful manner." At first agents and publicists alike refused to return calls from segment producers. But when John Goodman agreed to participate in the pilot, then other celebs started volunteering. "I'm on a special diet," the portly actor stated—"low salt and high colonics." The program is sponsored by Starbucks to help promote their new coffee enema, the Anal Latte.

The Reality Café—Viewers will find this documentary series truly riveting, what with the ups and downs of a posh specialty restaurant which serves only those items that have been eaten by contestants on shows such as *Fear Factor*.

The menu includes grubs, worms, huge hissing cockroaches, rancid cheese teeming with maggots, rat stew, reindeer testicles and horse rectums.

Laugh Track—Even diehard sitcom fans have grown tired of listening to the reconstituted sound of an audience that had originally been laughing at *I Love Lucy* and is now ostensibly laughing at *Everybody Loves Raymond.* Virtually all of them are dead, but it's the only form of an afterlife that I can conceive. *Laugh Track* will present clips of all new laughter, with the only visual being that of the studio audience laughing. It will serve as must-see TV for those who want their own laughter to be stimulated only by pure peer pressure without any interference from content.

Godspin—Every Sunday morning, representatives from a variety of religions—including cult leaders and professional skeptics—will discuss spiritual matters in a lively fashion. Such topics as the following will be explored: "Does the Deity Have an Awareness of Itself?" "Can Blasphemy Be a Form of Prayer?" "What Motivates Suicide Bombers?" "Should 'Under God' in the Pledge of Allegiance Be Changed to 'Inside God'?" And, "Did Jesus Masturbate or Did He Merely Have Nocturnal Emissions?"

Law and Frivolity—Courtroom dramas of plaintiffs suing TV networks for forcing them to waste time, forgo reading, and remain poorly informed.

UNDER THE COUNTERCULTURE

Marijuana vs. Cigarettes

The war on drugs is really a war on *some* people who use *some* drugs.

In 2004, the White House anti-drug campaign spent $170 million on insidious propaganda, working closely with the Partnership for a Drug-Free America, which was founded and funded by tobacco, alcohol and pharmaceutical companies.

As long as any government can arbitrarily decide which drugs are legal and which drugs are illegal, then all those individuals who serve time behind bars for illegal drugs are actually political prisoners.

I am most likely one of the very few who actually believed that former president Bill Clinton was telling the truth when he said he had tried smoking marijuana but that he didn't inhale because he wasn't a cigarette smoker and didn't really know how to inhale. That's exactly what happened with me, a noncigarette-smoker, the first time I tried smoking pot, but of course I persisted until I got it right.

I've been a pot smoker for almost 40 years, but recently I stopped for a month, just as a change of pace, and I had no withdrawal symptoms. I was simply aware at first of all the times I felt tempted, out of habit, to enhance every experience with marijuana. I wanted to smoke a joint before eating dinner, before listening to music, before making love, before going to the movies and before rolling a joint.

On the other hand, according to Dr. James West, outpatient medical director at the Betty Ford Center, "Smoking cigarettes is probably the most difficult addiction to break. Most recovering alcoholics who quit smoking will say that it was harder to quit smoking than to quit alcohol. About 70% of alcohol-dependent individuals are heavy smokers—more than one pack of cigarettes per day— compared with 10% of the population. Alcoholics eventually die from lung cancer more often than from alcohol-related causes."

The priorities are insane. Cigarettes cause 1,200 deaths every day, in this country alone. Nearly 2,000 young people under the age of 18 become smokers every day in America. And yet, although the World Health Organization spent three years working out an agreement with 171 countries to prevent the spread of smoking-related diseases, particularly in the developing world, the United States opposed the treaty, including the minimum age of 18 for sales to minors. Around the globe, tobacco now kills almost five million people a year. Within a generation, predicts WHO, the premature death toll will reach ten million a year.

Whereas, with marijuana, the worst that can happen is maybe you'll have a severe case of the munchies and raid somebody's refrigerator.

Boston Globe columnist Ellen Goodman writes, "Americans are fighting tobacco addiction at home while our government is supporting it abroad. In fact, the administration thinks tobacco companies should be allowed to market overseas in ways that are prohibited here—with everything from free samples to sponsorship of youth events. When it comes to tobacco, we are standing outside the world community like a nicotine junkie on a city sidewalk, huffing and puffing away."

In October 2003, Health Canada released the results of a study which found that more teenagers smoke pot than cigarettes. Fifty-four percent of 15- to 19-year-olds said they had smoked marijuana more than once. Conversely, cigarette smoking has continued to decline among Canadian youths, with the latest national figures showing that only 22% of teens smoke regularly.

In December, Associated Press reported that, in the U.S., an annual survey known as Monitoring the Future (funded by the National Institute on Drug Abuse), tracked drug use and attitudes among 48,500 students from 392 schools, concluding that marijuana remains by far the most widely used illegal drug. It has been tried at least once by 46% of 12th graders and used by more than a third in the past year.

John Walters, director of the White House Office of National Drug Control Policy, stated at a news conference that surveys in 15 cities have found that more teens smoke marijuana than regular cigarettes. However, the drug czar added, "More kids are seeking treatment for marijuana dependency than all other drugs combined." And in March 2005, Associated Press reported, "Treatment rates for marijuana nearly tripled between 1992 and 2002, the government says, attributing the increase to greater use and potency. 'This report is a wake-up call for parents that marijuana is not a soft drug,' said Tom Riley, a spokesman for the White House Office of National Drug Control Policy. 'It's a much bigger part of the addiction problem than is generally understood.'"

Both Walters and Riley neglected to mention how many young "addicts" have sought treatment for marijuana dependency as their only alternative to prison time.

For those who are truly dedicated *tobacco* addicts, though, there's a porn Web site featuring *Smokin' Hot Sluts*—"the largest archive of gorgeous girls who love to smoke before, during and after sex." Internet seekers are invited to "Tell our live babes your deepest, nastiest smoking fantasies, and they'll fulfill your dreams."

But what could such smoking fantasies possibly be? I quote: "Fuck my smoldering hot ass!" "Lesbian smoke orgies!" "Slide your filter tip deep inside me!" And, as if intended specifically for Bill Clinton and Monica Lewinsky, "Inhale and swallow!"

PREGNANCY AND POT

Trent Lott, who had to resign as Senate Majority Leader for his racist blooper, was also heavily anti-reproductive rights. Concerning legislation banning abortion, he once vowed on the radio, "I will call it up, we will pass it, and the president willl sign it. I'm making that commitment—you can write it down." The trickle-down immorality of such a promise has been harassment, fake anthrax mailings, segragationist-modelled blockades, violence, death threats and assassination.

Recently, Bob Rowell of the South Jersey Clinic Defense Coalition, responded to a fluff piece about the local anti-choice movement, titled "Gentle Persuasion," in the *Courier-Post*. In a letter to the editor, he wrote:

"Many local 'gentle persuaders' have made statements that were supportive of the terrorists who bombed clinics and perpetrated fatal sniper attacks against doctors and staffs. The article was as misguided as publishing a feature on the gentle persuaders of al-Queda. In fact, one can easily compare the rhetoric of the 9/11 attackers and groups like Army of God, Missionaries To The Preborn, and Life Dynamics (supporters of anti-choice sniper James Kopp) and see for themselves."

Of course, the term pro-choice means exactly what it says. And, just as the Plaster Casters became infamous for immortalizing the erect penises of various rock stars, women who are expecting babies can now immortalize their expanded bellies in all their three-dimensional glory by making plaster belly casts. Proud-

Body, a Colorado company, sells a do-it-yourself kit that allows mothers-to-be to create a belly cast in less than an hour.

But let's say that, like a friend of mine, you're a pregnant woman living in Florida and you enjoy smoking marijuana. She wrote:

"If you test positive at your first visit to a hospital (when all pregnant women are given a blood test), then you must continue to be tested until you're negative. Furthermore, the hospital is required to test you again at the time of birth, and if it's positive, the HRS—that's like Children and Families, the health department—will take your baby and will not give it back until you test negative, and will then continue to give regular tests. This is just one of the state's stupid laws, passed because of the preponderance of crackheads we have here. For the first five months of my pregnancy, I smoked about half a joint a week, and then I didn't smoke at all. I tested negative at the time of delivery."

On the other hand, if you give birth at home with the aid of a contemporary midwife, it's quite possible that you will be passed a joint to enhance the experience.

In Great Britain, even if you're not pregnant, a motion proposed by female members of Unison—one of England's largest trade unions—called for the legalization of marijuana because it helps women chill out without gaining weight. The motion included this statement: "Cannabis can be used for women to relax and de-stress without calories, in contrast to alcohol or chocolate."

This is not a new idea. One hundred years ago, Morphine Tea Parties were popular with women. The practice originated in Paris, where there were female morphine clubs. A number of ladies would meet around 4 o'clock every afternoon—who knows, maybe even at 4:20—and tea would be served. The servants would be sent out of the room, and the door would be locked.

Then the guests would bare their arms, and the hostess would produce a small hypodermic syringe. She would administer an injection to each person one by one. Sharing needles was not a problem in those days. And if one injection was not sufficient to satisfy any particular guest, then a second or even a third injection was given.

Recently, however, the exceedingly proper *British Medical Journal* weighed in negatively on any such practice: "It is only too true that alcoholism, morphinism, cocainism, and other supposed means of getting beyond a monotonous daily life are becoming increasingly prevalent among women, and it is also only too true that there is no ruin so utter as a woman's ruin from such causes.

"Opium as a reliever of pain may still be regarded as 'the gift of the gods,' but for those who use it for its mental effect, it is fraught with the utmost danger, none the less because the one motive may merge so easily into the other, and none the less because of the ease with which the subject of a single administration may stumble into an enthralling habit, for the greater the relief from one, the greater is the danger from the other."

Meanwhile, the Eugene (Oregon) *Register Guard* reported that what sounded to angry residents like a war zone around dawn turned out to be, not a terrorist attack, but rather just another example of the inhumane insanity of the drug war. Police served a search warrant for the alleged growing of marijuana. They enlisted an armored personnel carrier and 45 SWAT team officers armed with shotguns and automatic rifles to raid a cluster of houses.

But, after throwing flash-bang grenades, kicking in doors, and handcuffing four people—including one nude woman and one woman dressed only in underpants and a T-shirt—for hours in a room in one of the houses, police came up completely empty-handed. The invaders also admitted to having placed a black bag over the head of one of the women until she agreed to cooperate with them. Ah, equality for women at last.

Lucky she wasn't pregnant.

BONG WARS: TOMMY CHONG
AIN'T THE ONLY ONE

"The business of America is business," said Calvin Coolidge, 30th president of the United States. No wonder it was the front page of the *Los Angeles Times* Business section that reported the DEA's recent cluster of raids on head shops and Internet sites selling drug paraphernalia, an industry estimated to be worth $1 billion a year.

Several weeks earlier, after tougher laws on paraphernalia went into effect, the California Department of Alcoholic Beverages wanted liquor licenses suspended at ten stores accused of selling "rose tubes"—4-inch-long glass tubes with miniature fake roses—to undercover agents who asked for crack pipes.

Even before then, the war was already escalating, and generating a ripple effect. One student was suspended from high school because he displayed a banner that said "Bong Hits 4 Jesus" although it occurred on a public sidewalk off school property. And a married couple was arrested for contributing to the delinquency of their teenagers because they gave them bongs for Christmas.

Consider the case of Chris Hill. In order to avoid a potential 20-year sentence on drug paraphernalia charges, he accepted a plea bargain and agreed to serve 14 months in prison. His firm, Chills, a distributor of pipe and tobacco accessories, had been named in *Inc* magazine as one of the nation's 500 fastest-growing companies, and prior to his arrest in August 2001, he was chosen as of of America's top 500 young businessmen by the National Republican Congressional Committee.

The DEA seized Chills pipes from three Iowa tobacco shops which also sold pro-marijuana posters and books. Agents next went to Florida, raided Hill's business and home, handcuffing him in front of two infant daughters. His home and all vehicles were confiscated, he was fined $500,000, lost his warehouse building and manufacturing equipment, and faced bankruptcy.

The prosecuting U.S. Attorney claimed that Hill's logo—which features a space alien with the words "World Domination"—was evidence of a criminal conspiracy to take over the world. He responded that the prosecutors had been watching too many James Bond movies, adding sarcastically, "Maybe I should get a little white cat and shave my head."

Since 1990, federal law has made drug paraphernalia violators subject to RICO—Racketeer Influenced and Corrupt Organization—and money laundering charges. Jerry Clark and Kathy Fiedler ran a shop called Daydreams, which turned into a nightmare when they were raided by the DEA, U.S. Postal Inspectors, local cops and sheriff's deputies—and the RICO act was used against them, so that they faced 10 to 12 years behind bars.

Under federal law, merely manufacturing, distributing or selling non-traditional pipes is enough evidence to be found guilty of paraphernalia offenses. Authorities insist that companies can no longer protect themselves by posting signs or Internet warnings which indicate that their products are intended for tobacco use only.

And so I hereby call to the attention of law enforcement officials an article in the January 27, 2003 issue of *Time* magazine, which states: "At cafés around UCLA and in college towns across the country, students are passing around the hookah, the ancient Middle Eastern water pipe filled with sweetened tobacco. . . .

[I]n the past couple of years, the hookah has been resurrected in youth-oriented coffeehouses, restaurants and bars. . . . The Gypsy Cafe, which has been in business for 15 years, serves up as many as 200 hookahs a night at $10 a pipe. At the Habibi, which opened two years ago . . . smokers have rented more than 500 hookahs in a night. . . . Young patrons of the lounges agree that part of the hookah's charm lies in its illicit associations. 'It looks illegal,' says [a] Gypsy customer, 18, with a grin, sucking on his hookah with the insouciance of the blue caterpillar in *Alice in Wonderland*, 'but it's not.'"

And, just in case you guys at the DEA missed it, a guest on *Late Night* gave Conan O'Brien a beautiful bong, and he kept it! Hurry, it's still in his possession. He plans to use it as a glass-eye holder, but that doesn't matter, you can still bust him.

The cruel absurdity of anti-paraphernalia laws is underscored by the creative substitutes, such as apples, soda cans, toilet-paper cardboard tubes and aluminum foil, tweezers used as roach clips, and don't forget those plain old, regular *tobacco* pipes. Indeed, in Fulton, Kentucky, police investigating a marijuana-smoking complaint, found pot burning on a backyard grill with a large fan on the other side of the house, sucking the smoke through the home, in effect, said the police chief, "turning the house into a large marijuana bong." Seize it immediately, boys!

At a press conference announcing the February raids, Attorney General John Ashcroft went out of his way to praise the DEA, which had been criticized earlier this year, in a White House budget office assessment of government performance, as being "unable to demonstrate its progress." Yes, the business of America is indeed business, and all that those DEA agents ultimately want is simply to keep their jobs.

THE TRIAL OF IRA EINHORN

As I write this, the trial of Ira Einhorn for the murder of his girlfriend, Holly Maddux, is scheduled to begin. I have no doubt that he did it, but whatever the verdict, here are several facts, most of which will not be revealed in the courtroom.

Einhorn claims that the CIA framed him because he knew too much about mind-control technology, top secret weapons and unidentified flying objects. Yet they didn't assassinate *him*. Instead, he insists, they bludgeoned *her* to death, stuffing her body into a padlocked steamer trunk in a locked closet in his apartment.

Downstairs neighbors complained that "bodily fluids" were seeping down through their ceiling and staining their kitchen wall. Einhorn never investigated the godawful smell in his own apartment during the 18 months before he was apprehended. But why bother? He already knew that the stench was caused by her decomposing remains. One witness heard noisy thumps and a scream around the time Maddux disappeared. Another was asked by Einhorn to help him dump the trunk, explaining that it contained "top secret" documents.

Einhorn had a reputation for being violent toward women. I was tripping on LSD the day I met him in 1968, and he reeked with vibes of manipulation. Later on, I dated one of his former girlfriends, and she verified for me what an egomaniacal control freak he had been.

The media reported that he founded Earth Day and was the master of ceremonies at their event in Philadelphia. In reality, his mission there was to seize the microphone and proceed to hog it for half an hour. This so-called hippie guru was really an opportunistic scam artist. He became the New Age advisor to mainstream powermongers, consulting with corporations and politicians alike.

His $40,000 bail money, which he jumped on the eve of his first pre-trial hearing, was put up and sacrificed by Seagram heiress Barbara Bronfman. She sent him thousands more while he was on the lam, and alerted him when authorities were closing in. She was not charged with aiding and abetting a fugitive. Einhorn claimed that the reason he fled the United States was because he would not have received a fair hearing since he had once organized demonstrations against the Vietnam war.

When the way was cleared for his extradition from France, he slashed his neck with a dull bread-knife. There were superficial cuts but heavy bleeding. He was in and out of the emergency room, his wound considered not life-threatening. Coincidentally, a psychiatrist on *The Sopranos* described such an act as a "suicidal *gesture* as opposed to a suicidal *attempt*—'small cutting' is the clinical term."

After Einhorn was back behind bars, the *Philadelphia Daily News* published an article:

"Right about now, those prized Jersey beefsteak tomatoes are maturing into plump, succulent fruits ripe for the picking. We recommend you leave them on the vine just a little bit longer . . . when they will be finished growing. And ready for throwing. By then, they should be overripe, thin-skinned, seedy, worm-rav-aged, and perhaps even a little smelly, just like some ex-fugitive-murderer we all know: Ira 'The Blade' Einhorn. You can still take a shot at a reasonable fac-simile of his smug mug laid out on a giant billboard. That's right, the second annual Ira Einhorn 'Killer Tomato' contest is less than two weeks away. . . .

"Owner of the homegrown tomato that best exhibits the characteristics of the killer—thin-skinned, ripe-smelling and seedy—wins a trip to Alcatraz. Oth-ers presenting tomatoes get a chance to toss their fruit at the billboard."

In response to a column in the *News*, local radio host Bob Rowell wrote:

"Einhorn got a brief taste of the media limelight during the first Earth Day event, but was anything but a 'counterculture hero' or 'darling of the left.' Even before the murder, he was widely perceived to be insincere, phony and a con. The column was obviously a cheap shot at a subculture that the writer clearly despises. Einhorn and Manson were two murderers who were never embraced by the counterculture. Actually, they had much more in common with the *con-tras* and homicidal elements of some law enforcement entities."

Time magazine published a photo of Einhorn with Abbie Hoffman, proclaim-ing them to be friends. Not true. They met only once, at a 1968 conference of col-lege newspaper editors in Washington. However, Einhorn did cultivate a relationship with Hoffman's co-founder of the Yippies, Jerry Rubin. Anita Hoff-man, the keeper of Abbie's image, wrote a letter of complaint to *Time*.

An episode of *South Park* included a character that was openly a parody of Ein-horn, repeatedly warning that "Republicans are ruining the world," and using brainwashing techniques to force children into celebrating Earth Day. Later, he chops a young child to pieces. Yes, "the bastard killed Kenny!"

Among David Letterman's *Top 10 Reasons to Flee* was this one: "If your new roommate says, 'No matter what you hear, don't open this trunk.'"

While teaching an alternative education course in the 1960s at the University of Pennsylvania, Einhorn once stripped naked and danced in the classroom after passing around marijuana to the students.

And finally, his ironic and irrelevant position on the drug war: "SWAT teams are not the solution to soft drugs. Compassion must rule wherein medical mar-ijuana is concerned. Hemp should flourish, along with free energy and the UFO information that would allow people to create it."

Postscript: Ira Einhorn was found guilty by a jury, and he is currently serving a life sentence.

HIPPIES WITH CELL PHONES

At first I thought the Oregon Country Fair would be like a mainstream state fair, with greased pigs and gigantic tomatoes and bumper cars. But I was wrong. This was the 33rd annual fair, celebrating the continuity of countercultural values, a weekend oasis at lush campgrounds near Eugene, peaking with 18,000 attendees.

It was the first year that there would be speakers in addition to music, crafts, food and creative tomfoolery. A headline in the statewide daily, the *Oregonian*, announced: "Ram Dass, Krassner Will Talk at Country Fair." The article included the following:

"Ram Dass, the former Harvard psychologist who became a psychedelic pioneer and an admired spiritual teacher, will speak at the fair at 1:45 p.m. Sunday. Paul Krassner, a writer and comic who says he's taken LSD with Ken Kesey, Dass, Timothy Leary and Groucho Marx (among many others), also will speak on Sunday afternoon and is scheduled to introduce Dass. That could be interesting, especially because a note on Dass' Web site takes issue with a recent profile of Dass that Krassner wrote for *High Times* magazine. In it, Krassner wrote that Dass has retracted a story about how Dass once gave Maharaj Ji (his guru) a high dose of LSD and nothing happened.

"'Just to set the record straight,' reads the note on the Web site, 'it is Krassner's allegation which was fiction. Ram Dass was shocked by the statement in the article, and vehemently denies it. Krassner attributes the statement to some unnamed source, and admits that he did not check it with Ram Dass before publication.' In other words, Dass says he did not give Maharaj Ji a high dose of LSD and nothing happened. The amazing thing about this episode is not that these people are arguing about who gave how much LSD to whom, but that they can even remember any of it."

Ram Dass and I have been friends for four decades, and I wrote a personal apology to him—"I hope you understand that in the context of a totally positive article, my intention was to reveal what I thought was a true example of the rascal aspect of your personality"—and a public retraction in *High Times*. We hadn't crossed paths since, and now I was slightly nervous, but he greeted me with a smile and a warm embrace.

"I know you love me," I said, "but do you forgive me?"

Ram Dass laughed and replied, "There's nothing to forgive."

He re-tells that story about giving acid to his guru in an illuminating 2002 documentary, *Ram Dass: Fierce Grace*. Producer-director Mickey Lemle says, "When I first met Ram Dass 25 years ago, one of his messages that touched me was that we are both human and divine and that we must hold both simultaneously. He would explain that if one goes too far in the direction of one's humanity, one suffers. If one goes too far in the direction of one's divinity, one runs the risk of forgetting one's postal [Zip] code.

"So his stories and teachings were funny, self-effacing, and with an extraordinary grasp of the metaphysical. In form and content, his stories are about living on those two planes of consciousness, and the tension between them. His explorations took an unvited turn when he suffered a massive stroke in February 1997. Now, he has been forced to live his teachings in a way he had not expected. He uses his current predicament to help others—one can see why he is considered one of the great spiritual teachers of our time, and how he is able to see his stroke as grace, *fierce grace*."

In the documentary, Ram Dass comments: "This isn't who I expected to be—my expectation didn't have this stroke in it. Suffering comes when you try to hold onto continuity. I can't shift my car. It's so captivating to the consciousness, like I wanna see how the stroke capitulates my mind and then I wanna pull my consciousness out and be free in the middle of the stroke—an experiment in consciousness.

"I feel like an advance guard that calls back to the baby boomers, and now I call back about aging and things like stroke that are going to be in their present much sooner than they think. . . . My guru said suffering brings me so close to God. I was galumphing through life before the stroke, and I kind of thought that was it, that was all there was, but the stroke, it's like a whole new incarnation."

At the country fair, on stage in his wheelchair, Ram Dass talked about his current struggle to love George W. Bush, and I had a flashback to thirty years ago, when he talked about his struggle to love Richard Nixon. He explained that he loves Bush's *soul* and that Bush just happened to get a terrible incarnation this time around.

Ram Dass advised the audience to "take the ambiance of this fair into our lives because the instrument of greatest social action is the individual heart. Heart to heart rescusitation."

At dinner, he described the fair as resembling "a medieval village."

"Except," I observed, "there are hippies with cell phones."

In fact, a group of environmentalists were walking around the campgrounds with a placard: "No Fair for Cell Phones Near Schools and Homes." They went past a woman who was talking on a cell phone, but she stopped for a brief moment.

"No worries," she assured the group, "I am not a school or a house."

Organizer Laura Stewart told me. "This event is definitely into its second and third generation. Children learn that it is okay to have fun with their parents, be passionate about life, and live with an open heart. The bliss from the Oregon County Fair flows into the surrounding communities all year round. Those who participate know that we are not alone in our beliefs and values. We are stronger, louder and more visible because of our unity in celebration."

This particular year, the fair had a theme: to honor the memory of Ken Kesey.

"There are those," I told the audience, "who now envision Kesey on that Great Psychedelic Bus in the Sky, with Neal Cassady at the wheel, Jerry Garcia on guitar, and Timothy Leary on acid. But Kesey's little grandchild, upon learning of his death, only wondered, 'Now who will teach us how to hypnotize the chickens?'"

The Merry Pranksters had parked the descendant of their psychedelic bus, "Furthur," outside the entrance, and they were selling posters to help raise money for a statue of Kesey in the town square. There were two factions in Eugene. One wanted the statue to be Kesey sitting on a bench, reading a book to his three grandchildren. The other wanted the statue to be Kesey sitting on a bench, toking on a joint. The first statue won out.

"I don't care," insists the sculptor of the pot-smoking statue. "I'm gonna do it anyway."

ONE HAND JERKING

WELCOME TO THE MASTURBATE-A-THON

This is for Ronald Castle, Sr., a supervisor with the Department of Social Services in upstate New York. A county employee for more than 30 years, he has been indefinitely suspended without pay while he is under investigation for harassment, criminal nuisance and public lewdness. He had been masturbating into the coffee cups of fellow employees. It gives new meaning to an old romantic song, "You're the Cream in My Coffee." Plus, Ronald Castle, *Jr.* is blessed with a renewed sense of gratitude that he is alive today, instead of having been burned to death at the moment of ejaculation and then swallowed by some unknowing caffeine addict.

But this was a case of self-love combined with other-hate, and if Castle is convicted, I believe he should be sentenced to a new kind of community service, where he can actually whack off for altruistic reasons. It started a few years ago when Good Vibrations, a shop in San Francisco specializing in sex toys, erotic books and adult videos, declared the month of May to be National Masturbation Month. A tradition was born. Since then, those in the know have been encouraged to obtain pledges from individuals and stores who sponsor their masturbatory events in cities across the country. The funds raised have been donated to various sex-positive causes.

Good Vibrations' online customers were reminded: "Make sure you're well-rested, with ready hands and plenty of batteries and lube—it's Masturbate-a-thon weekend! You still have time to sign up your friends and family to help you raise money for every minute you spend masturbating this weekend. Spread the message of healthy self-love and collect funds for some excellent charities, all with a big ol' smile on your face. Download the pledge from from our web site . . . Wank on!"

Gonzo sex writer and educator Theresa Reed, known as Darklady, organized and promoted—almost exclusively online—the first Masturbate-a-thon in Portland, Oregon. Her invitation stated, "Our special location will be revealed when you join the elite Benevolent Society of Masturbators (BOOM). Come dressed erotically (and patriotically?) . . ." There was indeed a patriotic theme: "Mastur-

bate Your Way to Freedom." Artist Steve Hess contributed the logo—an American Eagle clutching a vibrator and a tube of lube—and Darklady wore an Uncle
Sam jacket, a top hat and an American flag which did *not* say, "Don't come on me!"

The co-ed party—benefiting the National Coalition for Sexual Freedom, the
Center for Sex and Culture, and Planned Parenthood—would feature free food
and beverages, condoms and lubrication, DJ's and live bands, strippers and porn
stars, door prizes and streaming video onto the Internet. The ThrillHammer
Orgazmatron machine proved to be a most popular competition. The woman
who rode it the longest became the winner. She was crowned Miss Masturbate-
a-thon 2002 and was presented with a lovely tiara, not to mention the afterglow
of multiple orgasms galore.

There was a silent auction of goods donated by local businesses and national
sex celebrities. Although the Masturbate-a-thon provided its own redeeming
social value, informative literature was also available so that guests could learn
more about the charitable groups they were helping to support. Promotional
material from sponsoring companies was prominently displayed. Hey, can you
even remember when masturbation used to be considered a taboo subject and
shameful practice?

"Originally," Darklady told me, "I planned on hosting this party at my home,
as I've had many large sex parties there. However, when I began talking to the
ThrillHammer people, we decided something bigger would be in order. Being
online fanatics, we definitely wanted to go beyond the more grassroots, humble
'masturbate-at-home' events being held elsewhere. We held the party at the
wonderfully pro-sex space at Ascension Dungeon and had some of the most
agreeable and competent security folks I've had the privilege to work with.

"I was very impressed by the enthusiastic turn-out and the innovating things
people did. One man brought a pyramid-like sex swing, local cable host Harry
Lime came along with his camera crew to videotape the ThrillHammer fun, and
people flocked to both the camera-friendly and camera-free rooms. We had no
unpleasant incidents and everyone seemed to have a great time."

The doors to the Masturbate-a-thon opened at 6 p.m. and the party ended at
2 a.m. Guests had to sign a liability waiver "in case you slip in your own spunk."
The main room was masturbation-free. Beyond that was a large open space with
the Orgazmatron. "ThrillHammer excitement will be broadcast live on the Internet," Darklady announced, "but the shy and saucy can protect their identity and
still get a good internal massage by wearing one of the lovely masks generously

donated by Bad Attitude. A modesty screen will also shield the especially shy from view. Please limit yourself to masturbation as this is, after all, a celebration of self-love."

But May was not only National Masturbation Month. It was also officially designated as Teen Pregnancy Prevention Month. Isn't it nice when different causes can work together like that?

Virtual Rape on the Internet

Although the California Supreme Court has declared that a man may be convicted of rape if his sexual partner first consents but later changes her mind and asks him to stop, a victim of date rape is unable to take advantage of that ruling. As a preventive measure, however, there is now a product on the market—paper coasters which theoretically test for date rape drugs—that is ringing up more than $20 million a year in revenue. These coasters have test spots which are supposed to turn dark blue in 30 seconds if a splash of alcohol contains the drugs that are often used to incapacitate victims.

When Andrew Luster, the millionaire great-grandson of cosmetics tycoon Max Factor and recently captured fugitive, was on trial for date rape, his defense lawyers attempted unsuccessfully to prove that he was actually an aspiring porn producer who was merely practicing his craft when he directed films in which women were only pretending to be asleep while he had sex with them, and that Luster actually intended to sell his porn flicks on the Internet.

The attorneys were foiled in their attempt to show excerpts of Luster's home-made movies in order to counter testimony from women who would testify that they were drugged and raped at his beach house. Ironically, though, there are *actual* porn producers who merchandise rape videos, and they *too* claim that the women who are sexually assaulted are merely pretending to be raped. They may really be raped, who knows, but these companies are simply attempting to cover their *own* asses.

Scream and Cream, for example, includes this blatantly misspelled disclaimer on their Web site: "All models herein depicted were over 18 at the time of depiction and were copmensated [sic] for their play. We do not condoce [sic] non-done [sic] non-nocensual [sic] sex. This site is forced sex *fantasy* only."

Another Web site, *Forced Girls*, can't even spell their own name, as they promote "The #1 forsed [sic] site on the net." And here is their come-on: "Tired of seeing teens all over the net that look older than your mum? We are too, this is why we created this site jam packed with only the youngest, barely legal girls forced to fuck and suck, prosecuted [sic] by their capturers and brutally punished."

The *Shocking Extreme* Web site states, "Warning: Exclusive Content," as though exclusivity were something kinky and forbidden. "She has no hope of escape," they boast. "These guys are pro's [sic]."

Uncensored Russian Rapes describes itself as a "Unique Russian rape site with fully exclusive Russian content. Different rape situations, pictures like rape with weapons, rape in the cars, gang rape, teen rape, amateur rape plus hundreds of real rape movies."

There is an urban myth in Russia that having sex with a virgin will cure AIDS. This dangerous myth has resulted in an epidemic of HIV infected males violating virgins, especially teenagers, because of the insane belief that the younger the virgin, the more potent the cure.

"Do you want to rape a virgin too?" asks the site. "Enter at your own risk."

Although I don't believe that those who download child pornography should be arrested, I do think that those who *produce* kiddie porn should get busted. Likewise, although I don't believe that those who download sexual assault pornography should be arrested, I do think that those who *produce* rape porn should get busted—but only if it can be proven that the sex was non-consensual, and that ain't easy. In fact, it's virtually impossible.

In the *Village Voice*, Johnny Maldoro wrote about a video by porn director Lizzy Borden: "Part fictional snuff, over-the-top gore, and violent hard-core porn, *Forced Entry* won't be taking home any *AVN* awards, and might even force the mainstream media to momentarily focus on our country's largest entertainment industry. . . .

"To prove that her actresses knew what they were signing up for, Borden tacks a bunch of bloopers onto the end of *Forced Entry*. Veronica Caine's wig comes off! Other wacky antics on the set prove the non-exploitative and even friendly relations between cast and crew members! For instance, Taylor St. Claire is totally 'not pregnant.' Those guys weren't jumping on a *real* fetus."

In Pakistan, the main human rights group reveals that in 2002, at least 461 women were slain by family members in so-called "honor killings." In such cases, women are murdered to protect the "family honor" for "offenses" such as dating, talking to men, having sex outside marriage, cooking poorly—and being raped.

Whereas, here in the United States, there was a TV documentary about a church sponsored "Hell House"—which was intended to scare religious teenagers out of engaging in *any* kind of sexual activity—and one girl's reaction is worth placing in a time capsule for future reference.

"The rape scene is the best," she said, "because you get to dance."

MAILER ON MATING AND MASTURBATION

When Norman Mailer wrote his first novel, *The Naked and the Dead*, he used a euphemism—"fug"—for fuck. The first time I encountered Mailer, I asked him if it was true that when he met actress Tallulah Bankhead, she said, "So you're the young man who doesn't know how to spell fuck." With a twinkle in his eye, Mailer told me that he replied, "Yes, and you're the young woman who doesn't know how to."

I saw Mailer again at City Hall Park in New York at the height of the Cold War. We were both among a thousand citizens committing civil disobedience against the law that required us to seek shelter during an air raid drill. Umbrellas bearing the legend *Portable Fallout Shelter* were held up while the crowd sang "America the Beautiful."

As soon as the air raid siren sounded, the chief of police announced, "Officers, arrest those persons who do not seek shelter!" The cops seized those persons who were nearest to them, including Mailer. Then the all-clear siren sounded, and the rest of the protesters began to disperse.

When I originally launched *The Realist* in 1958, I had requested an interview with Mailer. He declined, but in 1962, after I published an interview with Joseph Heller when *Catch 22* was released, Mailer called me. He was finally ready. We met at his home in Brooklyn Heights. Mailer sat in a chair, poised like a prize-fighter. And I was his sparring partner.

In 1963, I performed stand-up at Town Hall. When I introduced Joseph Heller, somebody else stood up, but since the audience didn't know what Heller looked like, they applauded. "That's not Joseph Heller," I said from the stage. "This is right out of *Catch 22*."

Then I introduced Norman Mailer, and again somebody else stood up. This time it was a young woman. "I'm a friend of Norman's," she called out. "He couldn't come tonight."

"That's the story of his life," I responded. It was a cheap shot, but I couldn't resist. "He's writing another book about it," I added.

In my interview with Mailer, we had been talking about the mating process of two individuals. "It's mutually selective," he said. "You fall in together or go in together." Little did I dream that I would end up "falling in together" with that young woman in the audience, Jeanne Johnson. We got married and had a daughter, Holly.

At one point in the interview, Mailer stated that "a native village is bombed, and the bombs happen to be beautiful when they land; in fact, it would be odd if all that sudden destruction did not liberate some beauty. The form a bomb takes in its explosion may be in part a picture of the potentialities it destroyed. So let us accept the idea that the bomb is beautiful. If so, any liberal who decries the act of bombing is totalitarian if he doesn't admit as well that the bombs were indeed beautiful."

Q. "Aren't you implying that this beauty is an absolute?"

A. "Well, you don't know. How do you know beauty is not an absolute?"

Later, a whole segment of our interview had to do with masturbation. Now, 40 years later, in Mailer's new book, *The Spooky Art: Thoughts About Writing*, he reprints from the interview almost that entire section, but leaves out my favorite part:

Q. "Is it possible that you have a totalitarian attitude toward masturbation?"

A. "I wouldn't say all people who masturbate are evil, probably I would even say that some of the best people in the world masturbate. But I am saying it's a miserable activity."

Q. "Well, we're getting right back now to this notion of absolutes. You know—to somebody, masturbation can be a thing of beauty—"

A. "To what end? Who is going to benefit from it?"

Q. "It's a better end than the beauty of a bombing."

A. "Masturbation is bombing. It's bombing oneself."

Q. "I see nothing wrong if the only person hurt from masturbation is the one who practices it. But it can also benefit—look, Wilhelm Stekel wrote a book on auto-eroticism, and one of the points he made was that at least it saved some people who might otherwise go out and commit rape."

A. "It's better to commit rape than masturbate. Maybe, maybe. The whole thing becomes difficult."

Q. "But rape involves somebody else."

A. "Just talking about it on the basis of violence: one is violence toward oneself; one is violence toward others. Let's follow your argument and be speculative for a moment—if everyone becomes violent toward themselves, then past a certain point the entire race commits suicide. But if everyone becomes violent toward everyone else, you would probably have one wounded hero-monster left."

Q. "And he'd have to masturbate."

A. "That's true. . . . But—you use that to point out how tragic was my solution, which is that he wins and still has to masturbate. I reply that at least it was more valuable than masturbating in the first place. Besides, he might have no desire to masturbate. He might lie down and send his thoughts back to the root of his being."

Mailer concluded that "The ultimate direction of masturbation always has to be insanity." He didn't mention anything about going blind or becoming a hunchback or growing hair on the palm of one's hand.

THE ONANIST QUARTET

During the trial of fertilizer salesman Scott Peterson, the prosecutor presented evidence that, three weeks after Peterson's wife Laci disappeared, he added a couple of hard-core porn channels to the programming on his satellite dish. Defense attorney Mark Geragos called this "as great a form of character assassination as I don't know what." His client was on trial for the murder of his pregnant wife.

Peterson had added the Playboy channel two weeks after Laci's disappearance. Geragos argued, "There is nothing different in the Playboy channel that isn't on HBO at night"—the couple already had HBO—but prosecutor Rick Distaso pointed out that, one week later, Peterson "canceled the Playboy channel and ordered two hardcore pornography channels."

Geragos asserted that, without being able to show that Laci didn't want porn in their home, the fact that her husband ordered it after she disappeared is irrelevant and "It's meant to inflame the jury." The jury convicted him, though not for porn.

But at least Peterson jerked off in the privacy of his own living room. In Creek County, Oklahoma, 57-year-old Judge Donald Thompson was accused of frequently masturbating under his robes while his court was in session, using a special device for enhancing erections. He admitted that he had a penis pump under the bench during a murder trial, claiming that it was a gag gift from a friend for his 50th birthday.

He was also charged with firing Lisa Foster, who had been his court reporter for 15 years, after she cooperated with investigators.

"On one occasion," the complaint stated, "Ms. Foster saw Judge Thompson holding his penis up and shaving underneath it with a disposable razor while on the bench."

Several witnesses—including jurors in his court and police officers who testified in trials—said that they had heard the "swooshing" sound of a penis pump duriing trials and that they had seen the judge slumped in his chair, with his elbows on his knees, working the device. They said that the pump sounded like a blood pressure cuff being pumped up.

Thompson, who had been a judge for 22 years, has since retired, though he denied the charges and didn't refer to them in his letter of resignation. He receives a full pension.

"But even the president of the United States," sang Bob Dylan, "sometimes must have to stand naked." Dylan didn't mention anything about masturbating but, according to Monica Lewinsky in the *Starr Report*, Bill Clinton jerked off into a sink after she performed incomplete fellatio. Clinton had previously fired Surgeon General Joycelin Elders for suggesting that we give our children sex education which would include some information about masturbation. The joke about Clinton was that at Oxford he jerked off but he didn't come.

Finally, a decade ago, I was at the home of a friend when someone visited him in order to borrow some pornography—it was the late Francis Crick, who in 1962 won the Nobel Prize in medicine for his seminal (yes, I said *seminal*) discovery with James Watson of the double-helix structure of DNA. In a bestselling 1968 book, *The Double Helix*, Watson wrote that Crick was so elated on the day of that discovery that he announced to the patrons of a local pub that the pair had just discovered "the secret of life."

That discovery in 1953 helped launch the modern field of molecular genetics, with far-reaching implications for understanding our biology, as well as spin-offs ranging from genetic engineering to DNA fingerprinting, not to mention DNA imprinting to be found in blood, saliva and hair follicles. Certainly, to reveal that Crick liked to play with himself is not "as great a form of character assassination as I don't know what."

Of course, despite the fact that I have waited until after Crick's death to write about this, the seemingly incongruous image of a Nobel Prize winner masturbating to porn in no way diminishes his accomplishments. There is not the slightest bit of inconsistency between his jerking off and being described by Caltech professor Christof Koch, his collaborator for many years, in these words: "He was the living incarnation of what it is to be a scholar: brilliant, rational, dispassionate and always willing to revise his own opinions and views in light of the actions of a universe that never ceased to astonish him. He was editing a manuscript on his deathbed, a scientist until the bitter end."

An obituary in the *Los Angeles Times* stated: "An inveterate collaborator and gatherer of thinkers about him, Crick mused over the years on questions as varied as why people dream, where life came from and whether much of the DNA in our cells was parasitic junk." Ironically, in recent years, DNA has become a euphemistic synonym for semen.

And so, a fertilizer salesman, a judge, a president, a Nobel laureate—together they serve as a monument to masturbation as the great equalizer.

Make Me Laugh

HOMER SIMPSON SUPPRESSED

The voice of Homer on *The Simpsons*, Dan Castellaneta, and I have long been fans of each other's work. I was impressed by his versatility as an actor on *The Tracy Ullman Show*, as well as his live appearances with an improvisational troupe and his own one-person, multi-character show. He in turn enjoys my writing and has attended several of my stand-up performances. So, when Danny Goldberg, who ran Artemis Records, invited me to do another album, I felt comfortable asking Castellaneta if he would consider introducing me in Homer's voice.

He said it would be "an honor and a pleasure." I was very excited. We agreed that the best approach would be for him to do the introduction from an offstage microphone, so that the audience could maintain their image of good old blustery Homer Simpson while they listened to Dan's disembodied voice. And then he would hand me the mike and I'd walk onstage. At the taping of *Irony Lives!* at Genghis Cohen in Los Angeles, I sat next to Dan/Homer as he was introducing me, and I felt as though I was being sucked mysteriously into Cartoon World.

I've always preferred apologizing in retrospect rather than asking for permission, since I've never had any assets that I could be sued for, but understandably Artemis Records felt it necessary to ask Fox TV for permission to include Homer's introduction. At the beginning of my performance, I mentioned that the introduction might not be on the album because attorneys for the Fox network wanted to hear the *entire* album before granting permission. I explained that Fox owned Homer's voice when it was done by Dan.

But they kept holding off making a decision. Then, when Fox asked for *seven* copies of the advance CD, I realized that they would most likely refuse to grant permission. The word in the industry is, "Never mess with Fox lawyers, they're worse than Disney."

Fox continued to stall, and release of the CD had to be postponed. Finally, I was informed by an attorney for Artemis Records that, "Unfortunately, Fox declined our request, and in doing so failed to go into any detail as to what their reasons were." I assume that it was because the album includes such tracks as "Terrorist Attacks," "In the Guise of Security," and "My Cannabis Cup Runneth Over." Well, Fox TV may own Homer's voice, but not the following transcript of what he said. And so now I'd like to introduce Dan Castellaneta introducing me:

Hello. Hello. May I have your attention, please. This is Homer Simpson. I have been asked to introduce our performer tonight.

There have been many great counterculture heroes that I have admired over the years. Steve McQueen, Dr. Demento, Dr. Denis Leary, and Wavy Gravy. Mmmmm, gravy.

But even some counterculture heroes go much too far and step over that line between dissent and in-dissent . . . sentcy. I'm speaking of Paul Krassner.

The first problem I have with Paul Krassner is that the only song I like that he wrote for the Jefferson Airplane was, "Crown of Creation." And even then his name is spelled K-a-n-t-n-e-r even though it is pronounced Krassner.

Second, I have a problem with the fact that he is an atheist. If there is no God, then who has placed a pox upon me and mocks me every day? Of whom do I live in fear and mortal terror? Buddha? I think not. He's way over in China where thankfully he can't get at me.

I also have a problem with his constant use of words such as "penis," "Larry Flynt," "premature," "ejaculation," "CIA," and on several occasions he has been known to use the words "Bush" and "Bush Jr." in mixed company. Did I mention "penis"? Yeah, here it is—"penis." (*Laughs*) Heh heh heh. (*To self*) Penis.

Let's see, where was I? I mentioned, "penis," "gravy," "Buddha," "God," "Jefferson Airplane." No. That's it.

Will everyone please put their hands together for that raving, unconfined nut—let's hope that he opens with "Crown of Creation"—Paul Krassner!

––––––––––

This kind of censorship by Fox was not a First Amendment issue, since it wasn't being done by the government. Nevertheless, I couldn't just ignore it. So I leaked the suppressed introduction to Real Audio on my Web site, then spread the word exponentially, and in the first five days there were 58,000 hits; at the peak they were coming in at the rate of 2,300 an hour. At this writing, there have been 505,604 hits. I daresay that more people will have heard Homer's introduction this way than would have heard if it were on the CD.

The irony of *Irony Lives!* is that Fox's attempt to disassociate themselves from the album has already begun to backfire. But the question remains: Who ever thought that some day Homer Simpson would become an intellectual property? And, answering my own question, I slap my forehead with the heel of my hand, uttering Homer Simpson's sacred mantra: "D'oh!"

Harry Shearer Still Hears Voices

Twenty years ago, producer Scott Kelman was watching the final nails being hammered at his new theater in downtown Los Angeles. It was opening night for my performance, *Attacking Decency in General*. (The name came from a memoir by the late ABC News anchor, Harry Reasoner, who wrote, "Krassner not only attacked establishment values; he attacked decency in general.") Later, Kelman produced Peter Bergman's show, *Help Me Out of This Head*. Kelman thought that *Peter, Paul and Harry* would be a great title for a few weeks' run of an evening of political satire at the Museum of Contemporary Art, only he didn't know of any satirist named Harry.

"Harry Shearer," I suggested. "He's brilliant. Let's do it."

And so the fantasy became a reality. As a warm-up before each show, Peter would look in the mirror and make strange operatic sounds; I would hide behind a theatrical prop and smoke a joint; and Harry would be transformed into then-President Ronald Reagan by his personal make-up artist, imported from Iowa. *Peter, Paul and Harry* got great reviews, and it was held over for two extra weeks.

"If I had been named after my *other* grandfather," Harry said, "this show would never have happened."

He became an actor at the age of seven, at the urging of his piano teacher. As a kid on *The Jack Benny Show*, when the cast was doing a read-through, there was one line in the script where, Harry told me, "I just got it in my mind to do it with a slight Brooklyn accent, and when I did that, Benny just started howling, banging the table and laughing."

That moment was an auspicious omen of Harry's future career. Today, foremost among his many talents is an uncanny ability to mimic the voice, mannerisms and point-of-view of countless public figures—entertainers, politicians, newcasters—with satirical precision, on his radio program, *Le Show*—now in its 21st year—broadcast every Sunday morning on KCRW in Santa Monica

("From the edge of America, from the home of the homeless") and syndicated to 70 stations around the country. But no longer in New York City.

"It took an age and a half to get *Le Show* carried by WNYC in the first place," he told me, "and then the broadcast landed at the distinguished hour of midnight Sunday. Which was just theoretically in compliance with the only contract provision we apply to affiliates—the program has to be broadcast on Sunday. (*Le Show* is given to stations free, so I don't think one onerous condition is too many.) After a few months, the program was moved to 1 a.m., which, last time I looked, was actually Monday. Then, a few months later, it was moved again, to 2 a.m. At that point, I lost patience with them. On a broadcast, I had Ralph the Talking Computer play the role of WNYC's manager, and I fired the station on the air (although I guess they got tipped off, not on *their* air)."

In the tradition of Lenny Bruce, Harry plays all the characters in little theatrical productions that serve as a vehicle for his incisive humor. He occasionally presents a phone conversation between George W. Bush and his father, taking the part of both and capturing the nuances of each. On the eve of Bush's trip to England, he confides to the former president:

"You know, this protest stuff is just a lot of hype cooked up by our friends in the liberal media to distract Americans from the good news that I'm having tea with the queen. I mean, I've been thinking about it. One day I'm sucking Jack Daniels off a frozen trailer hitch, ten years later I'm having tea with the frigging Queen of England! You know, that's the same kind of transformation the Iraqis are gonna experience if we play with our cards right. . . ."

On another occasion, in his own voice, referring to Bush's crusade to stamp out global terrorism, Harry observed, "It's like the war on drugs. It's a totally metaphorical war in which some people get killed. I expect the Partnership for a Terrorist Free America to start soon."

One of the voices he does on *Le Show* is CBS News anchor Dan Rather. When the Museum of Radio and Television honored Rather, he personally invited Harry to attend. Harry wanted to talk about issues, but Rather wanted to discuss *Spinal Tap*, the classic rock'n'roll mockumentary where Harry played Derek Smalls, the bassist in the band.

Ironically, that band, "Spinal Tap," which was put together and existed only for the sake of the movie, ended up going on tour, just as the three folksinging groups invented for the mockumentary *A Mighty Wind* have similarly been touring. During Spinal Tap's London appearance, Harry entered the brunch place at the hotel where they were staying—looking like his character, Derek, with fake hair extensions but a real beard—and he was awe-stricken by a gifted vocalist, Judith Owen.

"That's all your music, isn't it?" he asked after her set.

She was thrilled that somebody wasn't coming up and saying, "Do you know anything from *Cats*?" Harry describes her singing style as "equal parts early Elton John, late Joanie Mitchell, a little bit of Stevie Wonder—the first record she ever bought was *Songs in the Key of Life*—and with a tinge of the classicism of Procol Harum."

Eventally they got married, and now divide their time between Santa Monica and New Orleans. Sometimes when Judith has a gig, Harry accompanies her on the electric bass. And, in keeping with his eclectic taste in music and his keen sense of nepotism, he often plays her albums on *Le Show*.

Harry also does the voice of NBC News anchor Tom Brokaw, and went through a phase of counting—and recording for a radio montage—the number of times Brokaw said the word "tonight" in his newscasts. The record was 13. However, I started counting the number of times Harry used the expression "Ladies and gentlemen" on *Le Show*, and the record was 15. For example, he recalls asking a waitress, "Excuse me, what flavor ice creams do you have?" Adding, "And her reply, ladies and gentlemen, was 'Today?'"

Another example: Reading an article in the *Washington Post* about a military intelligence expert: "He defended the administration's pre-war position. 'The idea that we didn't have specific proof he was planning to give a biological agent to a terrorist group doesn't really lead you to anything, because you wouldn't expect to have that information even if it were true.' Run that around your mind a little bit. 'You wouldn't expect to have that information even if it were true,' ladies and gentlemen."

Harry has a few "copyrighted features" on *Le Show*. I won a bet with Nancy that they're not *really* copyrighted, and perhaps as a result of that bet, he recently introduced "Tales of Airport Security," where he reads listeners' accounts of such misadventures, calling it "a copyrighted feature of this broadcast, and when I say that, of course I am lying. That's full disclosure, ladies and gentlemen."

Sample tale: "Every time the female security guard swept her wand past my breasts, the wand would buzz. She sort of felt me up a few times, and I told her I was wearing an underwire bra. She took one last probing feel, and then it was determined I was telling the truth. Then came my lower abdomen. She instructed me to open up the top of my zipper. She then put her hand under my pants. Later, in flight, when I was digging in my purse for some lipstick, what should I find in my purse but somethng I use in my job as a supervisor of a department store restocking team—a box cutter."

Another "copyrighted feature"—"If it ain't copyrighted," said Harry, "who knows the difference?"—is "Apologies of the Week," ranging from the creator of a comic strip, *Get Fuzzy*, apologizing for suggesting that Pittsburgh smells bad, to the president of Serbia apologizing for evil committed during the war in Bosnia. From Brazil's government apologizing to the country's senior citizens for forcing them to show up at Social Security offices to prove they're not dead, to Burger King apologizing to a woman who was ordered by a franchise employee to stop breast-feeding her baby or leave, because it made a customer uncomfortable.

"Yeah," Harry observed, "it brings you down seeing somebody eating better than you at a Burger King."

When Rush Limbaugh was outed as an addict to prescription painkillers and went to rehab, Harry did his version of Rush ranting there, which resulted in some hate mail. "Rush is doing a radio show in his head in detox," he explained to me, "so first Bill Clinton calls him, in this nightmare—one of Rush's trademark lines is, 'With talent on loan from God'—then John Ashcroft calls him, and the first thing he says is, 'Rush, this is John Ashcroft, God wants his talent back.' That set them off."

Limbaugh *seems* like a cartoon character, but Harry also does the voices of several *actual* cartoon characters on *The Simpsons*, though it's possible that more Americans know who Ned Flanders is than John Ashcroft. Since Harry does both Mr. Burns and Smithers, I asked, "When you're taping *The Simpsons*, do you just stand there and talk to yourself?"

"Yes," he said, "and that happens a lot. When Hank [Azaria] plays Apu and Chief Wiggum, he'll talk to himself, and when Dan [Castellaneta] plays Homer and his dad, he'll talk to himself."

I sent Harry a report that Fox News had threatened legal action after an episode of *The Simpsons* on Fox Entertainment poked fun at the channel by featuring a "Fox News Crawl" at the bottom of the screen, reading: "Pointless news crawls up 37% . . . Do Democrats cause cancer? Find out at foxnews.com . . . Rupert Murdoch: Terrific dancer . . . Dow down 5000 points . . . Study: 92% of Democrats are gay . . . JFK posthumously joins Republican Party . . . Oil slicks found to keep seals young, supple . . . Dan Quayle: Awesome . . . Ashcroft Declares breast of chicken sandwich 'obscene' . . . Hillary Clinton embarrasses self, nation ... Bible says Jesus favored capital-gains cut ... Stay tuned for Hannity and Idiot ... Only dorks watch CNN ... Jimmy Carter: Old, wrinkly, useless ... Brad Pitt + Albert Einstein = Dick Cheney ... Right wing of chicken ..."

"Somebody asked me about this story," Harry told me, "and it sounded like utter hogwash to me—except for the part about misleading people into thinking the crawl was real—[Orson Welles'] *War of the Worlds* rule and all. I've advocated that Rupert do many things to himself, but suing wasn't one of them."

According to *Simpsons* creator Matt Groening, "Fox fought against it and said they would sue the show. We called their bluff because we didn't think Rupert Murdoch would pay for Fox to sue itself. So, we got away with it. But now Fox has a new rule that we can't do those little fake news crawls on the bottom of the screen in a cartoon because it might confuse the viewers into thinking it's real news."

Fox crawled out of the lawsuit but, Harry asked on the air, "What if there had been a suit?" And he proceeded to present the trial, with Nancy Grace from Court TV as prosecutor, F. Lee Bailey as defense attorney and Lance Ito (from O. J. Simpson's trial) as judge. Rupert Murdoch testified, "The fact that I brought this action against myself is proof enough to the average man that I *do* care about my news network's good name."

Harry is obviously not afraid to bite the hand that feeds him. Nor is he afraid to poke fun at the power structure that nauseates him.

"I'd always known about the Bohemian Grove, growing up in California and being a political junkie," he said. "The Grove is a retreat for the richest, most powerful white men in America, who go every summer for a week-long romp where they act like college sophomores on an unlimited budget. *Teddy Bear's Picnic* [the film he wrote and directed] is basically a comedy about grown-ups with too much power and what happens when the secrecy of their yearly romp is threatened."

Coincidentally, he was invited to be a guest at one of their big shows. I asked how he differentiates between him performing at the Bohemian Grove and Al Franken writing jokes for the Democrats.

"It was just sort of Quixotic orneriness," he said, referring to the material he chose to do at the Grove. "But I wasn't there being their court jester. I wasn't there to pander to whatever their brand of politics might have been at that particular gathering. Al is, of course, *literally* a Democratic court jester. Basically, the jest is going away. You can call people idiots and morons and fatsos just for a certain period of time before it stops being ironic in any sense.

"The other thing is, nobody at the Grove at that time was a candidate for anything that I was endorsing. Franken clearly wears his endorsements where his wit should be. I'm a satirist. My job is to make fun of *all* of them. People who supposedly practice the art of satire and then retire to the councils of power to write jokes for their leaders—people like Al Franken—really ought to have their satirist cards revoked."

[*Author's note*: Franken has since stated he was "seriously thinking about" running for senator in Minnesota; I think he'd be a worthy successor to Paul Wellstone.]

Harry's philosophy of comedy is, "Comedy is good, reality is better." His all-time favorite example:

"Well, I would say my object of idolatry in that regard would be the tape of Richard Nixon just before he makes his resignation speech. You can't beat that. [*In Nixon's voice*] 'Ollie there, he's always trying to take another picture of me, but he's always trying to get one of me picking my nose. You wouldn't do that, would you, Ollie? That's enough now.' Just the lunacy of him kidding around with this crew that you can actually see on the tape, they don't know what to make of this, and a guy who entered a field where one of the primary qualifications is the ability to make charming small talk, and then at this climactic, penultimate moment in Nixon's fall, what does he choose to do but walk in and make this insane small talk? That to me is one of the great comic choices ever."

"As a thoroughgoing news junkie," I asked, "you must know too much. So are you optimistic or pessimistic about the future?"

"Whose future?"

"The future of civilization, I suppose."

"There's that famous quip of Gandhi: 'When you speak of Western civilization, I think it would be a good idea.' Ultimately, you know, we're gonna be destroyed."

"You mean as individuals?"

"No, as a race. The planet will get eaten up by some process in the solar system, or in the universe, and the thing regenerates, so in the sense that I think a lot of liberals' pessimism translates as panic, I don't have that. I think I'm intellectually pessimistic and emotionally optimistic. I think the worst is gonna happen, probably, but in terms of my own behavior, in terms of the way I live my life, I don't act that way. A necessary distinction can be mainly to get up in the morning, if you see clearly what's going on. It's also the distinction between the individual and the larger—the two can have difference trajectories."

"So since we're gonna be totally destroyed anyway," I asked, "it doesn't make any difference whether you're optimistic or pessimistic?"

"I don't think the universe cares what your attitude is. Most choices you make are based on intellectually what you know and think, and on the other hand—I don't know, I always try to puzzle this out because I know that in terms of my behavior, I've always behaved as if I were optimistic, at least about me and the people around me. For example, I never, ever, as a child of the Cold War, aside from maybe an hour during the Cuban missile crisis, I never believed that we were gonna get blown up, never believed *that* was gonna be nuclear war, I never lived under the 'shadow of the bomb.'

"Certainly, it's not because I believe in the competence of most people, because I don't, I believe the opposite. That's where comedy comes from, is showing how fucked up people are. But it just didn't seem, on an emotional basis—obviously I knew what the dangers were—and you know, I have taken some joy in reminding people in the recent period when people are walking around as if *this* is the greatest threat that's ever faced the U.S., well, you know, 20 years ago, what, 20,000 missiles were aimed on a 3-minute warning system at the U.S. We got through that. In the forefront of my mind, whatever I'm facing in my time is so much less horrific than what my parents had and their familes faced in their time that it's a joke."

"Final question: Is there something you'd like to apologize for?"

"There are a bunch of performances I want to apologize for, but I'm not gonna single them out in case somebody happened to have liked them, and then they feel betrayed by me."

THE TRANSFORMATION OF DENNIS MILLER

Full disclosure: Several years ago, Dennis Miller called and invited me to be a writer on his HBO series. He requested that I send him some jokes and a rant. I did. Never heard back. After a few weeks, I wrote to ask if he'd made a decision.

Again, rudely ignored. Although I needed the money, and rationalized that I was on common ground with Miller on many issues, I actually felt relieved not to get the job.

I would've had to change my lifestyle—working at home in my Venice Beach cottage—plus I would have been writing for someone whose personality is snide ("Lenny Bruce was a heroin addict, and I could care less about heroin addicts") and whose humor has a streak of meanspiritedness, increasingly tainted by reactionary intolerance, with early tremors such as his disdain for the ACLU. A staff writer confided that Miller considered me too radical.

I still respected him for apologizing publicly to a sick child whose photo he had made fun of the previous week. And, more recently, I thought it was courageous of him to perform before an audience of 1,500 at Davies Symphony Hall in ultra-liberal San Francisco. Miller himself was shocked that anybody had shown up, and he admitted on stage, "I thought I was *persona non grata* in San Francisco."

James Sullivan, pop culture critic for the *San Francisco Chronicle*, wrote: "Once the arcane-reference comic darling of the cynical eggheads of the adult counterculture, the 50-year-old professional cynic has made a hard right turn of late that has some corners of his constituency up in arms. He is now considered a Bush administration apologist ('I guess I'm seen as a hawk now,' he commented), which made his first local appearance in years a litmus test of sorts for a man some Southern California power brokers would like to coerce into a Senate run. . . ."

Miller's material ranged from a defense of Operation Iraqi Freedom—poking fun at the left's fixation on the administration's failure to rally international support—to recasting the film title *Fitzcarraldo* as a verb in an old routine about Post Office inertia, which prompted me to pose the following query to Sullivan:

"So many comedians rely on easy joke references that will be recognized by the largest common denominator, and since there's nothing intrinsically funny about them, the audience applauds rather than laughs because they're really applauding themselves for recognizing the reference. On the other hand, Dennis Miller is infamous for his obscure references that will be recognized by fewer folks, but the result seems to be the same. What comment do you have on this phenomenon?"

His response: "I'd say that Miller's fans tend to think of themselves as smarter than the average bear, if you know what I mean. Certain fans of all kinds of entertainment pride themselves on being the ones 'in the know,' the ones who have done a little cultural research beyond whatever new video release is on sale this week at Target. There are cult bands and cult movies and cult TV shows. And

Dennis Miller is a cult comedian, albeit one who has managed to develop a considerable national audience. . . ."

In May 2003, the *Wall Street Journal* invited Miller to write an opinion piece reacting to Norman Mailer's commentary in the *London Times* the previous week. Mailer had written, "With their dominance in sport, at work and at home eroded, Bush thought white American men needed to know they were still good at something. That's where Iraq came in. . . . The great white stars of yesteryear were for the most part gone, gone in football, in basketball, in boxing, and half-gone in baseball. . . . On the other hand, the good white American male still had the Armed Forces."

Miller attempted to skewer Mailer with pedantic insults while missing his point with a politically correct sermon: "You know something, the only 'race' that really occurred to me during the war was our Army's sprint to Baghdad. Conversely, Mr. Mailer appears to see just race in our armed forces, right down to the 'Super-Marines,' as he calls them. It seems that Mr. Mailer notices color in people even when they're wearing camouflage. He then goes on to speak about racial subsets in the world of sports. Now, when I watch baseball, football and basketball, I see uniforms and skills. Mr. Mailer evidently sees races and nationalities. . . .

"And as Mr. Mailer's prostate gradually supplants his ego as the largest gland in his body, he's going to have to realize, as is the case with all young lions who inevitably morph into Bert Lahr, that his alleged profundities are now being perceived as the early predictors of dementia. . . ."

Does Miller's allusion to "young lions" indicate that he thinks Irwin Shaw wrote *The Naked and the Dead*? A few days later, the *Journal* published Mailer's response:

Dear Dennis,

Just because the two big guys who flanked you on *Monday Night Football* took away your balls and left you with a giggle in replacement doesn't mean you have to suck up to the *Wall Street Journal*. But thanks for appreciating my fine use of 'keen.' Keen up, then, to my piece and read it again without panic. You're too good to become squalid and kiss-ass for so little.

Cheers, blessings,

Norman Mailer

Talking Presidents, the toy company that manufactures talking action figures at $30 each, is now marketing a Dennis Miller doll, to go along with the George W. Bush doll ("You're working hard to put food on your family"), the Bill Clinton doll ("It depends upon what the meaning of the word *is* is"), the Donald Rumsfeld doll ("I believe what I said yesterday—I don't know what I said, but I know what I think and I assume that's what I said") and the Ann Coulter doll ("Swing voters are more appropriately known as the 'idiot voters' because they have no set of philosophical principles—by the age of 14, you're either a conservative or a liberal if you have an IQ above a toaster").

Anyway, Miller supplied comments for his doll in both family-suitable and explicit-language versions. Here are some of its 21 utterances:

"The world should remember that the United States does have a long fuse, but at the end of the day, it is connected to a *big* friggin' bomb!"

"And quit bringing up our forefathers and saying they were civil libertarians. Our founding fathers would've never tolerated *any* of this crap. For God sakes, they were blowing people's heads off because they put a tax on their breakfast beverage. And it wasn't even coffee."

"Of course, that's just my opinion—I could be wrong."

"The only way we were gonna get the French to go into Iraq is to tell them we thought there were truffles in there."

"Guess what, folks—that's the news, and I am outa here."

And where did he go? For a ride in George W. Bush's limousine, and in Air Force One, referring to himself as "a Rat Pack of one for the president in Hollywood." Miller has morphed himself from "Bush can't walk and fart at the same time" to "George W. is a genius." He promises that on his new CNBC show, he won't aim any barbs at Bush.

"I like him," he says. "I'm going to give him a pass. I take care of my friends."

Miller says that his political perspective changed when he kept hearing people comparing Bush with Adolf Hitler, and he didn't think that was fair.

"People say I've slid to the right," he explains. "Well, can you blame me? One of the biggest malfeasances of the left right now is the mislabeling of Hitler. Quit saying Bush is Hitler. *Hitler* is Hitler. That's the quintessential evil in the history of the universe, and we're throwing it around on MoveOn.org to win a contest. That's grotesque to me."

Out of 1,500 entries in the MoveOn political ad competition, there were only two that made the Hitler/Bush comparison (just an example of Miller sacrificing perspective for the sake of agenda), so if Tony Blair was George Bush's poodle, then Dennis Miller is his mynah bird. And yet, paradoxically enough, I'm now convinced that Dennis Miller is correct. There's a *vast* difference between Hitler and Bush. Hitler was elected.

THE BALLAD OF LENNY THE LAWYER

PROLOGUE

Robin Williams, Penn and Teller, Margaret Cho, and Tom and Dick Smothers were among the signers of a petition addressed to New York Governor George Pataki. It stated: "A pardon now is too late to save Lenny Bruce. But a posthumous pardon would set the record straight and thereby demonstrate New York's commitment to freedom—free speech, free press, free thinking." In 1964, Bruce had been convicted of obscenity for his performance at the Cafe Au Go Go in Greenwich Village.

The petition—also endorsed by First Amendment scholars, lawyers and Bruce's daughter, Kitty—was submitted at a press conference by the coauthors of *The Trials of Lenny Bruce*, Ronald Collins and David Skover, in May 2003. In July, Pataki was still giving this blatant no-brainer "serious consideration." Finally, in December, he granted the posthumous pardon. But Lenny would have been simultaneously outraged by the hypocrisy and amused by the irony that the governor had pardoned him in the context of justifying the invasion of Iraq.

"Freedom of speech is one of the great American liberties," Pataki said, "and I hope this pardon serves as a reminder of the precious freedoms we are fighting to preserve as we continue to wage the war on terrorism."

Pataki's pandering monument to opportunism was merely the tip of a satirical iceberg. In the words of former drug czar William Bennett, "Hypocrisy is better than having no values at all."

In 1959, I published an interview with Lenny Bruce in *The Realist*. It had been conducted totally by mail. Here's a sampling:

Q. *Could you be bribed to do only "safe" material from now on?*

A. What's the bribe? Eternal lfe? A cure for cancer? $45,000,000? What's the difference what I take? I'd still be selling out.

Q. *Do you think there is any sadism in your comedy?*

A. What a horrible thought. If there is any sadism in my work, I hope I—well, if there is, I wish someone would whip me with a large belt that has a brass buckle.

Q. *What would you say is the role of a comedian?*

A. A comedian is one who performs words or actions of his own creation, usually before a group of people in a place of assembly, and these words or actions should cause the people assembled to laugh at a minimum of, on the average, one laugh every 15 seconds—or let's be liberal to escape the hue and cry of the injured and say one laugh every 25 seconds—he should get a laugh every 25 seconds for a period of not less than 45 minutes, and accomplish this feat with consistency 18 out of 20 shows. . . . Now understand, I'm discussing comedy here as a craft—not as an aesthetic, altruistic art form. The comedian I'm discussing now is not Christ's jester, Timothy; this comedian gets paid, so his first loyalty is to the club owner, and he must make money for the owner. If he can upgrade the moral standards of his community and still get laughs, he is a *fine* craftsman.

When Lenny came to New York for a midnight show at Town Hall, he called me that afternoon, and we met for the first time at the Hotel America. He was staying there with Eric Miller, a black guitarist who worked with him in certain routines. In "How to Relax Colored People at a Party," Lenny would play the part of a "first-plateau liberal" trying to make conversation with Miller, playing the part of an entertainer at an otherwise all-white party. Lenny's character would spout one racial cliche after another. A critic had blasted him for "the insulting way in which he rididuled races and creeds."

Miller lamented, "They just don't understand."

At this point in his career, Lenny was still using the euphemism *frig* on stage. Although his irreverence was already being translated into "sick comic" by the media, he had not yet been branded "filthy." I handed him the new issue of *The Realist* featuring my interview with psychologist Albert Ellis, who described "the campaign which I have been waging, with remarkable lack of success, for many years, in favor of the proper usage of the word *fuck*. My premise is that sexual intercourse, copulation, fucking or whatever you wish to call it, is normally, under almost all circumstances, a damned good thing. Therefore, we should rarely use it in a negative, condemnatory manner. Instead of denouncing someone by calling him "a fucking bastard," we should say, of course, that he is an "unfucking villain" (since *bastard*, too, is not necessarily a negative state and should not only be used pejoratively)."

"I can see this scrawled on subway posters," I said. "*Unfuck You!*"

I didn't want to insult the readers' intelligence by resorting to asterisks or dashes, as other magazines did, but my printer wouldn't set in type that portion of the interview unless I brought a note from my lawyer. Lenny was amazed that I could get away with publishing it.

"Are you telling me this is legal to sell on the newsstands?"

"Absolutely. The Supreme Court's definition of obscenity is that it has to be material which appeals to your prurient interest—"

Lenny magically produced an unabridged dictionary from the suitcase on his bed, and he looked up the word *prurient*. "Itching," he mused. "What does that *mean*, that they can bust a novelty-store owner for selling itching powder along with the dribble glass and the whoopie cushion?"

"It's just their way of saying that something gets you horny."

Lenny clenched his jaw, nodding his head in affirmation of a new discovery: "So it's against the law to get you *horny*."

He asked me to give out copies of *The Realist* with the Ellis interview in front of Town Hall before his concert that night. He brought a copy on stage and proceeded to talk about it. As a result, he was barred from performing there again.

"They'll book me again," Lenny said. "They made too much on that concert. I'd have more respect for them if they *didn't* ever book me again. At least it'd show they were keeping their word."

But he was right. They *did* book him again.

———

I was able to subsidize *The Realist* by doing interviews for *Playboy*'s new feature, the Playboy Panel, which wasn't *really* a panel. I had to interview each person separately, then follow up with questions to give the illusion of interplay, and finally weave all the material into a discussion until I was convinced that we had all been sitting at a table together in the same room. For a panel on "The Hip

Humorists" in 1960, I flew to Milwaukee to interview Lenny. He was staying at the YMCA. After checking in, I went to his room. We talked for a while. As we were leaving, he asked furtively, "Did you steal anything?" I took my watch out of my pocket (I didn't like to wear it on my wrist) and placed it on the bureau. Lenny laughed—one loud staccato "*Ha!*"—and kissed me on the forehead.

That evening, three plainclothes police walked into his dressing room at the club where he was working. They told him not to discuss politics or religion or sex, or they'd yank him right off the stage. The previous night, a group of Catholics had signed a complaint about his act. The cops told him that he shouldn't say "son-of-a-bitch" in his impression of a white-collar drunk. Lenny was nervous, and did two slightly toned-down shows. We went back to his room and took turns naming all the books we had *not* read—even though we both used references from them—from James Joyce to Harold Robbins, from Franz Kafka to Kahlil Gibran.

"People use *The Prophet* to get laid," Lenny said.

Critics had written about each of us that we were in the tradition of Jonathan Swift and Mark Twain, but neither of us had read any of their books. Coincidentally, though, we were both reading books by Nathanael West. I was reading *Miss Lonelyhearts* and he was reading *The Dream Life of Balso Snell*, which had a line about an old actress with much-shaved armpits, prompting Lenny to improvise on what eventually developed into a routine about a popular singer who flashed her *un*shaved armpit to the audience. We stayed up till morning, discussing the subjectivity of humor.

At breakfast in the YMCA cafeteria, a man sitting at our table told how he had slapped his daughter because she wanted to see *Psycho*. He had seen it and didn't want her to witness a kissing scene between a partially disrobed couple. He didn't mention the violence of repeatedly stabbing a woman in the shower, but the contradictions in that conversation would work their way into Lenny's performance that night.

I was fascinated by the way he played with ideas, and inspired by how he weaved taboo comedic targets—nuclear testing, teachers' low salaries, drug laws, abortion rights, organized religion—into stream-of-consciousness vignettes. I was intrigued by the way he did show-and-tell with his audiences. When he heard "There Is a Rose in Spanish Harlem" on the radio, he bought the record, came on stage with a phonograph and played it. "Listen to these lyrics. This is like a Puerto Rican *Porgy and Bess.*" And when Gary Cooper died, he brought the *New York Daily News* on stage to share a headline: "The Last Roundup!"

"I found this today," he would say, introducing a bizarre concept as though it were as tangible as a record or a newspaper. Then, in each succeeding performance, he would sculpt and resculpt his findings into a theatrical context, playing all the parts, experimenting from show to show like a jazz musician, with a throwaway line evolving from night to night into a set routine. Audience laughter turned into applause for the creative process itself.

"Please don't applaud," Lenny requested. "It breaks my rhythm."

But sometimes he'd become so serious that the laughs wouldn't come every 15-25 seconds. I reminded him of this apparent inconsistency with his definition of a comedian's role.

"Yes," he said, "but I'm changing."

"What do you mean?"

"I'm not a comedian. I'm Lenny Bruce."

———————

Lenny's first arrest occurred in September 1961, ostensibly for drugs—for which he had prescriptions—but actually because he was making too much money and the local officials wanted a piece of the action. He was working at the Red Hill Inn in Pennsauken, New Jersey. Cops broke into his hotel room to make the bust. That night an attorney and bail bondsman came backstage and told him that $10,000 was all it would take for the judge to dismiss the charges. A beatnik-looking young lawyer friend witnessed this attempted extortion. In court, Lenny pleaded not guilty.

"Incidentally," he added, "I can only come up with $50."

The judge dismissed the case against him.

In October, Lenny was arrested for obscenity at the Jazz Workshop in San Francisco for using the word *cocksucker* to describe a cocksucker. He got busted for aptness of vocabulary. The officers said they came because of an anonymous phone call the previous night, although the doorman insisted that there had been no complaints or walkouts.

"We're trying to elevate this street," a sergeant told Lenny. "I took offense because you broke the law. I can't see any way you can break that word down. Our society isn't geared to it."

"You break it down," Lenny replied, "by talking about it."

Two decades later, Meryl Streep would get an Academy Award for saying "cocksucker" in *Sophie's Choice*, and if she didn't, then fellow nominee Jessica Lange would've won the Oscar for saying "cocksucker" in *Frances*.

Lenny was writing his autobiography—*How to Talk Dirty and Influence People*—which *Playboy* would serialize, then publish as a book, and they hired me as his editor. We hooked up in Atlantic City, where Lenny drove a rented car. We passed a sign warning, CRIMINALS MUST REGISTER, and Lenny decided to dedicate his book "to all the followers of Christ and his teachings; in particular to a true Christian—Jimmy Hoffa—because he hired ex-convicts as, I assume, Christ would have."

Lenny was taking Dilaudid for lethargy, and sent a telegram to a contact, with a phrase—DE LAWD IN DE SKY—as a code to send a doctor's prescription. Now he got sick while waiting for it to be filled. Later, while we were relaxing on the beach, I hesitatingly brought up the subject.

"Don't you think it's ironic that your whole style should be so free-form, and yet you can also be a slave to dope?"

"What does that mean, a slave to dope?"

"Well, if you need a fix, you've got to stop whatever you're doing, go somewhere and wrap a lamp cord around your arm—"

"Then other people are slaves to *food*. 'Oh, I'm so famished, I must have lunch immediately or I'll pass out.'"

"You said yourself you're probably gonna die before you reach 40."

"Yeah, but—I can't explain—it's like kissing God."

"Well, I ain't gonna argue with *that*."

Later, he began to get paranoid about my role: "You're gonna go to literary cocktail parties, and you're gonna say, 'Yeah, that's right, I found Lenny slobbering in an alley, he would've been nothin' without me.'"

I denied any such intention, but he demanded that I take a lie-detector test, and *I* was paranoid enough to take him literally. I told him that I couldn't work with him if he didn't trust me. We got into an argument, and I left. I sent a letter of resignation to *Playboy* and a copy to Lenny. A few weeks later, I got a telegram from him that sounded as if we had been on the verge of a divorce—WHY CAN'T IT BE THE WAY IT USED TO BE?—and I agreed to try again.

In December 1962, I flew to Chicago to resume working with Lenny. He was performing at the Gate of Horn, and now he was asking the whole *audience* to take a lie-detector test. He recognized my laugh.

Lenny had been reading a study of anti-Semitism by Jean-Paul Sartre, and he was obsessed by the implications of a news item with a statement by Adolf Eichmann that he would have been "not only a scoundrel but a despicable pig" if he *hadn't* carried out Hitler's orders. Lenny wrote a piece for *The Realist*, "Letter From a Soldier's Wife"—namely, *Mrs.* Eichmann—pleading for compassion to spare her husband's life. Now, on stage, he credited Thomas Merton's poem about the Holocaust, requested that all the lights go off except one dim blue spot, and then began speaking with a German accent:

> My name is Adolf Eichmann. And the Jews came every day to what they thought would be fun in the showers. People say I should have been hung. *Nein.* Do you recognize the whore in the middle of you—that you would have done the same if you were there yourselves? My defense: I was a soldier. I saw the end of a conscientious day's effort. I watched through the portholes. I saw every Jew burned and turned into soap. Do you people think yourselves better because you burned your enemies at long distance with missiles without ever seeing what you had done to them? Hiroshima *auf Wiedersehen.* [*German accent ends.*] If we would have lost the war, they would have strung Truman up by the balls, Jim. Are you kidding with that? Not what kid told kid told kid. They would just *schlep* out all those Japanese mutants. "Here they did; there they are." And Truman said they'd do it again. That's what they should have the same day as Remember Pearl Harbor. Play them in unison.

Lenny was arrested for obscenity that night. The cops broke open his candy bars, looking for drugs. One of the items in the police report complained: "Then talking about the war he stated, 'If we would have lost the war, they would have strung Truman up by the balls.'"

"I guess what happens," Lenny mused, "if you get arrested in town A and then in Town B, with a lot of publicity, then when you get to Town C they *have* to arrest you or what kind of shithouse town are *they* running?"

Chicago was Town C. Lenny had been released on bail and was working again, but the head of the vice squad warned the manager: "If this man ever uses a four-letter word in this club again, I'm going to pinch you and everyone in here. If he ever speaks against religion, I'm going to pinch you and everyone in here. Do you understand? You've had good people here. But he mocks the pope—and I'm speaking as a Catholic—I'm here to tell you your license is in danger. We're going to have someone here watching every show."

And indeed, the Gate of Horn's liquor license was suspended. There were no previous allegations against the club, and the current charge involved neither violence nor drunken behavior. The only charge pressed by the city prosecutor was Lenny's allegedly obscene performance, and his trial had not yet been held.

Chicago boasted the largest membership in the Roman Catholic Church of any archdiocese in the country. Lenny's jury consisted entirely of Catholics. The judge was Catholic. The prosecutor and his assistant were Catholic. On Ash Wednesday, the judge removed the spot of ash from his forehead and told the bailiff to instruct the others to do likewise. The sight of a judge, two prosecutors and 12 jurors, all with a spot of ash on their foreheads, had the surrealistic flavor of a Lenny Bruce fantasy.

After the first week of the trial, Lenny flew to Los Angeles—Town D—where he was promptly arrested on suspicion of narcotics possession. Years later, the arresting officer went to prison himself, for drug smuggling. When the Chicago case resumed, the jury found Lenny guilty. The judge gave him the maximum penalty—a year in jail and a $1,000 fine—"for telling dirty jokes," explained a network newscaster.

A week later, the case against the Gate of Horn was dismissed, but it had become obvious that Lenny was now considered too hot to be booked in Chicago again. In San Francisco, the jury found him *not* guilty of obscenity. Arresting officers admitted that his material didn't arouse their prurient interest. But in Chicago, the judge refused to permit that line of cross-examination by the defense. Nor would he allow the head of the vice squad to take the stand, on the grounds that his testimony would be extraneous to the issue before the court.

"Chicago," said Lenny, "is so corrupt it's thrilling."

In less than two years, Lenny was arrested 15 times.

"There seems to be a pattern," he said, "that I'm a mad dog and they have to get me no matter what—the end justifies the means." It became a news item in *Variety* when he *didn't* get arrested one night. While the Chicago verdict was on appeal, he was working at the Off-Broadway in San Francisco. The club's newspaper ads made this offer: "No cover charge for patrolmen in uniform."

Since he always talked on stage about his environment, and since police cars and courtrooms had lately *become* his environment, the content of Lenny's performances began to revolve more and more around the inequities of the justice system. "In the Halls of Justice," he declared, "the only justice is in the halls." But he also said, "I love the law." Instead of an unabridged dictionary, he now carried law books in his luggage. His room was always cluttered with tapes and transcripts and photostats and law journals and legal briefs. Once he was teasing 10-year-old Kitty by pretending not to believe what she was telling him.

"Daddy," she said, "you'd believe me if it was on tape."

Lenny's jazz jargon was gradually being replaced by legal jargon. He had become intimate not only with the statutes concerning obscenity and narcotics, but also with courtroom procedure, and his knowledge would be woven into his performances. "Query," he'd begin. "If a tape recording is my voice, are they using me to testify against myself, since it's my voice that would indict me?" As club owners became increasingly afraid to hire him, he devoted more and more time and energy to the law. When he finally got a booking in Monterey, he admitted to me, "I feel like it's taking me away from my work."

One time we were fooling around with a tape recorder, and Lenny began spinning out quaint, absurd imagery:

> I will confess to some experiences that I've had. Forbidden sights I have seen. The most beautiful body I've ever seen was at a party in 1945. I was in the bedroom getting the coats. The powder room door had been left intentionally ajar, and I viewed the most perfect bosom peeking out from the man-tailored blouse above a tweed pegged skirt.
>
> "You like what you see? They *are* nice, aren't they?" she said, caressing the area near her medallion.
>
> "Yes, they are very nice."

"Would you like to touch them?"

"I'm—I'm—"

"You're shocked," she said, "aren't you?"

Indeed I was. Eleanor Roosevelt had the prettiest tits I had ever seen or dreamed that I had seen.

"I've got the nicest tits that have ever been in this White House, but because of protocol we're not allowed to wear bathing suits, you know. I get a million offers for pictures, but being saddled with the Girl Scout coordinators has left me with only a blind item in a gossip column: *What Capitol Hill biggie's wife has a pair of lollies that are setting the Washington-go-round a-twitter?*"

Lenny's problem was that he wanted to talk on stage with the same freedom he exercised in his living room. That harmless little bit of incongruity about Eleanor Roosevelt would show up in his act from time to time. It certainly didn't fall within the definition of hard-core pornography which the Supreme Court had ruled was not protected by the First Amendment. Nevertheless, Lenny was arrested in supposedly sophisticated New York at the Cafe Au Go Go for giving an indecent performance, and at the top of the police complaint was "Eleanor Roosevelt and her display of tits."

Ultimately, Lenny fired all his lawyers in the New York trial and defended himself. He was found guilty, even though the law stated that to be obscene, material must be *utterly without any* redeeming social importance; therefore, if *one single person* felt that Lenny's performance had *the slightest bit* of redeeming social importance—and there were several witnesses who so testified—then he should've been found not guilty.

Lenny hadn't been able to get work in six months. Club owners were afraid to book him. He almost got an engagement in Philadelphia, but the deal fell through when the district attorney demanded that Lenny show up a couple of days early and take a Naline test to prove there was no morphine in his system. Plus he was told to present his material in advance. CRIMINALS MUST REGISTER. He performed at a club in Westbury, but on his way to the parking lot after the first performance, a district attorney warned him, "If you do another show like the one did tonight, I'll arrest you." Then the D.A. told the club owner, "If you let him go on, I'll pull your license."

Lenny went before the Court of Appeals in New York, seeking an injunction that would prevent district attorneys from arresting him in the future. The three-judge panel was headed by Thurgood Marshall, former chief counsel for the NAACP, who would later become the first black justice appointed to the Supreme Court. Lenny pleaded that he was like a carpenter whose tools were being taken away. He compared the denial of his rights to "a nigger who wants to use a toilet in Alabama."

"You're not a Negro, Mr. Bruce," said Judge Marshall.

"Unfortunately not, Your Honor."

And Lenny's request was denied. A week later, he was due to be sentenced. Once again, he would act as his own attorney. In court, he borrowed a watch, because he planned to state for the record what time he began and ended his argument—"so that the judge can't close me out for taking too long." Lenny spoke for a solid hour. He did everything in this one-time-only matinee performance short of applying burnt cork to his face, donning white gloves, getting down on his knees and singing "Nobody Knows De Trouble Obscene," but his most relevant argument concerned the very obscenity statute which he'd been accused of violating.

As his legal homework, Lenny had obtained the legislative history of that statute from Albany, and he discovered that back in 1931 there was an amendment proposed which *excluded from arrest* in an indecent performance: stagehands, spectators, musicians and—here was the fulcrum of his defense—*actors*. The law had been misapplied to him. Despite opposition by the New York Society For the Suppression of vice, the amendment was finally signed into law by then-Governor Franklin D. Roosevelt.

Lenny had complained that prosecutor Richard Kuh tried to do his act in court. A friend of mine who dated Kuh swears that he took her back to his apartment and played Lenny Bruce records for her. Maybe someday he would play for her the sound-track album from the movie *Lenny*, with Dustin Hoffman doing Lenny's act on stage where he complains about the district attorney doing his act in court. But now, before sentencing, Kuh recommended that no mercy be granted because Bruce had shown a "lack of remorse."

"I'm not here for remorse," Lenny responded, "but for justice. The issue is not obscenity, but that I spit in the face of authority."

The face of authority spat back at Lenny that afternoon by sentencing him to four months in the workhouse. Then, in the press room of the Criminal Courts building, a reporter asked, "Do you believe in obscenity?"

"What do you mean?" asked Lenny. "Do I believe we should *pray* for obscenity?"

As we walked into the lobby, a man came up and said, "Listen, I have some stag films and party records that you might be interested in." Lenny and I went for some pizza instead. Then we headed for his hotel room where, to help unwind from the day's tension, he played some old tapes, ranging from a faith healer to patriotic World War II songs.

"Ignoring the mandate of Franklin D. Roosevelt," observed Lenny the lawyer, "is a great deal more offensive than saying Eleanor has lovely nay-nays."

On October 2, 1965, Lenny visited San Francisco FBI headquarters. Two days later, they sent a memo to the FBI director in Washington, describing him as "the nightclub and stage performer widely known for his obscenity" and stating that "Bruce, who advised that he is scheduled to begin confinement, 10/13/65, in New York State as a result of a conviction for a lewd show, alleged that there is a conspiracy between the courts of the states of New York and California to violate his rights. Allegedly this violation of his rights takes place by these lower courts failing to abide by decision of the U.S. Supreme Court with regard to obscenity. . . ."

On October 13, Lenny's 40th birthday, instead of surrendering to the authorities in New York, he filed suit at the U.S. District Court in San Francisco to keep out of prison, and he got himself officially declared a pauper. He also asked the federal court to protect him from harassment by police in New York, Chicago, Los Angeles and San Francisco, to determine how much money he had lost since his conviction in New York, and to order the police department there to pay him damages.

Since his first arrest for obscenity in San Francisco, his earnings had plummeted from $108,000 to $11,000, and he was $15,000 in debt. Under great emotional and financial stress, he had not yet filed a proper appeal in his New York case. Au Go Go owner Howard Solomon had been convicted of the same charge, and that ruling *was* reversed on appeal.

On May 31, 1966, Lenny wrote to me: "I'm still working on the bust of the government of New York State." And he enclosed his doodle of Jesus nailed to the cross, with a speech balloon asking, "Where the hell is the ACLU?" Lenny hadn't identified with Christ's jester, but now he did seem to be identifying with Christ himself.

On August 3, he received a foreclosure notice on his home. Lenny died that day from an overdose of morphine. His death was on the cusp of accident and suicide. In his kitchen, a kettle of water was still boiling. In his office, the electric typewriter was still humming. He had stopped typing in mid-word: *Conspiracy to interfere with the 4th Amendment const*

Constitutes *what*, Lenny?

At the funeral, his roommate and sound engineer, John Judnich, dropped Lenny's microphone into his grave before the dirt was piled on. But, like any pioneer, Lenny's legacy continues on. I asked a few thoughtful stand-up comics how he had influenced them.

Barry Crimmins: "I think about him almost every day and he really, really, really has kept me honest on the stage. I don't get fucked with because of what he did. Speech became a lot freer, thanks to Lenny. I have never had to worry about local police officials monitoring my shows. The only true censorship I've faced has been commercial in nature."

Paul Provenza: "He influenced me in a big way, now more than ever. I didn't realize that I would politicize comedically until I grew to a point where I can come out with the truth. When I was first listening to Lenny, all I was thinking about was comedy, and I realize now that it was the other way around. His comedy was about what he was thinking and feeling."

Veteran comedian George Carlin sums it up: "Lenny Bruce opened the doors for all the guys like me; he prefigured the free-speech movement and helped push the culture forward into the light of open and honest expression. I like to find out where the line is drawn, and then drag the audience across the line with me, and make them happier for the experience. Lenny opened all the doors, or kicked them down."

Among the doors Lenny kicked down were the traditional targets of stand-up performers—airplane food, Chinese waiters, their wives' cooking, driving and frigidity—and instead he went after, in Carlin's words, "the powerful people, to puncture the pretentiousness and pompousness of the privileged."

A documentary, *Lenny Bruce: Swear to Tell the Truth*, was nominated for an Academy Award in 1999, but as producer Robert Weide told me, prophetically, "If there's a documentary about the Holocaust, it will win."

"You don't think you have any chance at all?"

"The odds against *my* film winning are six million to one."

Lenny really would've appreciated that.

Epilogue

When rock star Bono received an award at the Golden Globes ceremony in 2003, he said, "This is fucking brilliant." However, the FCC ruled that he had *not* violated broadcast standards, because his use of the offending word was "isolated and nonsexual." You see, it was merely an adjective.

But then Justin Timberlake exposed Janet Jackson's breast during the half-time extravaganza at the Super Bowl. I had never seen the media make such a mountain out of an implant. The incident served as an excuse to crack down on indecency during this election year.

So, in February 2004, the FCC reversed the Bono decision, contending that his utterance was "indecent and profane" after all.

And has Governor Pataki now decided to revoke his posthumous pardon of Lenny Bruce?

Gay Rights and Wrongs

BEFORE THERE WAS SAME-SEX MARRIAGE

In November 2002, an appeals court ruled that Louisiana's 197-year-old anti-sodomy law did not discriminate against gays and lesbians. The state Supreme Court had previously claimed that the law against oral and anal sex did not violate the right to privacy, based on an appeal, but then plaintiffs, the Louisiana Electorate of Gays and Lesbians Inc., challenged the law, asking the appeals court to consider the trial judge's ruling that the law did not amount to *unconstitutional* discrimination.

So it was good news a month later when the United States Supreme Court agreed to decide whether the Constitution permits states to enforce anti-sodomy laws exclusively against same-sex couples. Until then, the Court had hesitated to admit that such discrimination violated the 14th Amendment, which guarantees "equal protection of the laws." There was fear that if they overturned a Texas law which criminalized "deviate sexual acts" between people of the same sex, it could affect state laws on adoption, foster care, marriage, and employment.

In fact, back in 1986, the Supreme Court *upheld* Georgia's outlawing of consensual homosexual sodomy. That story made front page headlines. A few months later, however, there was only a small news item on the inside pages when that same Court refused to reinstate a law in Oklahoma that outlawed consensual *heterosexual* sodomy. This meant that if Sandra Day O'Connor participated in a threesome with Justices Antonin Scalia and Clarence Thomas during recess, indulging in an infinite variety of positions, only the two men could be arrested.

In an anthology, *Take My Advice: Letters to the Next Generation From People Who Know a Thing or Two*, filmmaker Bruce LaBruce writes: "I'm still the reluctant pornographer, but in this era of rampant assimilationism and gay conservatism, I see pornography as the last refuge of gay radicalism." Let us hope, then, that legislation in America will eventually catch up with the porn industry.

It should not be forgotten that, during his first term as Senate Republican majority leader, Trent Lott publicly compared homosexuality to kleptomania; voted yes on prohibiting same-sex marriage; voted no on prohibiting job discrimination by sexual orientation; blocked the nomination of openly gay philanthropist James Hormel as a U.S. ambassador; and was lambasted for ignoring a surge in anti-gay hate crimes even after the horrific murder of Matthew Shepard became international news.

Although skin color cannot be changed—except perhaps for Michael Jackson—there is currently a movement to transform gays into straights. Ironically, Robert Spitzer, a professor of psychiatry at Columbia University, was a central figure in persuading the American Psychiatric Association to de-pathologize homosexuality in 1973, but he recently reported the results of a study in which two-thirds of a gay and lesbian sample successfully went through "conversion therapy."

Dr. Spitzer defends himself: "What I found was that, in the unique sample I studied, many made substantial changes in sexual arousal and fantasy—and not merely behavior. Even subjects who made a less substantial change believed it to be extremely beneficial. Complete change was uncommon. My study concluded with an important caveat: that it should not be used to justify a denial of civil rights to homosexuals, or as support for coercive treatment. I did not conclude that all gays should try to change, or even that they would be better off if they did. However, to my horror, some of the media reported the study as an attempt to show that homosexuality is a choice, and that substantial change is possible for any homosexual who decides to make the effort."

But, in *The Advocate*, a national gay news magazine, Michelangelo Signorile points out that "conversion therapies have been shown to be harmful. A five-year study of 150 people published in the *Journal of Gay & Lesbian Psychotherapy* in 2001 strongly concluded that 'participants in conversion therapies are plagued by serious psychological and interpersonal problems after termination.' These findings were consistent with several other papers published in journals during the 1990s.... With religious right-backed 'ex-gay' groups promoting conversion therapies in full-page newspaper ads for several years now—and recently in in ads in Washington, D.C. subway stations—the time for the vast majority of psychologists to take a stand would seem to be at hand."

And when Bill Clinton became president in 1992, it was thought that discrimination against gays in the military would finally end. But then Colin Powell—the first African-American to become head of the Joint Chiefs of Staff—acted to prevent such progress. In my dreams, I confronted him:

"General Powell," I said, "you insist that sharing the barracks with a gay soldier would make the other men uncomfortable, but didn't they used to say the same thing about *blacks* in the military?"

"Well, yes," he replied, " but we never *told* anybody we were black."

This was the forerunner of "Don't ask, don't tell."

WHAT DOES BILL O'REILLY REALLY WANT?

An associate producer of Fox TV's *The O'Reilly Factor*, hosted by professional curmudgeon Bill O'Reilly, has accused him of sexual harassment, claiming that he pressured her to have phone sex and tried to engage her in conversations about masturbation, vibrators, oral sex, threesomes and foreplay involving a loofah, which O'Reilly also called "the falafel thing [that] I'd put on your pussy . . ." But there's one flaming desire he didn't bring up with her, which he *did* proclaim when Dan Savage was a guest on his program.

Savage writes an outrageously rational sex advice column, "Savage Love," online and in alternative papers, from the *Village Voice* in New York to the *Orange County Weekly* in California. We met when he was a member of a panel discussion about "Sex and Humor." I was the moderator. He referred to heteros like me as "breeders." I have a biological daughter, but since Savage and his male partner have adopted a child, I appreciate where he was coming from.

A reader once wrote to Savage, "I am a mature teenage girl with a question for you. My brother was watching a porno site with one of his friends and claims he saw a video clip of a man sticking his entire head up a woman's pussy! I say it's impossible! The woman would die! My brother says that if a woman can give birth, she can get a man's head up there. Set us straight, Dan." It was signed, "Can U Now Talk?"

Savage replied: "If your brother wants to win this argument, CUNT"—readers know that Savage uses the initials of their pseudonyms—"all he has to do is take you to the porn site where he saw this video clip. If he can't, well, then he's clearly lying. As for your brother's argument, anyone who's taken a high school health class should be able to see through it. Baby's skulls are small and soft, while full-grown men's skulls are big and hard. Still, I'm reluctant to tell you that it's impossible for a man to stuff his entire head into a woman's pussy. There may actually be a video clip out there somewhere of a tiny man sticking his teensy head into a big woman's huge vagina. If someone out there has a video clip of this, please *do not* send it to me. So let's just file this sex act under unlikely-bordering-on-impossible."

Promoting his book, *Skipping Towards Gomorrah: The Seven Deadly Sins and the Pursuit of Happiness in America*, Savage did a guest stint on *The O'Reilly Factor*. He defended pot smokers and sex educators. But then Bill O'Reilly asked what he thought about gay bathhouses. O'Reilly must have already known how he would answer, since Savage has been bashing bathhouses for a decade in his column.

"And, guys," he had written, "are gay bathhouses even necessary these days? Web sites such as gay.com have basically turned every gay man's apartment into a virtual/potential gay bathhouse, so do we really need to go to the real thing anymore? Why eat out when you can order in?" So now, Savage answered O'Reilly, "I hate gay bathhouses, and I think they should be closed."

O'Reilly shouted, "I want to go to a gay bathhouse!" He kept repeating it: "I want to go to a gay bathhouse! I want to go to a gay bathhouse!"

Savage recalls, "I was stunned. There I was, sitting across the table from the darling of the American right, and he was shouting at me about wanting to go to a gay bathouse. I didn't know what to say. If Bill O'Reilly wanted to go to a gay bathhouse, well, who was I to tell him he shouldn't?"

As if reflecting Savage's future recollection, O'Reilly continued: "If I want to pursue happiness in a gay bathhouse, shouldn't I be free to do that, Mr. Savage?"

Savage told O'Reilly that he was right and admitted that his urge to close gay bathhouses was inconsistent with his do-whatever-feels-good positions on drugs and sexual acts. "You win," he said then, "but really," he says now, "I was thinking, 'Get me the hell away from this guy before he shouts *I want to go to a gay bathhouse* again!' Picturing gay men in a gay bathhouse is revolting enough, but picturing Bill O'Reilly in a gay bathhouse? That could put a gay guy off gay sex for the rest of his unnatural life."

If the Make-a-Wish foundation were to grant O'Reilly's request, he would learn that in March 2004, a federally-funded study indicated that newly diagnosed HIV infections among bathhouse and sex club customers were twice as high as in the gay population and seven times higher among bathhouse patrons than in the general population. In September, the Los Angeles County Board of Supervisors approved a law that would require bathhouses to obtain a health certificate, which could be revoked if patrons are permitted to indulge in unprotected sex. Now, unannounced inspections during peak hours would be allowed.

No bathhouse owners testified against the rule, although Steve Afriat, a lobbyist hired to fight tougher regulation, said, "When you start regulating whether or not people can have safe sex, maybe one day you'll regulate whether people of the same sex can have sex with each other at all." The Supreme Court's recent decision on sodomy has rendered that fear moot.

When San Francisco ordered its bathhouses shut down in 1984, angry activists demonstrated at City Hall, and the city's public health director received so many death threats that he wore a bullet-proof vest for the next few months. Unlike San Francisco, officials in Los Angeles allowed its bathhouses to remain open, but passed an ordinance requiring owners to instruct patrons in safe-sex practices, and to not only provide condoms, but also to make their use mandatory.

According to a Los Angeles County study, about 36 percent of respondents reported using drugs before going to gay bathhouses and sex clubs, which health officials say encourages unsafe behavior. Among the most widely used drugs are methamphetamine together with Viagra, a combination that loosens inhibitions and enables patrons to have sex repeatedly with different partners. One of the few gay leaders calling for more regulation is Michael Weinstein, president of the AIDS Healthcare Foundation. "The debate always seems to counterpoise civil liberties to public health," he said. "But if you are earning money in a commercial establishment from creating a sex environment, then you should be required to make that environment as safe as possible, or you shouldn't be allowed to operate."

However, when an editorial in the *Los Angeles Times* called for the closing of sex clubs, Weinstein complained that "Prohibition didn't work for alcohol, and it won't work for safer sex. Closing the bathhouses in San Francisco did not have a significant impact on new infections and . . . there are many places where bathhouses operate and promote safer sex."

In July 2004, Dr. Jonathan Fielding, Los Angeles county health director, called for the licensing of the county's eleven gay bathouses and sex clubs. The new rules include a requirement that require such establishments to be well-llighted so that inspectors can see what patrons are doing. Hey, isn't that Bill O'Reilly there, the guy who's putting on a red-white-and-blue condom?

If you search for *The O'Reilly Factor* on the Internet and then find the archive link to Dan Savage, you'll notice that the second half of their interview has been erased. Instead of hearing Bill O'Reilly shout, "I want to go to a gay bathhouse," you'll hear three minutes of a test pattern.

When informed of this, Savage commented, "Either Bill O'Reilly doesn't want people to think that he wants to go to a gay bathhouse, or the folks at Fox News don't want DJs all over the world sampling O'Reilly and making 'I Want to Go to a Gay Bathhouse!' a dance sensation this winter in Ibiza. Well, it's too late. I know of three or four DJs who are already hard at work on Bill O'Reilly's breakthrough dance track. Stay tuned."

9/11 and the Invasion of Iraq

THREATS AGAINST THE PRESIDENT

Groucho Marx said in an interview with *Flash* magazine in 1971, "I think the only hope this country has is Nixon's assassination." Yet he was not subsequently arrested for threatening the life of a president. In view of the indictment against David Hilliard, chief of staff of the Black Panther Party, for using similar rhetoric, I wrote to the Justice Department to find out the status of their case against Groucho. This was the response:

> Dear Mr. Krassner:
>
> Responding to your inquiry of July 7th, the United States Supreme Court has held that Title 18 U.S.C., Section 871, prohibits only "true" threats. It is one thing to say that "I (or *we*) will kill Richard Nixon" when you are the leader of an organization which advocates killing people and overthrowing the Government; it is quite another to utter the words which are attributed to Mr. Marx, an alleged comedian. It was the opinion of both myself and the United States Attorney in Los Angeles (where Marx's words were alleged to have been uttered) that the latter utterance did not constitute a "true" threat.
>
> Very truly yours,
> James L. Browning, Jr.
> United States Attorney

At the time, I was the host of a radio talk show on ABC's FM station in San Francisco. Naturally, I went on the air and read that letter. And then I added, "Well, *I'm* an alleged comedian. Kill Richard Nixon." But I would never get away with doing something like that in these ultra-fearful times.

In July 2003, the *Los Angeles Times* published a Sunday editorial cartoon by conservative Michael Ramirez. Depicting a man pointing a gun at President Bush's head, it was a takeoff on the Pulitzer Prize-winning photo from 1968 that showed a Vietnamese general executing a Viet Cong lieutenant at point-blank range. In the cartoon, the man with the gun was labeled "Politics" and the background was labeled "Iraq."

"I thought it was appropriate," said Ramirez, "because I was drawing a parallel between the politization of the Vietnam war and the current politization that's surrounding the Iraq war related to the Niger uranium story." He said that he was not advocating violence against Bush. "In fact, it's the opposite." He explained that he was trying to show that Bush was being undermined by critics who said the president overstated the threat posed by Iraq and lied in his State of the Union speech about Saddam Hussein's alleged effort to illegally obtain uranium from Africa for nuclear weapons. Bush has since admitted that the accusation was based on faulty intelligence. "President Bush is the target, metaphorically speaking," he said, "of a political assassination because of sixteen words that he uttered in the State of the Union. The image, from the Vietnam era, is a very disturbing image. The political attack on the president, based strictly on sheer political motivations, also is very disturbing."

Nevertheless, the cartoon was enough to prompt a visit the next day by a Secret Service agent who asked to speak with Ramirez. He was turned away by an attorney for the *Times*. The agent had called Ramirez and asked if he could visit. Ramirez assumed it was a hoax and jokingly said yes.

"How do I know you're with the Secret Service?" he had asked.

"Well," replied the agent, "I've got a black suit and black sunglasses and credentials."

"Sure, come on down, and make sure you bring your credentials."

The agent arrived half an hour later. However, in an interview by Brooke Gladstone on WNYC radio, Ramirez said, "The firestorm began actually with Matt Drudge's report on Sunday evening, which was a little interesting because he had the headline on his report that said that I was being investigated by the Secret Service. And I really wasn't contacted by the Secret Service until the next morning at 10:30."

Gladstone: "Sounds like he has a line in to the Secret Service."

Ramirez: "I think Matt Drudge is *with* the Secret Service."

Gladstone: "Now, threatening the president is against federal law, and it's the Secret Service's job to protect the president against potential threats. Do you think that Bush's security detail should have felt threatened by your cartoon?"

Ramirez: "No, I think that this is a pretty famous image, and I think the use of the metaphor [is justified] especially in light of the fact that it really is a cartoon that favors him and his administration."

That irony aside, if Bush were actually assassinated, then Vice President Dick Cheney would be demoted to the presidency.

Other examples of the thought police in action:

A man who shall remain anonymous sent Bush a letter saying that if he required a smallpox shot for the troops, he should get a shot himself. He was visited by a Secret Service agent.

Another man, Richard Humphreys, happened to get into a harmless barroom discussion with a truck driver. A bartender who overheard the conversation realized that Bush was scheduled to visit nearby Sioux Falls the next day, and he told police that Humphreys—who was actually making a joke with a Biblical reference—had talked about a "burning Bush" and the possibility of someone pouring a flammable liquid on Bush and lighting it. Humphreys was arrested for threatening the president.

"I said God might speak to the world through a burning Bush," he testified during his trial. "I had said that before and I thought it was funny."

Nevertheless, he was found guilty and sentenced to more than 3 years in prison. He decided to appeal, on the basis that his comment was a prophecy, protected under his right to freedom of speech.

In August, Donnie Johnston, a reporter for the *Free Lance-Star* in Fredericksburg, Virginia, wrote about the trickle-down effect of such official repression:

"A few days ago, a public official called me over to his car to discuss his displeasure with the war in Iraq and the way the Bush administration is handling the nation's economy. This well-respected man would talk only from his vehicle, saying he was fearful of criticizing the president or his policies in public. Before our conversation ended, the man told me of other public officials who also are fearful of speaking out. 'You have to be careful what you say in public these days,' he added. . . . Almost daily, someone informs me that he is scared of openly expressing his views. Even those who do dare to speak out do so in hushed tones, fearful of what ears might overhear. In the politically charged atmosphere that exists in America today, having the wrong person hear criticism of the government can lead to trouble. That became evident recently when an entertainer [a singer] who innocently joked that President Bush had 'chicken legs' was banned from performing further at Borders Books and Music in Fredericksburg."

The nation continues to gallop toward a police state in the guise of security. And, in the process, rampant paranoia has now become our Gross National Product. Some elementary schools have even gone so far as to ban parents from bringing cameras to record their children performing in the annual Christmas pageant, because authorities are afraid that those videotapes might somehow find their way into the horny hands of breathless pedophiles.

PROPAGANDA WARS

"The propagandist's purpose is to make one set of people forget that certain other sets are human."
—Aldous Huxley, 1937

The capture of Saddam Hussein is serving as an orgasmic propaganda victory justifying American imperialism. But propaganda is a many-splendored thing.

Image Manipulation: George Bush gave a speech in Indianapolis to promote his economic plan. White House aides asked people in the crowd standing behind him to take off their ties so that they would look more like the ordinary folks that Bush said would benefit from his tax cut.

Demonization of Enemy: Alternet reports about the police beatings of demonstrators against corporate globalization: "For months beforehand, Police Chief John Timoney had portrayed protestors as terrorists and the gathering in Miami as a siege of the city. Not only were the public and media frightened by Timoney's depiction of the planned protests, there's little doubt that the police themselves buy the propaganda. Having been thoroughly indoctrinated on the threat posed by protesters, and emboldened with new quasi-military equipment, the police were, to say the least, overeager to lunge at protesters."

Obfuscation of Issues: Defense Secretary Donald Rumsfeld has won the 2003 "Foot in the Mouth Award" for his comment on the search for weapons of mass destruction in Iraq: "Reports that say something hasn't happened are always interesting to me, because as we know, there are known knowns, there are things we know we know. We also know there are known unknowns. That is to say, we know there are some things we do not know. But there are also unknowns—the ones we don't know we don't know."

Ulterior Motivation: The *New York Times* reports that "a leaked CIA report warned that resistance to the U.S. occupation is growing among ordinary Iraqis, leading to a new U.S. plan to speed up transfer of power to Iraqis. . . . Even long-time CIA and Pentagon operative Ahmed Chalabi is accusing Bush of letting his re-election concerns determine policy in Iraq, saying, 'The whole thing was set up so President Bush could come to the airport in October [2004] for a ceremony to congratulate the new Iraqi government. When you work backwards from that, you understand the dates the Americans were insisting on.'"

Covering Up Reality: Referring to the president's surprise visit on Thanksgiving day to U.S. troops in Iraq, Mike Littwin reports in the *Rocky Mountain News*: "Before the press was herded into the giant hangar in advance of George W. Bush's pep rally/photo op with the Fort Carson troops, we were given the rules. No talking to the troops before the rally. No talking to the troops during the rally. No talking to the troops after the rally. . . . But even here, or maybe especially here, a soldier or two might have, in conversation, questioned the need for the war in Iraq. This is not exactly a welcome notion in the White House. The Bush campaign has put up an ad in Iowa saying that certain of his opponents are 'attacking the president for attacking the terrorists,' as if opposing the war in Iraq is the same as opposing the war on terror."

The book *Weapons of Mass Deception: The Uses of Propaganda in Bush's War on Iraq* is by the co-editors of *PR Watch* and co-authors of *Trust Us, We're Experts!* and *Toxic Sludge Is Good For You!* Since the production of propaganda is accelerating so rapidly these days, I wondered what they would like to have included in their book if it hadn't already gone to press.

"The main thing that stands out in my mind," Sheldon Rampton told me, "has been the progressive unraveling of the propaganda campaign and the efforts by the government in Britain, Australia and the United States to paper things over. On the one hand, there has been a steady trickle of whistleblowers [who] have come forward and declared that the intelligence information was selectively interpreted, manipulated, cooked, and falsified. The Bush and Blair governments have responded by retreating into minutae and by attempting to re-spin these exposures as a simple question of whether they 'lied' or not. . . .

"Other things that I find interesting from a propaganda perspective recently: The renaming of 'Total Information Awareness' as 'Terrorism Information

Awareness'; and Bush's repeated charge that his critics are trying to 'rewrite history.' I find this phrase interesting at several levels: First, it says something about the shallowness of the man that he thinks of events from only a few months ago as 'history.' Secondly, it is a patent attempt at reversal, since the Bush administration has been trying to rewrite history by shifting attention away from the issue of weapons of mass destruction (one of the core claims of its argument for war). What Bush is really trying to do is claim that as the winner of the war in Iraq, it is his prerogative to write the history. Of course, he really *hasn't* won the war yet. . . .

"I was struck recently by reading a letter to the editor in an Arizona newspaper by a woman named Carol Drew. She began by complaining that the people of Iraq are 'selfish and thankless' for 'crying and whining about how little food and water there is, and blaming it on America.' She then went on to say that she has a niece stationed in Iraq as a soldier. 'The soldiers are suffering diarrhea,' she reported. 'They sleep on the ground in ditches to cover themselves from constant gunfire from the Iraqis. . . . She has lost 15 pounds and is weak from lack of proper nutrition and water, but is adamant about being there to do the job that her government has required her to do.'

"The first time I read the letter, I was rather angry that a woman in Arizona would attack the people of Iraq as 'selfish and thankless,' after all they've been through. As I reread it, though, I began to feel more appreciation for what she must be going through as she worries about her niece. But it also struck me as a powerful example of how effective the propaganda campaign in the United States has been at shaping the thinking of many people in the United States. It seems that even 'constant gunfire' from the Iraqis isn't enough to wake her up to the fact that the Iraqis don't want us there."

I also asked about the relationship between gossip and propaganda.

"Gossip can serve as effective propaganda," John Stauber replied, "in the hands of a skilled 'perception manager,' another word for a PR flack. Gossip is undocumented information spread popularly from person to person, that may or may not be true. It is often malicious, and started by an individual to smear or undermine an enemy or opponent. Gossip is very difficult to defend against because the very act of denial seems incriminating. Gossip puts the burden on the victim to prove an often anonymous charge to be false, rather than requiring that the gossipers prove an allegation to be true. Gossipers are an anonymous mob, passing on allegations that by the very act of passage are granted some invisible authority. Gossip can be very harmful, even if at some point it is exposed as false and malicious.

"Skilled propagandists can plant gossip and, if it takes root and spreads successfully, it can serve a useful propaganda purpose. For instance, gossip has helped spread the false propaganda that Jews stayed home from work at the World Trade Center on 9/11 because they were warned of the attacks in advance. This is an outrageous lie, but that has not stopped it from being spread and believed by those predisposed to so believe. Critical thinkers reject gossip and rumor, but popular media promotes it. Imagine the tabloid or entertainment press without it; it's impossible. Propaganda and gossip are both enemies of critical thinking and democracy. Propagandists can exploit the part of human nature that embraces gossip to plant and promote rumors that serve their purposes."

CONDOLEEZZA, LINDA AND MONICA

What was it again that Condoleezza Rice testified she couldn't remember telling George Bush? About sleeper cells in the United States? Or was it stem cells? Does any reasonable person believe she really forgot? If she didn't tell Bush, she's covering her ass. If she did tell him and he did nothing, she's covering *his* ass. Maybe the 9/11 Commision should've offered her HT-0712, the "Mind Viagra" pill that restores memory in fruit flies and mice. But would that make any difference if Condi was consciously resorting to blatant deception in the guise of false memory-loss syndrome?

Just as there's selective memory, there's selective deception. The infamous Oklahoma City bomber, frontman Timothy McVeigh, was a frequent guest at the home of co-conspirator Terry Nichols. He shared with Nichols an unspeakable act of domestic terrorism. And yet, Nichols' wife, Marife Torres, testified at his state murder trial that she eventually became jealous of McVeigh because Nichols spent more time with him than he did with her and their daughter, but that during one of McVeigh's visits, she had an affair with him—which, of course, McVeigh kept secret from Nichols.

In order to best deceive others, one must deceive oneself until that deception becomes a reality. A Bush family member was quoted in the *Los Angeles Times:* "George sees this as a religious war. His view is that they are trying to kill the Christians. And the Christians will strike back with more force and more ferocity than they will ever know."

That's virtually interchangeable with this utterance by Abu Bakar Bashir, an Islamic cleric and accused terrorist leader: "America's aim in attacking Iraq is to attack Islam, so it is justified for Muslims to target America to defend themselves."

And so it came to pass that, after four mercenaries—oops, I mean contractors—were slaughtered in Fallujah, and consequently U.S. Marines bombed mosques where weapons of individual destruction had been stored, they also shot bullets into copies of the Koran. Which only increases the perception of a religious war that Muslims must avenge. And, with provocation like that, who needs friendly fire?

Recently I told my friend Avery Corman, the author of *Kramer vs. Kramer* and *Oh God*, that I was finally working on my first novel.

"It's really hard writing fiction," I said. "You have to make everything up."

"Oh, come on, Paul, you've been making up stuff your whole life."

"Yeah, but that was journalism."

So I was prepared to believe that "Deep Throat"—the secret source of Bob Woodward and Carl Bernstein in their investigation of the Watergate break-in—was actually a composite of several sources, invented for the sake of dramatic effect. In any case, that code name was a seminal point in the pornographication of news.

On NPR, commentator Daniel Schorr referred to it as "recycling the title of a movie." He didn't mention that it was a *porn* movie. *Deep Throat* has become such a mainstream reference that you don't even have to *know* that the Linda Lovelace character's clitoris was embedded deep in her throat, so that performing fellatio on a man was her only way of achieving orgasm.

I was also prepared to believe that Woodward only *imagined* that he snuck into CIA head William Casey's hospital room and obtained exclusive deathbed confessions.

But Homey don't play that game no more. Or does he?

In the *St. Louis Post-Dispatch*, Harry Levins wrote about Woodward's new book, *Plan of Attack*: "Can a book that reconstructs events without naming its sources be trusted as real history? Woodward's book re-creates private conversations between decision-makers word for word, even though no reporters were present. Except for a few on-the-record interviews, the book makes no mention of who told Woodward what had been said at these meetings. . . . In fact, said Professor Mark Hanley of Truman State University in Kirskville, Mo., 'Woodward's book isn't history. It's a book by an investigative reporter who's enormously important—and who knows what will make his book interesting.'"

History or not, it's revealing how Woodward's *on*-the-record interviews have instigated a mini-goldmine of ass-covering lies.

Item: The *New York Times* reported that "Secretary of State Colin Powell disputed Woodward's account . . . he said that he had an excellent relationship with Vice President Dick Cheney, and that he did not recall referring to officials at the Pentagon loyal to Cheney as the 'Gestapo office.'" Who among us would be unable to recall uttering such an epithet? Indeed, Powell later apologized for it.

Item: Donald Rumsfeld said—referring to the impending attack on Iraq—he didn't remember assuring Saudi Ambassador Prince Bandar, "You can take that to the bank." Then Woodward produced a transcript of the taped interview, and there it was.

Item: Appearing together before 9/11 commission members—in private and not under oath—Bush and Cheney inspired several editorial cartoons showing Cheney as a ventriloquist and Bush as his dummy; one caption stated, "No wonder Cheney talks out of the side of his mouth." My inside source, "Green Door," tells me that Cheney was asked, "Did you inform Prince Sadar, 'Saddam is toast'?" To which Bush-dummy responded, "No, he said, 'Saddam *likes* toast.'"

Woodward had previously written a book—*Bush At War*, about the attack on Afghanistan—that was favorable to George W. Bush, which is why Bush *requested* him to write a book about his entry into the Iraq war, granted him permission to interview White House officials, and instructed them to cooperate.

Referring to *Plan of Attack*, Larry King asked Woodward, "Did they expect a more favorable book?"

"I think they expected a more favorable *war*," he replied.

In *Against All Enemies*, Richard Clarke had written: "Just before going to the meeting [in 1998 with Bill Clinton], I read a CIA report from a source in Afghanistan that bin Laden and his top staff were planning a meeting on August 20 to review the results of their attacks [on the American embassies in Tanzania and Kenya] and plan the next wave. Terrorist coordinators from outside Afghanistan had been summoned back for the session. As we sat down in the Cabinet Room, I slipped the report to George Tenet, who was sitting next to me. On it, I penned, 'You thinking what I'm thinking?' He passed it back with a note on it, 'You better believe I am.'

"We had both come to the conclusion that this report meant we had the opportunity not merely to stage a retaliatory bombing, but also a chance to get bin Laden and his top deputies, if the President would agree to a strike now during the white-hot 'Monica' scandal press coverage. . . . Although we had been going after al Qaeda for several years, now it would be the top priority to eliminate the organization. The President asked National Security Advisor Sandy Berger to coordinate all of the moving parts necessary for a military response, tentatively planned for August 20, six days later. . . . 'Listen, retaliating for these attacks is all well and good, but we gotta get rid of these guys once and for all,' Clinton said, looking seriously over his half glasses at Tenet . . . 'You understand what I'm telling you? . . .'

"All of this was taking place against the backdrop of the continuing Monica scandal. Like most of his advisors, I was beyond mad that the president had not shown enough discretion or self-control, although from what I knew of Presidential history, marital infidelity had also been a problem for several of his illustrious predecessors. I was angrier, almost incredulous, that the bitterness of Clinton's enemies knew no bounds, that they intended to hurt not just Clinton but the country by turning the President personal problem into a global, public circus for their own political ends. Now I feared that the timing of the President's interrogation about the scandal, August 17, would get in the way of our hitting the al Qaeda meeting.

"It did not. Clinton made clear that we were to give him our best national security advice, without regard to his personal problems. 'Do you all recommend that we strike on the 20th? Fine. Do not give me political advice or personal advice about the timing. That's my problem. Let me worry about that.' If we thought this was the best time to hit the Afghan camps, he would order it and take the heat for the 'Wag the Dog' criticism that we all knew would happen, for the media and congressional reaction that would say he was using a military strike to divert attention from his deposition in the investigation. . . . Ironically, Clinton was blamed for a 'Wag the Dog' strategy in 1998 dealing with the real threat from al Qaeda but no one labeled Bush's 2003 war on Iraq as a 'Wag the Dog' move even though the 'crisis' was manufactured and Bush political advisor Karl Rove was telling Republicans to 'run on the war.'"

Poor, naive Monica Lewinsky. *The Starr Report* disclosed her fantasy about being together with Clinton more often when he was out of office. She quoted him as saying, "I might be alone in three years." In that same section of the report, she quoted Clinton as saying, "Well, what are we going to do when I'm 75 and I have to pee 25 times a day?" And it must have been embarrassing for Clinton to hear the tape that Linda Tripp made, where Monica told her what she had said to him on the phone: "I love you, Butthead." Fortunately, he didn't respond, "I love you, Beavis."

Clarke wrote, "The American public's reaction to the U.S. retaliation . . . was about as adverse as we could have imagined. According to the media and many in Congress, Clinton had launched a military strike to divert attention from the Monica scandal. . . . Our response to two deadly terrorist attacks was an attempt to wipe out al Qaeda leadership, yet it quickly became grist for the right-wing talk radio mill and part of the get Clinton campaign. That reaction made it more difficult to get approval for follow-up attacks on al Qaeda, such as my later attempts to persuade the principals to forget about finding bin Laden and just bomb the training camps."

Who could possibly have predicted that Monica Lewinsky—who had merely been performing oral sex on Bill Clinton while Yassir Arafat was waiting in the Rose Garden for their appointment—that years later she would be considered as ultimately responsible for the 9/11 attacks and the unrelated invasion of Iraq? Not me, babe.

I FORGET THE TITLE OF THIS

Ronald Reagan's funeral was a week-long series of photo-ops, a most appropriate postscript to a presidency that was an eight-year celebration of government by public relations. There was that photo of Ronnie and Nancy posing with Michael Jackson. Then there was Nancy, sitting on Mr. T's lap—he was dressed in a Santa Claus costume and she was kissing him on the cheek. And there was Ronnie and the pope—the Great Communicator meets the Great Excommunicator.

When Reagan ran for re-election in 1984, a network TV correspondent presented a hard-hitting report about the White House ducking issues for the sake of a "feel good" campaign. Yet a Reagan aide phoned and said, "Great piece, we loved it," explaining to the confused correspondent, "We're in the middle of a campaign, and you give us 4-1/2 minutes of great pictures of Ronald Reagan. And that's all the American people see."

Reagan used to wear only one contact lens when he appeared before crowds. Whenever his speech-writer Ken Khachigian tried to shorten his stump speech by eliminating a line, Reagan replied, "Have you seen the way people respond when I say that?" The eye with the contact lens would read the speech, and the other eye would study faces in the audience for their reaction.

When he testified before the committee investigating the Iran/*contra* scandal, he was unable to recall whether he had approved trading weapons for hostages, testifying 130 times that "I don't remember." During his 1980 campaign, there had been rumblings of senility, and Reagan publicly offered to take a senility test if the proper authorities concluded that he had become senile, but nobody ever took him up on it. Perhaps his convenient losses of memory were actually early tremors of the Alzheimer's disease that plagued him for the last ten years of his life.

Nowadays, of course, there are other excuses. A reader wrote to the column "People's Pharmacy" by Joe and Teresa Graedon in the *Los Angeles Times*:

"I took Lipitor for more than a year, and I thought I was doing great. My cholesterol levels dropped significantly with no side effects. Then I began having problems remembering names. Sometimes it took me till noon to gather my scattered thoughts enough to work. I couldn't put a complete sentence together, and I began avoiding situations that required meeting with people. I'm in the advertising and marketing business, but I avoided clients and preferred to work by e-mail. After reading one of your articles that linked Lipitor to memory problems, I immediately contacted my doctor, and he agreed to a holiday from Lipitor. It took a few months, but my memory has returned. Memory problems should be listed as a side effect of Lipitor."

And the answer: "Amnesia is listed as an infrequent side effect of Lipitor, and memory loss is noted as a potential side effect of other cholesterol-lowering drugs such as Lescol, Mevacor, Pravachol and Zocor." (Pravachol promises to prevent your first heart attack *and* to prevent your second heart attack, so that when you do have your first heart attack you'll think that it's really your third.) "Although this seems to be rare, we have heard from readers who have had difficulty with names, numbers and concentration while taking one of these. Some have even reported episodes in which they could not remember their address, spouse or occupation."

But how to account for the current epidemic of memory loss among Bush administration officials testifying before investigating committees?

The May 24, 2004 issue of *Newsweek* stated that a memo written by White House counsel Alberto Gonzales after the September 11th attacks may have established the legal foundation that allowed for the abusive treatment of Iraqi prisoners. *Newsweek* reported that in January 2002, Gonzales wrote to President Bush that, in his judgment, the post 9/11 security environment "renders obsolete [the Geneva Convention's] strict limitations on questioning of enemy prisoners and renders quaint some of its provisions."

According to *Newsweek*, Secretary of State Colin Powell "hit the roof" when he read the memo, and he fired off his own note to Bush, warning that the new rules "will reverse over a century of U.S. policy and practice" and have "a high cost in terms of negative international reaction." But then, on *Meet the Press*, he claimed that he did not recall the Gonzales memo. Huh?

There is an explanation, though. In November 2003, Powell was interviewed by Abdul Rahman Al-Rashed, an American correspondent for a London-based Saudi newspaper. Referring to Powell's description of his international killer schedule, Al-Rashad asked, "So do you use sleeping tablets to organize yourself?"

"Yes," Powell replied. "Well, I wouldn't call them that. They're a wonderful medication. How would you call it? They're called Ambien, which is very good. You don't use Ambien? Everybody here uses Ambien."

So I decided to check out the side effects of Ambien: "Sleep medicines may cause the special type of memory loss known as amnesia. When this occurs, a person may not remember what has happened for several hours after taking the medicine. This is usually not a problem, since most people fall asleep after taking the medicine. Memory loss can be a problem, however, when sleep medicines are taken while traveling, such as during an airplane flight, and the person wakes up before the effect of the medicine is gone. This has been called 'traveler's amnesia.' Memory problems are not common while taking Ambien. In most instances memory problems can be avoided if you take Ambien only when you are able to get a full night's sleep (7 to 8 hours) before you need to be active again. Be sure to talk to your doctor if you think you are having memory problems."

If you remember to talk to your doctor, that is.

A study in the May 27, 2004 issue of *Neuron* confirms previous models of memory recall that found sensory-specific components of a memory are preserved in sensory-related areas of the brain. The hippocampus can draw on this stored sensory information to create vivid recall. Which is why, even after you've returned from a vacation, you may still fully recall the sights, sounds, tastes and smells of some of its particularly memorable moments. For their study, the researchers mapped brain activity in human volunteers who sampled different odors and viewed pictures of various objects. As for short-term memory loss, Wes Nisker writes in *The Big Bang, the Buddha, and the Baby Boom: The Spiritual Experiments of My Generation*:

"Recent research in molecular biology has given us a clue to the connection between THC, the psychoactive ingredient in marijuana, and the actual experience of getting high. It turns out that our body produces its own version of THC and that the human brain and nervous system have a whole network of receptors for this cannabinoid-like substance. That means you've got a stash inside of you right now, and nobody can even bust you for it. Our body's natural THC was discovered by Israeli neuro-scientists, who named it anandamide, from the Sanskrit word for 'inner bliss.' The scientists believe that our system produces this THC equivalent to aid in pain relief, for mild sedation, and also to help us forget. It is very important that we forget, because if we remembered everything that registers in our senses from moment to moment, we would be flooded with memory and could not function. So anandamide helps us edit the input of the world by blocking or weakening our synaptic pathways, our memory lanes."

So, the next time somebody reminds you, "Don't bogart that joint," at least you'll have a scientific explanation, if you can only remember what it is.

THE WAR ON INDECENCY

ARNOLD, MADONNA, DOONESBURY AND
AN INTERNET PORN SCAM

I think maybe I should start selling "I Told You So" T-shirts.

In the '90s, I published this item in *The Realist*: "Here's a story about the arrogance of power even the tabloids won't publish. At a dinner party, Arnold Schwarzenegger told a young woman he would give her $1,000 if she would stick her finger up her ass and then let him smell it. She refused. Later, he followed her into the bathroom and forcibly stuck his own finger up her ass. He did not pay her. She is an actress and has not brought a lawsuit because she fears it would hurt her career in Hollywood."

But now Arnold has replaced Bill Clinton as America's generic sex-joke reference. The morning after California's recall election, on *The View*, Meredith Viera demonstrated to Joy Behar the governor-elect's special handshake. Viera simply placed her right hand on Behar's left breast. Amidst laughter and applause, Behar asked, "Can I please have my nipple back now?" It was a perfect example of television's ever-expanding sense of permissiveness.

Even if you didn't happen to catch the open mouth kiss between Madonna and Britney Spears during the MTV Music Video Awards—"It wasn't a publicity stunt," explained Britney, "we just did what felt right"—you certainly must have seen a photo of that smooch, which appeared on the front page of newspapers around the country.

This incident evoked the most public discussion since Michael Jackson kissed Lisa Marie Presley on the MTV Awards to prove that their marriage wasn't a public relations gesture, and Al Gore kissed Tipper at the Democratic convention to prove that he wasn't like that wife-cheating Bill Clinton. Indeed, the *Atlanta Journal Constitution* was deluged with complaints from readers about the Madonna-Brittany photo, and their managing editor apologized, saying that it should not have been published on the front page, but rather on the inside.

On a weekly media discussion program, *News Watch*, on the Fox network, moderator Eric Burns criticized the TV news and entertainment programs for showing clips of the kiss "over and over again," though I counted a total of ten lingering displays of the kiss on *News Watch* itself.

"What's next," wondered conservative columnist Cal Thomas, "full frontal nudity?" Or, worse yet, presidential candidates "Joe Lieberman kissing Howard Dean?" Thomas was particularly concerned about newspapers arriving on the front doorstep and children bringing them into their homes.

The controversy was brought into focus by former *Saturday Night Live* cast member Jon Lovitz when he was a guest on *Late Night with Conan O'Brien*. He complained that the televised kiss wasn't long enough, because by the time he pulled his pants down to his ankles, it was already over.

But Lovitz could easily have gone on to pleasure himself simply for the sake of his own future health. The British magazine *New Scientist* had reported on a study in Australia which concluded that the more men ejaculate between the ages of 20 and 50, the less likely they are to develop prostate cancer. Apparently, ejaculation prevents carcinogens from building up in the gland. As if men need such encouragement to jerk off.

The *New Scientist* article was reported on in England, India, South Africa and New Zealand, as well as wire service coverage in the United States, not to mention providing fodder for morning radio shock jocks and late night talk show monologues.

On a recent Sunday, Garry Trudeau's comic strip *Doonesbury* depicted Reverend Scot Sloan reading a newspaper at breakfast: "Incredible. . . . There's a new study that suggests that regular masturbation prevents prostate cancer."

Boopsie responds, "Hey! . . . Enough of that!"

"Enough of what? It's in the paper."

"I don't care! Talk like that makes me uncomfortable! People shouldn't sit around talking about sex like it's the weather! It's just not appropriate!"

"You're dating yourself, Boopsie."

Zonker enters: "Hey, did you guys hear self-dating prevents cancer?"

Doonesbury has previously caused controversy. Trudeau pulled a 1985 series about abortion, and a 2001 strip poking fun at President Bush a few days after 9/11 (drawn before the terrorist attacks). In 1998, some papers refused to run a strip about accusations that President Clinton had sex with a White House intern and, just before the 2000 election, a strip that accused Bush of cocaine abuse. But this was the first time Trudeau allowed his syndicate to offer a substitute strip—one that was a year old, but with the current date.

Trudeau said the strip, which was censored by 400 out of 1400 papers, "isn't really about masturbation or cancer, but about the shifting nature of taboos and the inabiity of two adults to have a certain kind of serious conversation. It's a *South Park* world now, and younger readers are unlikely to be shocked or confused by anything they find in *Doonesbury*. Besides, our general experience is that most children don't understand *Doonesbury* in any event, and thus sensibly avoid it."

However, any children who were innocently trying to log on to a Web site—such as Disneyland, Bob the Builder, Teletubbies, Anna Kurnikova or Backstreet Boys, among many others—but who misspelled a name, would have been automatically misdirected to hard-core porn sites that they could not avoid, courtesy of "typo squatter" John Zuccarini. He was arrested for registering several thousands of Internet addresses and earning $1 million a year from porn Web site operators who paid him between 10 and 25 cents for each hit he sent their way.

This is the first prosecution under a new clause in the Amber Alert law, making it a crime to use "misleading" domain names to lure children to porn. But the Amber Alert legislation was originally intended only to combat *physical abduction* by sending out immediate information to aid in the safe recovery of a child. It was intended only for time-critical child abduction cases, where the victim is in imminent danger of bodily harm or death.

In December 2003, Zuccarini pleaded guilty and agreed to a prison term of 30 to 37 months. In a culture permeated by corporations misleading potential customers, he is among the sleaziest. He registered 15 variations of the popular children's cartoon site, cartoonnetwork.com, and 41 variations on the name of teen pop star and Madonna-kisser Britney Spears. A child who typed cartoonjoe.com instead of joecartoon.com would wind up at an explicit sex site. Zuccarini was charged with "enticing children to pornography."

"Although this man's method of making a bunch of money is abhorrent," said porn star Jenna Jameson, "I fail to see how he is responsible for enticing children into pornography. Why not charge the teachers and parents for not properly beating their children into correctly spelling 'Barney'? Hell, why not charge the child too? The man is scum . . . that's for sure, but should he be charged as enticing children into porn? No. False advertising, yes. I'm tired of people using the umbrella of 'It's for the children' to cover everything they find morally reprehensible."

There's an irony here that must be acknowledged. Somewhere a child has a homework assignment to write a composition about President Bush (our misleader-in-chief) but, instead of typing whitehouse.gov, this child types white-house.com—the very same porn site where Jenna's statement appeared.

BLOW JOB BETTY

As a friend of Lenny Bruce as well as the editor of his autobiography, *How to Talk Dirty Dirty and Influence People*, I would've preferred this little story to have been included in the book from Lenny's point of view rather than mine, but any-way. . . .

I remember sitting in an office with a few *Playboy* attorneys. They were anxious to avoid libel, so they kept changing the name of any person in the original manuscript who might bring suit. For example, Lenny had mentioned an individual called Blow Job Betty, and the lawyers were afraid she would sue.

"You must be kidding," I said. "Do you really believe anybody would come out and *admit* that she was known as Blow Job Betty?"

The book ended with a montage of Lenny's life experiences, cultural icons, folklore and urban myths:

"My friend Paul Krassner once asked me what I've been influenced by in my work.

"I have been influenced by my father telling me that my back would become crooked because of my maniacal desire to masturbate; by reading 'Gloriosky, Zero' in *Annie Rooney*; by listening to Uncle Don and Clifford Brown; by smelling the burnt shell powder at Anzio and Salerno; torching for my ex-wife; giving money to Moondog as he played the upturned pails around the corner from Hanson's at 51st and Broadway; getting hot looking at *Popeye* and *Toots and Caspar* and *Chris Crustie* years ago; hearing stories about a pill they can put in the gas tank with water but 'the big companies' won't let it out—the same big companies that have the tire that lasts forever—and the Viper's favorite fantasy: 'Marijuana could be legal, but the big liquor companies won't let it happen'; Harry James has cancer on his lip; Dinah Shore has a colored baby; Irving Berlin didn't write all those songs, he's got a guy locked in the closet; colored people have a special odor.

"It was an absurd question. I am influenced by every second of my waking hour."

The lawyers edited Harry James and Dinah Shore out of that paragraph, but for some unfathomable reason, Irving Berlin remained. There was one incident which they decided to omit entirely from the book. Lenny had been working at Le Bistro, a night club in Atlantic City. During his performance, he asked for a cigarette from anyone in the audience. Basketball star Wilt Chamberlain happened to be there. He lit a cigarette and handed it up.

"Did you see *that*?" Lenny whispered into the microphone. "He nigger-lipped it. . . ."

Lenny and I had an unspoken agreement that there would be nothing in the book about his use of drugs. When I first met him, he would shoot up in the hotel bathroom with the door closed, but now he just sat on his bed and casually fixed up while we were talking. That's what we had been doing one time when Lenny nodded out, the needle still stuck in his arm.

Suddenly the phone rang and startled him. His arm flailed, and the hypodermic came flying across the room, hitting the wall like a dart just a few feet from the easy chair in which I sat uneasily. Lenny picked up the phone. It was Blow Job Betty, calling from the lobby. She came up on the elevator and went down on Lenny. In front of me.

Lenny had introduced us. "This is Paul, he's interviewing me." At one point, while she was giving him head, Lenny and I made eye contact. He looked at me quizzically, and his eyes said, "I'm not usually an exhibitionist."

My eyes replied, "And I'm not usually a voyeur."

A little later, Lenny said to her, "I really wanna fuck you now."

Blow Job Betty gestured toward me and said, "In front of *him*?"

"Okay, Paul," said Lenny, "I guess the interview is over now."

In retrospect, I understand the mindset of Bill Clinton when he testified under oath that he "never had sexual relations with that woman, Ms. Lewinsky." The president had simply made the same distinction between intercourse and oral sex that Blow Job Betty had made.

Incidentally, those *Playboy* lawyers insisted on changing Blow Job Betty's name to Go Down Gussie.

"I hope there actually *is* somebody out there named Go Down Gussie," I told them, "and I hope that *she* sues *Playboy* for invasion of privacy."

WHEN JUSTIN MET JANET

About 20 years ago, *People* magazine published a special feature on '60s activists. A full page photo showed Ken Kesey, Wavy Gravy and me, all sitting on top of "Furthur," the psychedelic relic of a bus that Tom Wolfe had chronicled in *The Electric Kool-Aid Acid Test*. We were told that *People* planned to put this photo on the cover, so I carefully held onto my crotch, a sort of private joke to keep myself pure.

However, the cover went to Michael Jackson. And *he* was holding onto *his* crotch. Our gesture was exactly the same, except that there was a glove on his hand. The magazine's motivation differed from mine—this shot of Jackson in the midst of performing was pragmatically selected out of hundreds in order to sell copies—but still, I had been beaten at my own game with a splash of irony.

I had a flashback of that incident when Roseanne Barr—just like baseball players do all the time—grabbed *her* crotch and spat on the ground after screeching *The Star Spangled Banner* before the game. If I had ingested LSD for the occasion, I would've been positive this was merely a hallucination. More recently, I had that same kind of flashback when rapper Nelly clutched *his* crotch while performing at the Super Bowl half-time festivites.

That gesture served as the warm-up act for the instantly infamous revelation of Janet Jackson's right breast by Justin Timberlake as the culmination of their sexed-up duet. Never before in media history had the mainstream audience been fed and re-fed an image so many times.

Reuters reported that a woman in Tennessee has filed a class action suit against Jackson, Timberlake, CBS, MTV and Viacom, claiming that millions of people are owed monetary damages for being involuntarily exposed to lewd conduct.

Nevertheless, according to the search engine Lycos, Jackson's internationally seen flash of flesh has become the most searched for event in the history of the Internet. Previously, the attacks on September 11th were the most sought after topic in a one day period.

The biggest spike in TiVo activity during the Super Bowl game occurred at the end of the half-time show. Someone in almost every single one of the 20,000 TiVo households that were tracked during the game rewound and replayed that segment at least once.

The Daily Show presented the titillating image over and over and over again, each one from a different news or entertainment program, as Jon Stewart described the varieties of pixilation that had been used to cover up Jackson's apocalyptic nipple.

Comedian Tom Dreesen, speaking at a Southern California Sports Broadcasters luncheon, commented that "Timberlake should have gone for two." And on the *Tonight* show, Jay Leno said that Timberlake "is now qualified to run for political office."

A correspondent for *The Economist* observed that George Bush missed the earth-shaking moment because he turned off the game after the first half and went to bed, that John Kerry expressed how delighted he was that the New England Patriots won, and that Howard Dean said it was no big deal to him because as a docter he had seen *countless* breasts, so therefore with those three the whole thing had an aura of Sleepy, Happy and Doc.

Chicago Tribune columnist Clarence Page conducted an exclusive interview with Janet Jackson's bra. It began:

Q. "Thank you for agreeing to open up to our audience."

A. "You're welcome. I need the exposure."

At one point, the bra stated, "If you're looking for something to hide from the kids, how about the commercial for Cialis, the potency drug with its warnings about four hour erections? What do you say when your child asks, 'Daddy, what's erectile dysfunction?'"

And the correct answer could well be, "Something that would please superfeminist Andrea Dworkin." After all, the *New Republic* once published an article, "The New Porn Wars" by Jean Bethke Elshtain, which stated, "Dworkin has written that it is acceptable for women to have sex with men as long as the man's penis isn't erect."

No wonder Clint Eastwood's little daughter in the film *Tightrope* wanted to know, "Daddy, what's a hard-on?"

As a result of Timberlake's snatching off half of Jackson's red bra along with part of her black leather bustier, more than 200,000 complaints were filed with the Federal Communications Commission. Michael Powell, chairman of the FCC, has launched an investigation, as if to divert attention from the facts indicating that his father Colin had lied to the UN about the necessity for invading Iraq.

Janet Jackson also lied when she told the press that the bare tit action had not been planned by her and was simply a spontaneous happening. If that were true, though, she could have sued Justin Timberlake for sexual molestation. I mean, there were certainly enough witnesses.

THE CRACKDOWN

When I was a kid, I heard a song on the radio called "Paradise." There would be a line—for example, "And then she holds my hand"—always followed by humming. The song was banned because of what might be going on *during* those wordless segments. And that was just the beginning.

In the '50s, Rosemary Clooney's rendition of "Mambo Italiano" was banned because it it didn't meet the ABC radio network's "standards for good taste." They also banned Billie Holiday's version of Cole Porter's "Love for Sale."

In the '60s, the Rolling Stones were not permitted to sing "Let's Spend the Night Together" on the *Ed Sullivan Show* unless they desexualized it and sang "Let's spend some time together."

In the '70s, radio stations across the country banned Loretta Lynn's song, "The Pill," and Jesse Jackson unsuccessfully called for a ban of disco music because he felt it promoted promiscuity and drug use.

In the '80s, Tipper Gore and twenty wives of Washington politicians formed the Parents Music Resource Center because they were afraid of lyrics. And even though they were able to pressure the music industry into putting warning labels on album covers, they still couldn't stop the songs.

In the '90s, hip-hop had become an easy target of censorship, with every new rapper perceived by the establishment as an enemy combatant.

In 2004, when Vice President Dick Cheney told Vermont Senator Frank Leahy, "Go fuck yourself," the *Washington Post,* unlike other daily newspapers, published that physically impossible suggestion without resorting to asterisks or dashes. But, had a radio or TV news report failed to bleep the F-word, a stiff fine for indecency would surely have been levied.

In May, singer Avril Lavigne's performance was cut short by MTV producers after she flipped the bird—gesturing to the camera with her middle finger—

in response to interviewer Damien Fahey asking her what she thought about the labels that media critics apply to her.

An Indianapolis radio station owned by Emmis Communications used its so-called "dump button," an electronic delay device, to prevent the words *urinate*, *damn* and *orgy* from being heard by listeners during its broadcast of Rush Limbaugh's show.

Last year, KBOO in Portland, Oregon was fined $8,000 for broadcasting the hip-hop song, "Your Revolution" by Sarah Jones, that included the words *blow job*. KBOO spent $25,000 fighting the complaint, and Jones sued the FCC, which reversed its decision, based on evidence that Jones was invited to perform the song in high schools and junior highs.

This year, you won't be hearing Elton John's song, "The Bitch Is Back."

The reality TV show, *Elimidate*, in a pre-emptive strike, has eliminated from its shows in syndication, words such as *ass* and *bitch*, as have courtroom programs.

Bare asses shot at a nudist camp on the Fox network's *Simple Life 2* were covered by large happy faces. Not so with the forced display of pixilated buttocks by a pyramid of prisoners at Abu Ghraib prison in Iraq. Secretary of Defense Donald Rumsfeld called this abuse, as opposed to torture. What a relief.

The *Los Angeles Times* reported that one of the ringleaders "forced naked detainees to masturbate, showing them how to move their hands back and forth until 'one of them did it right.'"

Pompous legislators self-righteously perused the photos—here a man forced to wear women's panties on his head, there a naked man on the ground wearing a dog collar attached to a leash held by a female soldier—and these congressmen were plenty angry. Why? Because, for that kind of activity, *they* have to pay extra to those Washington hookers.

BOOK RELATED ACTIVITIES

The Secret Life of Walter Winchell

In 1953, I went to the office of *Expose'*—a free-speech tabloid, the forerunner of today's alternative press—to subscribe, and I ended up with a part-time job, stuffing envelopes for a dollar an hour. The editor, Lyle Stuart, was the most dynamic individual I'd ever met. He became my media mentor and my unrelenting guru. He and his wife Mary Louise became my role models and intimate friends. Lyle was working on a book, *The Secret Life of Walter Winchell*, having already published an article about the infamous gossip columnist in *Exposé*.

"Circumstance is a funny thing," Stuart recalls. "You miss a traffic light and your whole life changes. That's what actually happened to me when I was about 15. I was with two high school buddies on 6th Avenue [Avenue of the Americas]. In those days, from 42nd St. to about 45th St., there were a number of little auction shops. We went into one and became what they called "a tip"—the auctioneer offered some little wrapped packages to anyone who would bid a penny, so we bid a penny, and a black guy standing among us bid a penny too, and of course what that does is, it keeps you there for the whole length of the auction. You're part of the audience, and that draws people in.

"At the end, we got our prize, and it turned out to be a little pocket comb, probably worth about a penny. We left the auction place, walked to 42nd St., and we were about to cross, but the light changed. This black fellow followed us, and we were joking about our prize, and he was about to walk to Times Square to get the subway to uptown. We chatted a little bit and he said, 'How'd you like to come to my place for a drink sometime?' And, being young, adventurous kids, we said, 'Sure.' A couple of nights later, we went to Avant Keel's home in Harlem, and I began my lifetime friendship with him.

"All because of that one penny, spent in 1939, I became very much involved with black affairs, and it would eventually cost Walter Winchell his TV career decades later. Winchell was the most powerful journalist—not of his time, but probably of all time—because his column was of such great importance that he could make a stock rise or fall by mentioning it. He could make a show close by panning it, he could keep a show open as he did with *Hellzapoppin'* when all the critics were against it. Even the president of the United States, Franklin Roosevelt, would give him items."

Stuart's first contact with Winchell was when he started doing publicity and came up with a line about a stripper who was 6'4" and, purely as a publicity stunt, she married a midget. They had a real wedding and then separated. The line: "Lois Deefay and the midget broke up because they couldn't see eye to eye." Winchell sent a telegram saying it was the funniest line he'd heard all year. Stuart placed more and more material with him and later started ghosting complete columns, each on one subject.

(Ed Sullivan didn't use ghosted material. Rather, press agents had to play poker with him once a week, and they made sure to lose.)

Stuart was particularly sensitive about racism. One of his favorite books was *Kingsblood Royal* by Sinclair Lewis, about a white man who discovered that he had Negro blood. In fact, he felt so strongly about race that when he was courting Mary Louise, as a test he told her that he was "part Negro." Winchell published almost everything Stuart wrote, but when he submitted a column about blacks in the south, Winchell—who was gradually moving toward right-wing politics—decided Stuart was too liberal for him.

One night, Stuart picked up the next morning's *Daily Mirror* and, like most *Mirror* readers, automatically turned to Winchell's column. Winchell had been carrying on a campaign against dialect comics ("vomics," he called them), short-circuiting several careers in the process. He had also been repeatedly smearing internationally renowned black singer Josephine Baker, wrecking her career in America. But this time, at the top of his column, he presented a dialect story about Baker—supposedly she had wandered into the kitchen at a party and said something to the cook, who responded, "Honey, why don't yo speak the way yo really is?"—and this enraged Stuart.

He headed straight for his office and his typewriter. The entire second issue of *Expose'* would be devoted to exposing Winchell. But an ambitious attorney who had organized a phony union, the Newspaper Delivery Association, poured mimeograph ink over all 3,000 copies and notified Winchell about his action. Stuart had enough money to go back to press; then he an associate distributed the issue themselves. One Times Square newsstand alone sold 1,450 copies. Altogether, 85,000 copies were printed and distributed.

A publisher offered Stuart $1,000 to write a book about Winchell. While Stuart was working on it, thugs ambushed and beat him with blackjacks in order to ingratiate themselves with Winchell. When the book was published, it drove Winchell crazy. He had been attacking the Copacabana in his column because they fired one of his girlfriends from the chorus line, so the nightclub sent a limousine to *Expose'* and bought 50 copies every day and handed them out to their best customers each night. Winchell heard about this and never mentioned the Copacabana again.

But he continued to attack Stuart—in print, on radio and television—resulting in three successful libel suits against Winchell, enabling Stuart to start his own publishing company. In the third lawsuit, Stuart personally handed a summons to ABC-TV president Bob Weitman, who told Winchell that they would pay the damages but he would be responsible for the punitive. Winchell said he would resign if he didn't get a piece of paper indemnifying him for the punitive damages. To Winchell's surprise, Weitman accepted his resignation.

"So they used me," Stuart says, "to break his lifetime contract. Again, circumstance is a funny thing. Put a penny on a prize and become very interested in black affairs, leading to that Josephine Baker item in the column, which led to my anger at Winchell, and my doing to him what he had done to people all of his career, and recently we [Barricade Books] re-published *The Secret Life of Walter Winchell.*"

Expose' was way ahead of its time, dedicated to good old-fashioned muckraking, with articles such as "Cancer Research" and "The Telephone Monopoly." But the name *Expose'* got confused with the slick scandal magazines that were flourishing then—*Exposed, Confidential, Whisper, Secret*—so *Expose'* became *The Independent*, and I eventually became its managing editor.

When Lyle was originally writing the Winchell book, I helped a little with the research. I was still a college student, committed to working as a camp counselor that summer, and my mother would send me a collection of Winchell's columns each week. When Stuart sued *Confidential* for libel, he assigned me to serve a subpoena on the publisher, Robert Harrison. I succeeded on my first attempt, and then just stood there in Harrison's office, basking in my own naiveté.

"Okay, it's served," he snarled. "What the hell are you waiting for, a *tip*?"

It was a great moment of cringe.

OCCULT JEOPARDY

Along with sex, drugs and rock'n'roll, there was a spiritual revolution at the core of the 1960s counterculture. However, in his book, *Turn Off Your Mind*, Gary Lachman (who, as Gary Valentine, was a founding member of the group Blondie) writes, "There was a shadow side to all the love and peace that supposedly characterized the decade. Brotherhood and compassion were the face the sixties showed the world, but underneath was a different picture. The most obvious emblem of this is Charles Manson and his Family, responsible for the gruesome Tate-LaBianca killings that ended the naive optimism of the flower generation."

He is factually incorrect, reporting that Manson wrote a weekly column in the *Los Angeles Free Press*. "Not true," former *Free Press* publisher Art Kunkin told me. "I brought Ed Sanders out here to cover the trial, but Manson himself never wrote a column." Also, Lachman falsely asserts that after Timothy Leary escaped from prison, he "smuggled twenty thousand hits of LSD into Algiers, but Eldridge Cleaver wasn't interested." Actually, Cleaver did take an acid trip there, though he insisted on wearing his guns.

Lachman presents tidbits of truth, but fails to report interesting details. He discloses that Michael Hollingshead (who first turned Leary on) "dosed two undercover policemen," but omits the rest of that story: A pair of Scotland Yard agents had arrested Hollingshead and were extraditing him from Stockholm. During the flight he managed to slip LSD into their coffee; they were still disoriented and hallucinating when the plane landed, so he disembarked alone, breezed past Customs and called Scotland Yard, advising that Thorazine be administered to ease the agents' return to ordinary reality.

Turn Off Your Mind is essentially a chronological laundry list of references that could conceivably serve as an aid in preparing for a stint on *Occult Jeopardy*:

☞ This group had a professional *I Ching* consultant who was paid to toss the coins at their office every morning. (Who were The Beatles?)

☞ The Manson girls ran up a massive gonnorhea bill with his doctor. (Who was Dennis Wilson?)

☞ In 1970 this invidual received a bachelor's degree in magic from the University of California in Berkeley. (Who is Isaac Bonewitz?)

☞ He once attached a petrol-soaked sanitary napkin to a helium balloon, lit it and sent it across Lake Michigan, as a result of which police and local radio stations received reports of a flying saucer. (Who was Alan Watts?)

☞ He was introduced to witchcraft in his teens by his 74-year-old grandmother, who taught him the art by taking his virginity. (Who was Alex Sanders?)

☞ While on LSD he had paranoid visions of secret messages coming from Jack Benny and Doris Day on television. (Who was Timothy Leary?)

☞ His black mass included crushing a sugar cube soaked in LSD, urinating on marijuana, and hanging a picture of Leary upside down. (Who was Anton LaVey?)

☞ She called LaVey's Church of Satan philosophy "Kahlil Gibran with balls." (Who was Jayne Mansfield?)

☞ He wore a black armband to school, believing the rumor that Paul McCartney was dead. (Who is Gary Lachman?)

Lachman's fixation on fascism in *Turn Off Your Mind* taints his perception. He claims that, "With [Jerry] Rubin, [Abbie] Hoffman epitomized the new irrationalism that burst upon the radical scene in the late '60s. . . . The association of late-'60s radicalism with the Nazis isn't far fetched."

And this: "The abyss isn't some possibility in the future; it is 'here now,' whether it is the start of Germany's trip to the absolute elsewhere, or the mud-splattered abandon of Woodstock."

Of course, we all have the capability of surrendering to the forces of darkness within ourselves, but it's a matter of choice, and the positive side of the '60s is still alive and celebrating. The annual Rainbow Family Gathering attracts 20,000 people. In *The Cultural Creatives*, Paul Ray and Sherry Anderson estimate that 50 million Americans are broadly sympathetic to hippie values. It has been a few decades since the original Human Be-In at Golden Gate Park preceded 1967's Summer of Love—and, indicating the role of technology in the evolution of the counterculture—a worldwide Digital Be-In has now been scheduled.

Lachman chooses to focus on the negative aspects of a mass awakening that provided hope, inspiration, joyfulness and a sense of community to countless young people. In the process, he resorts to the kind of lying generalizations—"As in most ashrams and hippie households, the kids were abandoned and pretty much left to themselves"—that will surely appeal to the Fundamentalist Christians and '60s-bashing markets.

Unless you happen to be a hard-core enthusiast of occult esoterica, you'll probably find reading Lachman's book to be a chore rather than a pleasure. Marred by a dependence on secondary research, it is virtually devoid of humor, and even takes metaphors literally to express his prejudice: "A famous Zen injunction advises that if we see the Buddha on the road, we should kill him. Cassady and some of the other mentors of the Beats might have done just that."

Lachman writes, "Many believed that [Herman Hesse] received the Nobel Prize less for his great novel *The Glass Bead Game* than for the fact that he hadn't been a Nazi. Hesse had become the focus of every literate late adolescent with a bad case of *Weltscherz*," admitting that, "Needless to say, I was one of these." Ah, if only he had mentioned that *San Francisco Oracle* editor Allen Cohen was so enamored of Hesse's *Siddartha* that he changed his *own* name to Siddartha and moved to a commune, where everybody thought his name was Sid Arthur, and they all called him Sid.

TRASHING THE RIGHT TO READ

While serving five years in federal prison for growing medical marijuana in Los Angeles, Todd McCormick contributed a couple of stories—about his experiences with psilocybin and ketamine—to my collection, *Magic Mushrooms and Other Highs: From Toad Slime to Ecstasy*, and when it was published, I immediately sent him a copy.

But the warden rejected it "because on pages 259-261, it describes the process of squeezing toads to obtain illicit substances which could be detrimental to the security, good order and discipline of the institution." This was pure theater of cruelty. Federal correctional facilities do not have a toad problem, and outside accomplices have not been catapulting loads of toads over barbed wire fences to provide the fuel for a prison riot.

McCormick commented, "Can you believe this shit! I wonder how much we pay the guy/girl who actually sits and reads every book that comes in for offending passages. How about you tear out pages 259-261 and re-send this book back with a copy of the rejection and a notation that the offending pages have been removed."

Which is exactly what I did. This time, though, my cover letter to the warden was ignored, and the book was returned, stamped "Unauthorized." I had called their bluff. Obviously, McCormick was being punished simply because he happened to be a prisoner.

I then corresponded with several friends in prisons around the country to find out what *they* had not been allowed to read. I wanted to see other examples of arbitrary and frivolous censorship by prison personnel. Here are some results of my informal survey:

☞ "The Texas Department of Corrections blocked Bo Lozoff's *Breaking Out of Jail*, a book about teaching meditation to prison inmates."

☞ "Disallowed: *Trainspotting* because of its 'glorification of drug use.' Tom Robbins' *Still Life With Woodpecker* because it has a chapter that 'contains information about bombmaking.'"

☞ "An inmate couldn't get nude pictures of his wife sent to him but *could* get a subscription to *Playboy*. The rationale: A wife deserved more respect."

☞ "They kept out *The Anarchists Cookbook*. No kiddie porn, no tales or photos suggesting sex with a guard, no photos showing frontal or rear nudity—not even a wife or friend."

☞ "The Utah prison system banned *Rolling Stone* as being an anarchist publication."

☞ "*A Revolution in Kindness* is banned from the Louisiana State Penitentiary at Angola as 'a threat to internal security.' It was intended for Herman Wallace, who contributed an essay about how he organized a chess tournament on his cell block as a way of easing tensions and minimizing violence between inmates. Wallace is one of the Angola Three—Black Panthers who have been in solitary confinement for 31 years for trying to improve conditions in the 'bloodiest prison in America' in the early 1970s."

☞ "All hardback books forbidden, because the covers could be fashioned into weapons. Educational textbooks—a new rule precludes prisoners on death row [including this particular prisoner] or in lockdown from taking correspondence courses—and I've had a couple of books returned to sender on the claim they appeared to be for a course. *MAPS* [Multidisciplinary Association for Psychedelic Studies]—their publication was sent back several times because maps are not allowed in here. *High Times* was repeatedly denied because it posed a danger to the safe, secure and orderly operation of the institution. 'Smut mags' like *Hustler* are reviewed monthly."

☞ "There's a whole new genre of men's magazines—*Maxim, Stuff, For Him*—which show it all except for nipples and beaver. Now the feds want to ban *Maxim* due to 'security' reasons. The 'rejected mail' slip they send you when some verboten material arrives has a box to check (to specify offending matter) which says 'pubic hair.'"

☞ "Peace activist William Combs spent eight days in solitary confinement for receiving and sharing with other imates what federal authorities consider disruptive, if not subversive, political literature. The offending 'propaganda' included commentary by such extremists as Bill Moyers and Ellen Goodman, and included an article published in *Reader's Digest*. The common thread was that they all questioned the wisdom of government policy."

The name of the game is control in the guise of security—a microcosm of the nation outside prison walls—the practice of power without compassion.

After *Magic Mushrooms and Other Highs* was rejected for the second time, I appealed to the Regional Director of the Bureau of Prisons (as instructed by the warden) for an independent review. I also wrote to the ACLU. I heard back from neither. Todd McCormick was released from prison in December 2003. Among so many other things to catch up on, he would finally be able to read what he had written. However, he was discharged to a halfway house, where all his books and magazines were confiscated as "paraphernalia."

JEWS IN THE NEWS

It was ironic that a generation which considered leaving the Lower East Side to be a sign of advancement, was dismayed when their children began emigrating there to gain a sense of community. In 1966, the same year a section was rechristened the East Village, I moved to a loft above a bar on Avenue A.

As a stand-up comedian, I had a routine about comic-strip superheroes being Jewish. You could tell by their names: Superman, Batman, Hawkman, Spider-Man, Flashman, SkyMan, Doll Man. Captain Marvel was really a Jew *pretending* to be a Protestant; his power-word "Shazam!" was just a euphemism for "*Shalom!*"

However, in the film version of "Spider-Man," according to the Jewish weekly

The Forward, the trouble with Tobey Maguire's Spidey was "that he isn't Jewish enough." (Conversely, a top NBC executive originally dismissed the pilot of *Seinfeld* as "too Jewish.") Yet, in *From the Lower East Side to Hollywood: Jews in American Popular Culture,* Paul Buhle writes that Spider-Man's alter-ego, Peter Parker, is now "on his way to becoming sarcastic—yet another Jewish example of the vernacular aspiring uplift to something better."

Buhle, a Gentile columnist for the Jewish magazine, *Tikkun,* seems to be referring to himself when he calls comic artist R. Crumb "genetically Gentile, but cryptically Jewish." Of Bill Griffith, creator of *Zippy the Pinhead,* he states: "Not born with Jewishness, he was assimilated into it (no doubt with some help from his wife, Diane Newman, as Crumb has had help from his two Jewish wives)."

Griffith tells me, though, "I *always* thought I was Jewish, or some sort of Wasp version of a Jew, because all my friends were Jewish. Growing up in the suburbs, Levittown was a kind of dividing line for Jews and Italians. I knew I wasn't Italian because of my name. I was soaked with Yiddish humor from Harvey Kurtzman in the early Mad magazine. At one point I had a Jewish girlfriend, and her mother said that I must be Jewish because I was so smart. She didn't want me to *not* be Jewish. It was some way of ushering me in."

And Newman, wondering why Buhle labels her as Griffith's "talented, excessively self-conscious Jewish wife and fellow artist," says, "I never met the guy, so I don't know why he said that. It could be that he's talking about my art as opposed to my personality, but he doesn't really discuss my art in the book at all. I don't think my artwork is particularly self-conscious, I think it's satirical. *DiDi Glitz* doesn't seem like a self-conscious character to me, and it's not *me.* I seem to exist primarily to establish Bill as someone he can talk about with some kind of Jewish connection."

One of the Jewish connections that Buhle makes is the gay connection. On Broadway: "The historic Jewish subtext of musicals having now been replaced by a gay subtext . . . in the theatrical world, 'Jewish' and 'gay' so often flow into each other." On David Geffen: "[He] had a special feeling for gay rights. Nineties billionaire Geffen himself was gay, after all, and that might be the largest fact of change in Jewish-American entertainment business life." This connection can be explained by "a Jewish world where surviving or reviving Yiddish at once takes on a gay affect (the marginal re-embracing the marginal)."

Allen Ginsberg was, of course, the epitome of a gay Jew. Buhle writes, "Half-Jewish Lawrence Ferlinghetti, whose launching of City Lights (the store and the publisher) in 1953 brought the message to millions, including the similarly half-Jewish Diane di Prima, protofeminist queen of the Beats, also introduced City Lights' all-time champion author, Allen Ginsberg. . . . *Howl and Other Poems* (1956), in addition to being a sort of poetic declaration of Beatitude, was patently a recollection of Jewish left-wing memory held up against a crazed, postwar consumerist *goyishe* America."

I've had mini-dialogues with countercultural icons about various aspects of Jewishness.

Lenny Bruce told me, "I know some Jews who are so reformed they're ashamed they're Jewish." I asked Mort Sahl if he considered himself Jewish. "No," he said, "I belong to me. And that's *enough*. I don't consider myself *anything*. And I'm having a tough time finding any kinship. You know, you get along with people who have *ideas*, that's all." I asked Abbie Hoffman, "Do you think it's an ego trip for me to be concerned about whether my readers think I'm on an ego trip?" "That's because you're Jewish," he laughed. Timothy Leary said, "The Weather Underground was amusing. They were brilliant, brilliant Jewish Chicago kids. They had class and dash and flash and smash."

I asked Ram Dass, "If you and I were to exchange philosophies—if I believed in reincarnation and you didn't—how do you think our behavior would change?" He paused, and then: "Well, if you believed in reincarnation, you would never ask a question like that." Bob Dylan was a true minimalist. I asked why he was taking Hebrew lessons (in 1970), and he answered, "I can't speak it." And when I pointed an imaginary microphone at him and asked how he felt about the six million Jews who were killed in Nazi Germany, he simply said, "I resented it."

I asked Woody Allen if he agreed with the motivation of the Buddhist monks who set fire to themselves in Vietnam. "I don't think so," he replied. "No, I think that they don't know what they're doing. I think they're nuts. That's *not* the answer. When you're home at night, and you say to yourself, 'Tomorrow morning I'll get up at eight o'clock and set fire to myself,' there's something wrong. I wouldn't do it that way. I can see dying for a principle, but not that way. At the very minimum, if you are going to die for something you should at least take *one of them* with you. Go back to the Jews in Germany. If you have a loaded gun in your home, and the state comes to get you, you can at least get two or three of *them*. I'm not opposed to violence as a course of action in many instances. Sometimes passive resistance is fine, but violence in its place is a good and necessary thing. But setting fire to yourself is not the answer. With my luck, I would be un-inflammable."

Buhle associates Jews with progressive politics in general and the blacklist in particular. "In 1947," he recalls, "Representative John Rankin of the House Committee on UnAmerican Activities warned Congress about the true identities of various actors, including Danny Kaye, Eddie Cantor, Edward G. Robinson, and Melvyn Douglas. Like others using stage names, they were essentially parading under Gentile labels, a practice that Rankin considered *prima facie* evidence of their 'UnAmerican' intentions. . . .

"[T]he Committee Chair had opened the hearings to notorious anti-Semites on the premise that Jewish control of Hollywood demanded redress. By the later 1940s, internal FBI memos complained that the Jewish press failed to take up its patriotic duty of supporting the blacklist. . . . After hesitating, Hollywood's power brokers fell in line with the blacklist, conducting it themselves with the help of notorious anti-Semites and of some noted Jewish institutions alike."

There is something unsettling—but, I suppose, necessary for his book—about the way Buhle focuses on actors through Hebrew-colored glasses, from "There was something Jewish about John Garfield, even if only New Yorkers seemed to know for sure" to "Only a blind person could fail to see the Jewishness of Judy Holliday," from "At least [Montgomery] Clift was psychologically troubled, if not actually Jewish" to "Jose Ferrer in his dark looks and cerebral talk [was] almost definitely perceived as Jewish."

Should the fact that Irving Berlin wrote "Easter Parade" and "White Christmas" be considered a sign of assimilation?

Not even animated cartoon characters can escape the laser beam of Buhle's peripheral vision: "Betty [Boop] offered a total contrast to the shy but red-blooded Mickey [Mouse], himself modeled after the *goyishe* and anti-Semite aviator sensation Charles Lindbergh. . . . No one east of the Hudson, at least, would describe her as a Gentile: at times her parents have Yiddish accents, and Jewish in-jokes can often be heard (like the Samoan Islanders who greet her with a roaring *Sholem Aleichem!*), Hebrew lettering and all."

Although *From the Lower East Side to Hollywood* serves as an ambitious slice of Jewish-American cultural history, it certainly isn't a comprehensive one. For example, missing entirely from its pages except for footnotes are Jerry Lewis ("In the comedy trade, and apart from his charity grandstanding, he was best known for ridiculing women comics") and Jackie Mason ("The most famous or notorious Jewish story of the *Ed Sullivan Show* was the firing of Jackie Mason for acting 'too kikey' on camera").

I happen to be an e-mail recipient of an Internet anti-Semitic listserv, and many of Buhle's descriptions are uncomfortably similar, such as: "Film star Peter Coyote (not surprisingly the adopted name of a Jewish red-diaper baby)"; "Mama Cass Elliott was born Ellen Naomi Cohen"; "the very Jewish Jew, [Morey] Amsterdam"; ". . . the very often Jewish-inflected *Saturday Night Live*"; "the very Jewish Gabe Kaplan"; "the emphatically Jewish Roseanne Barr"; "Mel Brooks . . . one of the most blatantly Jewish [of successful filmmakers]." It is the ultimate irony of Buhle's book that it will appeal to Jews and anti-Semites alike.

A MELLOW HOWL

Remember that opening line of *Howl*: "I saw the best minds of my generation destroyed by madness, starving hysterical naked. . . ." Well, a new biography of Allen Ginsberg—*American Scream* by Jonah Raskin—has a surprising revelation:

"In the mid-1970s, in the midst of the counterculture he had helped to create, he promised to rewrite *Howl*. Now that he was a hippie minstrel and a Pied Piper for the generation that advocated peace and love he would alter *Howl*, he said, so that it might reflect the euphoria of the hippies. He would include a 'positive redemptive catalogue,' he said."

In 1982, there was a celebration of the 25th anniversary of Jack Kerouac's *On the Road*, at Naropa, a Buddhist college in Boulder, Colorado, where presumably they refer to his book as *On the Path*. I was invited to moderate a discussion, "Political Fallout of the Beat Generation." The panelists: Ginsberg, William Burroughs, Abbie Hoffman and Timothy Leary. We were all invited to sign posters for the event. Hoffman wrote his signature extra large, with great care.

"The guy who shot John Lennon," he explained, "complained that Lennon gave him a sloppy autograph, so I ain't takin' any chances."

Hoffman had recently "debated" Watergate conspirator G. Gordon Liddy, currently a radio talk-show host.

"Liddy," he shouted, "I got just one question for you. Do you eat pussy?" The audience cheered. This was really off the wall. "Come on, Liddy, answer me! *Do you eat pussy?*" Liddy couldn't respond over the roar of the crowd. Hoffman bleated over and over, *"Do you eat pussy? Do you eat pussy?"*—like some kind of sexual street fighter chanting his mantra—*"Do you eat pussy? Do you eat pussy? Do you eat pussy?"* The audience went wild. Hoffman was triumphant.

Finally, Liddy was able to reply: "You have just demonstrated, more than I ever could possibly hope to, the enormous gap which separates me from you."

Since Leary had also encountered Liddy in a series of debates, Hoffman now asked *him* if Liddy ate pussy.

"I can attest to the fact that he does," Leary replied. "At least he made it a point at some of our debates to announce that he is definitely *not* monogamous."

During the Beat Generation panel, Ginsberg said, "I think there was one slight shade of error in describing the Beat movement as primarily a protest movement. That was the thing that Kerouac was always complaining about. He felt the literary aspect or the spiritual aspect or the emotional aspect was not so much protest at all, but a declaration of unconditioned mind beyond protest, beyond resentment, beyond loser, beyond *winner—way* beyond winner—beyond winner or loser . . . but the basic thing that I understood and dug Jack for was unconditioned mind, negative capability, totally open mind—beyond victory or defeat. Just awareness, and that was the humor, and that's what the saving grace is. That's why there *will* be political aftereffects, but it doesn't have to win because having to win a revolution is like having to make a milliion dollars."

As moderator, I asked, "Abbie, since you used to quote Che Guevara saying, 'In a revolution, one wins or dies,' do you have a response to that?"

Hoffman: "All right, Ginzo. Poems have a lot of different meanings for different people. For me, your poem *Howl* was a call to arms."

Ginsberg: "A whole boatload of sentimental bullshit."

Hoffman: "We saw in the sixties a great imbalance of power, and the only way that you could correct that imbalance was to organize people and to fight for power. Power is not a dirty word. The concept of trying to win against social injustice is not a dirty kind of concept. It all depends on how you define the game, how you define winning and how you define losing—that's the Zen trip that was learned by defining that you were the prophets and we were the warriors. I'm saying that you didn't fight, but you were the fighters. And I'll tell you, If you don't think you were a political movement and you don't like winning, the fuckin' lawyer that defended *Howl* in some goddamn obscenity suit—you wanted *him* to be a fuckin' winner, I guarantee you that. That *was* a political debate."

Abbie would've been shocked to learn that Ginsberg had planned to rewrite *Howl* , this time beginnng with an upbeat line: "I saw the best minds of my generation turned on by music. . . ."

THE COMMUNAL TRUTH

Recently, I was a guest lecturer in a popular course at UCLA about the 1960s— "Agitational Communication," taught by Paul von Blum, who was active in the Berkeley Free Speech Movement. A student asked me, "Did you guys really believe what you were saying, or was it all just rhetoric?"

"Both," I answered. "Countless people were actually living their ideals, personally and in communal situations, but there was lots of rhetoric."

With the baby boomer generation coming of middle age and putting into perspective their own personal histories, innumerable autobiographies and memoirs have been glutting the literary market. Indeed, a *New Yorker* cartoon depicted an editor at a publishing house saying to a writer, "Congratulations! Your manuscript was the one-millionth personal memoir submitted to us this year."

In 1999, actor Peter Coyote's *Sleeping Where I Fall* survived that fierce competition, telling the story of his chosen journey from riches to rags—from being delivered to school in a chauffeur-driven, leather-roofed Cadillac limousine, to traveling with hippies in a truck named the "Meat and Bone Wagon," retrieving radishes, lettuce, tomatoes and squash from a garbage bin behind a Safeway supermarket.

It was with the San Francisco Mime Troupe that Coyote first experienced what was later to become his trademark theatrical pursuit: the dissolution of the boundaries between art and life. And it was there that he met a couple of life actors, Peter Berg ("perhaps the most radical and cranky member of the troupe, and arguably the most brilliant") and Emmett Grogan ("determined to be a life star . . . moving through a room with the detached concentration of a shark"). They formed the nucleus of what would become the Diggers, a loose confederation of friends who were part psychedelic social workers, helping supply local hippies and new arrivals to the Haight-Ashbury scene with food and shelter, and part practitioners of street theater.

In December 1967, the Diggers sponsored a parade called "The Death of Money." There they were, without a permit and 4,000 strong, chanting, "The streets belong to the people!" When the police arrested two Hells Angels, the coffin marked with dollar signs that marchers had been carrying was passed around and spontaneously filled with bail money, to the utter surprise of cops and bikers alike. In return, the Angels threw a party in Golden Gate Park on New Year's Day, footing the bill, with free beer and music by the Grateful Dead and Janis Joplin with Big Brother & the Holding Company.

As the Diggers operated at the edges of the counterculture, they expanded through combinations and alliances, such as the one with the Hells Angels. They referred to this larger, centerless coalition as the Free Family, a group that established a series of communes in the Pacific Northwest and Southwest. They sought to create an environment devoted to an alternative lifestyle, one not tied to the conventions of polite behavior.

But it quickly became obvious that the credo of "Do your own thing" didn't work in an overloaded household. Somebody would use someone else's toothbrush, and objecting to that might be regarded as bourgeois. Ideological conflicts invaded the communal spirit. One individual removed the bathroom door, asserting that the fear of being observed was a neurotic vanity to be banished. High aspirations were tainted by petty arguments. There was even a hair-raising public fight over a spoon. Their experiment in communal living continuted to unravel.

"The only reason to fix the trucks now," Coyote wrote, "was to escape from one another. Life continues after something dies, it simply does not continue in the same way. We maintained our chores and responsbilities, but the activity was pro forma. Everyone knew that the Free Family as a source of future security was a fiction."

By contrast, The Farm—a commune in Tennessee that also evolved out of a San Francisco community—succeeded in hanging together and working productively. I contacted founder Stephen Gaskin to find out The Farm's accomplishments and the secret of its success.

"As in the Japanese game of *Go*," he told me, "sometimes one consolidates one's forces in a citadel. Other times one sends out one's stones to larger territories that can be integrated later. We realize that we're doing both of those here on The Farm. We vote in the elections. We are good to our neighbors. We do work for, and are worked for by, the people in the neighborhood, and are seamless with the web of life in Tennessee. Sometimes a manager in one of the local stores will recognize me and tell me something like, 'No Farm person has ever bounced a check at this store.' We have Tennessee in-laws.

"On the other hand, we are citizens of the world who reach out for peace, for justice and support for Indians and all native peoples. We work for women's rights and against nuclear fuel cycles all over the world. We have organized a national peace effort from The Farm called Peace Roots Alliance—hippie roots, that is. We put up billboards in major cities and run educational meetings resisting the war in Iraq. This is our work."

The Farm's relief and development agency, Plenty International, founded in 1974, grew into an earthquake relief program in Guatemala that moved millions of Canadian International Development Agency dollars into kilometers of water-pipe between 1976 and 1981. The Farm organized water projects in South Africa and soy dairies in the Caribbean.

"On the way to doing these things," Gaskin said, "we learned how to sharpen a chain saw, shoe a horse, plow a field, how to deliver babies [his wife Ina May is the author of *Spiritual Midwifery*], how to take blood pressure, how to feed a thousand people, how to field an International Relief and Development Company, and all the lessons that result in The Farm, still here after 35 years.

"The things we had to learn to feed ourselves and deliver our babies were relevant in the small countries. I think the important factors in The Farm's long term survival was that we tried not to be doctrinaire. We were not Baptists, we were not macrobioticists or Marxists or Jains or Buddhists. We were hippies who wanted to live together and who would accept the level of organization that it took to achieve that. I think that allowed us to bend rather than break when heavy changes happened."

In 1967, Gaskin was a teaching assistant at San Francisco State College. Some students said they liked him but that he didn't know what was going on, and that they wouldn't be able to take him seriously until he saw The Beatles' movie, *A Hard Day's Night*. He did, and recognized the power of youth as represented by the hippies, resulting in the founding of his "Monday Night Class." The idea was to compare notes with other trippers about tripping and the whole psychic and psychedelic world. They began as a nucleus of a dozen folks and eventually grew into meetings of as many as 1,500. It was from among these seekers that a convoy to Tennessee was launched.

"The most important thing to come out of the Monday Night Class meetings," Gaskin writes in an introduction to a revised version of his 1970 book, *Monday Night Class*, "and the glue that held us together, was a belief in the moral imperative toward altruism that was implied by the telepathic spiritual communion we experienced together. Every decent thing accomplished over the years by the people of Monday Night Class and The Farm—its later incarnation— came from those simple hippie values. It was the basis for our belief in spirit, nonviolence, collectivity and social activism.

"I consider myself to be an ethnic hippie. By that I mean that the ethnicity I grew up with was such a white bread, skim milk, gringo experience that it wasn't satisfying for me. It had no moxie. Now, being a hippie, that's another thing. I feel like the Sioux feel about being from the Lakota Nation. I feel like Mario Cuomo feels about being Italian. It makes me feel close with Jews and Rastafarians. I have a tribe, too. I know that the hippies were preceded by the beatniks, the bohemians, the free-thinkers, Voltaire and so on, back to Socrates and Buddha, but the wave of revolution that spoke to me was the hippies. And rock 'n' roll lights my soul and gives a beat to the revolution."

Time magazine may have invented the shorthand term "hippies," but in reality those who participated in the counterculture that exploded out of the 1950s were surfing on an epidemic of idealism, displaying courage and imagination. There was a mass spiritual awakening—a movement away from western religions of repression toward eastern philosophies of liberation—a generation of young pioneers, traveling westward without killing a single Indian along the way.

In 1969, Vassar graduate Roberta Price got a grant to visit communes and photograph them. When she and her boyfriend David visited a commune, Libre, in the Huerfano (means "orphan") Valley in southern Colorado, its alchemy transformed them from observers into participants. In 1970, Roberta and David got married, left graduate school in Buffalo, moved to Libre and built a house around a huge boulder 9,000 feet high on the side of a mountain overlooking the valley. Roberta's book, *Huerfano: a memoir of life in the counterculture*, published in 2004, serves as a nice slice of countercultural history.

Several Huerfano Valley residents have gone to Barnes & Noble—the main bookstore in the Pueblo, Colorado area—and asked for a copy of *Huerfano*, only to be told that they don't have it. One clerk admitted that they do in fact have some copies, but they keep them hidden in the back, adding, "This book will never be put out." Blame it on the cover. It's an old photo of the author, standing in an isolated field, apparently nude—"apparently" because, except for her smiling face, arms, lower legs and bare feet, her body is blocked out by a treasure of freshly plucked weed that she's holding.

A review in the *Los Angeles Times* advised readers to "Ignore the picture on the cover of the naked woman hiding behind an enormous bundle of marijuana. This memoir of life in one of the great communes of the West is better than that—and for many people a road not taken that is fascinating to read about."

Nevertheless, the use of marijuana was an integral aspect of communal life. In fact, with the grant money alloted to produce the book, Roberta bought a Pentax Spotmatic and some film, and David bought a Corvair camper and a kilo of marijuana.

"We use every part of the marijuana plants we harvest," Roberta writes. "What to do with the stems and seeds is the biggest challenge and takes the most ingenuity." And she proceeds to describe a recipe for marijuana butter, to be used in making brownies.

At Libre, a variety of hallucinogens were smoked or ingested: Windowpane LSD and Owsley Orange Acid. Sticky black opium from Vietnam. THC iced tea. Psilocybin mushrooms. Peyote at a solstice gathering. MDA that had been developed by the U.S. Army to dose hostile populations, in order to make them docile and manageable. Marijuana that been smuggled into the country in stuffed alligators from Colombia. Hashish that had been molded and wrapped as Maja soaps from Spain.

"You know," someone observed while passing a pipe, "you don't have to smoke much hash to look at these cliffs and hear dinosaurs eating ferns."

I once asked Ken Kesey, in reference to a phrase he had uttered, "What's your concept of 'the communal lie'?"

"I remember delegates from two large communes," he replied, "stopping by once at my farm and negotiating in great tones of importance the trade of one crate of cantaloupes, which the southern commune had grown, for one portable shower, which the northern commune had ripped off of a junk yard. When this was over they strutted around in an effluvium of 'See? We're self-supporting.' Bullshit. A crate of melons and a ratty shower isn't enough summer's output for sixty-some people to get off behind. It was part of a lie that the entire psychedelic community, myself more than most, was participating in.

"When a bunch of people, in defense of their lifestyle, have to say 'Look how beautiful we were at Woodstock,' I can't help but ask, 'How was your cantaloupe crop this year?' Being beautiful or cool or hip is too often a clean-up for not pulling weeds. Woodstock was beautiful, and historic and even perhaps Biblical, but Altamont was far more honest. Success is a great spawning ground of confidence and camaraderie; bald truth is found more often up against the wall. Bullshit is bullshit and neither the length of the hair nor the tie of the family can make it anything else."

Libre was able to avoid that danger by the diligence of its inhabitants in developing self-sufficiency. Roberta writes:

"I wonder what to say on application forms . . . that after graduate school I acquired new skills? I can mix cement, blow dynamite, bank a fire, use a chain saw, split wood, milk goats, make yogurt and Parmesan cheese, bake donuts, ride bareback, hunt mushrooms, start fires, frame roofs, cure bacon, punch cows. That I've memorized the shapes of three thousand clouds, calibrated one hundred eleven rainbows, and watched five babies slide out into life? That big birds bring me messages, and I've stared straight into a cougar's yellow eyes? That I lived in the Orphan Valley for seven years with friends, crazies, and some who were both, that we were heroic fools or foolish heroes—I can't say which, and maybe it doesn't matter."

She makes reference to "raptograms" in the book. As she explained to me, "It was a point I was making on raptors being big birds, hawks and eagles. There are various parts of the book in which they brought me messages, or at least it *seemed* like they were bringing me messages at the time. So raptogram is a reference to those messages." Her sense of communication with other species was sharpened while riding her horse Rufus, who, she wrote, "turns when I think about it, before I tell him with reins or knees. I experiment more, thinking, not moving my hands or my body, and every time he anticipates my direction. I don't tell anybody about our telepathy."

In 1969, the first three couples at Libre got money from the National Institutes of Health, the federal government's medical research arm, in connection with a study to determine whether communal living facilitated psychic communication. I called Dean Fleming, one of those originals (after 20 years, Libre finally got telephones), and he described the experiment:

"Stanley Krippner came out to Libre, and he invited us to come to Maimonides Hospital in Washington, D.C., so we stopped there on our trip back east. The six of us went into this Dream Lab. It was basically a sensory deprivation chamber. It was completely dark, completely silent. He said, 'Okay, now, one at a time I want you to think of an image, and just think of it, and the other people will say what they get from that.'

"We were so absolutely right on that it was kind of terrifying. Unbelievable. I mean we caught it every time. It wasn't like, 'Oh, yeah, we know exactly what it is.' For example, one us thought of the Chrysler Building in New York, and somebody else said, 'I see the helmet of Kali.' I remember thinking of the Verrazano Bride, and then people said, 'Yeah,' they see this like horizontal line above another horizontal line, there's two of them, they're two different colors. It was pretty interesting, but it wasn't absolute, in the sense of saying, 'Oh, yeah, that's the Verrazano.'"

I contacted Stanley Krippner—co-author of *Dream Telepathy* and *Becoming Psychic*, and co-editor of *The Psychological Effects of War Trauma on Civilians*—and asked about his conclusions in that study.

He recalled saying something like this: "There is a great deal of anecdotal evidence that ESP experiences are reported more frequently by people who are emotionally or physically close to each other than people who are strangers or who live at considerable distances. Because commune members share emotional and physical proximity, it would be expected that they would report mutual ESP. Whether this is actual ESP or ordinary communication thought to be ESP is another question, of course. I probably did not mention that commune members often shared sexual 'closeness' as well, and lovers, or at least bedmates, report ESP more frequently than mere acquaintances."

For Roberta, sexual closeness was a strong learning experience:

"David was the only person I'd ever slept with. . . . I was an idealistic monogamist, but we'd talked about it some. . . . We frowned on hypocrisy and the stifling repression of our parents' generation. You have to follow your heart, but it's dangerous, unchartered territory. 'This is a consequence of freedom,' he said, 'and we need to support everyone.' 'How do you support people with conflicting lusts?' I asked. 'These are frontiers we're facing,' he explained, as if we were a New Age Lewis and Clark. 'We have to love them all.'

"In the year and a half we've been here," she wrote, "there's been a lot of bed-hopping among our comrades. There were those cataclysmic switches at the first Thanksgiving at Libre in 1969, between our first and second visits, even before we moved west—when Peter's wife, Judy, left Peter after he went off with Nancy at the Thanksgiving dinner, and Nancy's husband went back to Austin, and she moved in with Peter and stepped over a broom and got married to him. Linda left Dean that Thanksgiving and went off with Steve, who left Patricia. . . .

"So far, it doesn't seem as if any couple is holding up too well against free love. 'It doesn't mean I love you less, you know,' David said. 'We're capable of loving people in different ways at different times, and we shouldn't repress these feelings. . . . We have to overcome possessiveness and jealousy so that we can explore all the possibilities. If we love each other, we'll give each other this freedom.'"

One afternoon, Roberta brought a hand mirror to a Libre women's meeting: "We're going to look at our vaginas," she informed David. "Men see their sexual organs all the time, and it's, well, empowering for women to see theirs." She wrote that members of another commune, the Red Rockers, "are more on the cutting edge. . . . The men had a men's meeting, and they paired off and slept together, although they all kept their underpants on. . . .

"Open marriages bloom all around us, usually before the old marriages wither and die and newly passionate couples spring up. . . . Our attitudes have changed so much from those of the repressed society in which we grew up. If you feel any affection or attraction for someone, it's downright rude and quite awkward not to make love if the opportunity comes along. It's not much more than a handshake to some."

Finally, though, Roberta—who had a few flings herself—told David, "I want a monogamous relationship now or nothing." He chose the latter and, after seven years at Libre, she departed, leaving her extended family behind. She is now an attorney, specializing in intellectual property rights. She has recently represented some tribes on cultural/intellectual property issues, such as Pueblo of Zia and her decade-long attempt to protect their sacred Zia Sun symbol from tawdry commercial use, and there has been a change in Trademark Office protocol on Native American symbols, largely due to her efforts.

And Libre, now in its 37th year, with 15 members, continues to flourish. Dean Fleming tells me:

"The first wave is mostly all over the place. The second wave is still here, like David, and all those people who came in the early '70s and stuck it out. Part of it was the people who started it were all kind of crazed and pioneer-type people, and they're obviously gonna keep on doing things full time. I'm a painter and so I wanted to have a good studio. I was in New York before on Broome St., thinking what's the perfect studio, and I said it has to be really beautiful in the country and it'd have to be surrounded by friends. So that was the reason for the Libre community.

"And it's still unbelievably beautiful and it's still full of friends. Not nearly as crazed as it was in the '60s and '70s. But it's still frail. We had a situation where the land would not belong to any individual, belonged to the whole group. And likewise for houses, so people come and go, they can't just sell them off, the land belongs to all of us, and we kind of keep checks and balances on it. And now our kids that were born here are becoming members, and even if they're not here, they're beginning to come and take care of the place, and maybe we'll get another generation out of it before it's worn out."

Certainly, the Free Family had *its* evolutionary role. Peter Coyote wrote in *Sleeping Where I Fall* that "the Diggers understood fundamentals about the relationship between culture and imagination, and culture and politics, but our spurning of more traditional political alliances was, I believe, somewhat snobbish and counterproductive. The failure to curb personal indulgence was a major collective error. The ideas and moral positions that emerged during this period—the civil rights movement, feminism, holistic medicine, organic farming, numerous alternative physical and spiritual therapies and disciplines, and perhaps most important, bioregional or watershed political organization, were abetted by agents like the people remembered here: flawed and imperfect people certainly, but genuinely dedicated to creating more enlightened options for themselves and others."

He tells me, "I was just at my daughter's wedding, where her guest list included many members of that family who are not related to her by blood, but people that she considers her 'kin.' Our children (and their children) are still friends, still in close touch as we are. We're still all in touch, come to one another's aid when necessary, and are bonded by indelible experiences. The fact that one of our communes out of nearly a dozen collapsed is no more a death knell to the Free Family than the collapse of one star is to the rest of the universe."

In a recent episode of *Doonesbury*, triggered while watching the ultra-materialistic *Cribs* on MTV ("This is my bling-bling room," says a rapper, "where I put all my shiny, expensive stuff for my boys to envy!"), Boopsie's daughter asks her live-in babysitter, Zonker, "Did you really once live on a commune?"

He was only one of three million such participants.

Rebels With Causes

MAE, WE HARDLY KNEW YE

November 22, 2003 marks the 40th anniversary of the assassination of President John F. Kennedy, so I'd like to pay posthumous tribute to the queen of conspiracy research, Mae Brussell, particularly in view of a recent Op-Ed piece in the *Los Angeles Times* by Richard M. Mosk, who was a staff member of the Warren Commission.

"This year's decennial anniversary," he wrote, "may well be remarkable for what will be missing: myriad articles and discussions debunking the Warren Commision's conclusion that Lee Harvey Oswald acted alone."

Mae Brussell was the daughter of Edgar Magnin, senior rabbi at the Wilshire Boulevard Temple in Beverly Hills, and the granddaughter of I. Magnin, founder of the clothing-store chain. House guests ranged from Louis B. Mayer to Thomas Mann, from Jack Warner to Albert Einstein. She attended Stanford University, majoring in philosophy. She was married and divorced twice. In her forties, she had an affair with Henry Miller.

When JFK was slain, Mae was a suburban homemaker with five children. Her 7-year-old daughter Bonnie was concerned about Lee Harvey Oswald. She saw him on TV. He had a black eye and he was saying, "I didn't do it. I haven't killed anybody. I don't know what this is all about." Bonnie decided to send him her teddy bear. It was all wrapped up and ready to mail when she saw Oswald murdered by Jack Ruby on TV that Sunday morning, and then all day long, over and over again in slow-motion.

What then began as Mae's hobby would turn into a lifetime pilgrimage. One bit of research led to another—and another and another and another. Although the Ultimate Mystery would remain forever inconceivable, assassination research became her spiritual quest for truth. Conspiracy became her Zen grid for perceiving political reality, drawing her deeper and deeper into a separate reality that Carlos Castaneda never dreamed of. (Castaneda was, of course, one of the three tramps arrested at the Grassy Knoll.)

Mae started a weekly radio program, *Dialogue Assassination*, originating at KLRB in Carmel, California, and syndicated to half a dozen other stations. She purchased the *Warren Commission Report* for $86, studying and cross-referencing the entire 26 volumes, without the aid of a computer. It took her eight years and 27,000 typewritten pages. She was overwhelmed by the difference between the evidence and the conclusion that there had been only a single assassin.

"Lee Harvey Oswald was set up to take the fall," she said, "but the Warren Commission ignored physical evidence from the scene of the crime—bullets, weapons, clothing, wounds—and based its judgment that Oswald was just a disturbed loner on the testimony of some 30 Russian emigres in the Dallas-Fort Worth area. Most of them, according to the testimony, were affiliated with anti-Communist organizations that had collaborated with the Nazis during the war."

Next she began to study the history of Nazis brought to this country after World War II under "Project Paperclip" and infiltrated into hospitals, universities and the aerospace industry, further developing their techniques in propaganda, mind control and behavior modification. She observed how the patterns of murder in the U.S. were identical to those in Nazi Germany. It was as if an early Lenny Bruce bit—about how a show-business booking agency, MCA, promoted Adolf Hitler as a dictator—had actually been a satirical prognostication of the way Richard Nixon would rise to power. The parallels between the rise of Hitler and Nixon were frightening.

I first met Mae in February 1972. She was about 50, plump and energetic, wearing a long peasant dress patchworked with philosophical tidbits, knitting sweaters for her children while she breathlessly described the architecture of an invisible government. The walls were lined with 40 file cabinets containing 1,600 subject folders.

Every day Mae would digest ten newspapers from around the country, supplemening that diet with items sent to her by a network of researchers and young conspiracy students known as Brussell Sprouts, plus magazines, underground papers, unpublished manuscripts, court affidavits, documents from the National Archives, FBI and CIA material obtained through the Freedom of Information Act, and hundreds of books on espionage and assassination. Each Sunday she would sort out the previous week's clippings into various categories as though she were conducting a symphony of horror.

Mae had never been published before, but I gave her a double assignment for *The Realist*. One article would compare the rise of Hitler with the rise of Nixon—each resulting from a series of political assassinations. (Meanwhile, Nixon was having lunch with her father, Rabbi Magnin.) The other article would be on the function of Lee Harvey Oswald and other alleged assassins in achieving that purpose.

I stayed overnight, devouring material from Mae's massive fies. The next morning, my head was still swirling in the afterglow of a fresh conversion. Previously, my religion had been Coincidence, but now it was becoming tempered with Conspiracy. On the bus back home, I pondered the theological question Mae had posed: "How many coincidences does it take to make a plot?"

A few months later, I got a call from her. No wonder she was so excited. The attempted burglary of Democratic headquarters at the Watergate Hotel had suddenly brought her 8-1/2 years of dedicated conspiracy research to an astounding climax. She recognized names, *modus operandi*, patterns of cover-up. She could trace linear connections leading inevitably from the assassination of JFK to the Watergate break-in, masterminded by E. Howard Hunt, who had worked for the CIA for 21 years.

Three weeks later—while Nixon was pressing for the postponement of an investigation until after the election, and the mainstream press was still referring to the incident as a "caper" and a "third-rate burglary"—Mae completed a long article for *The Realist*, documenting the conspiracy and delineating the players, from the burglars all the way up to FBI Director L. Patrick Gray, Attorney General John Mitchell and President Nixon himself.

"The significance of the Watergate affair," she wrote, "is that every element essential for a political *coup d'etat* in the United States was asembled at the time of their arrest."

Believing that her documented article could prevent Nixon's re-election, she delineated the details of a plot so insidious and yet so logical that the typesetter wrote "Bravo!" at the end of her manuscript. However, instead of my usual credit arrangement, the printer insisted on $5,000 cash in advance before this issue could go to press. I didn't have the money, and had no idea how I would get it, but I was filled with an inexplicable sense of confidence.

When I got home, the phone rang. It was Yoko Ono. She and John Lennon were in town, and they invited me to lunch. At that time, the Administration was trying to deport Lennon, ostensibly for an old marijuana bust, but really because they were afraid he was planning to perform for protesters at the Republican convention that summer. I brought the galleys of Mae's article to lunch. Her account of the government's motivation and methodology provided a context for John and Yoko's current harassment. I mentioned my printer's ultimatum, and they immediately took me to a bank and withdrew $5,000 cash. The timing was so exquisite that Coincidence and Mysticism became the same process for me.

A year before the Watergate break-in, E. Howard Hunt had proposed a "bag job"—a surreptitious entry—into the office of psychiatrist Lewis Fielding, who had refused to cooperate with FBI agents investigating one of his patients—Daniel Ellsberg, leaker of the Pentagon Papers. It was the function of the White House "plumbers" to *plug* such leaks. The burglars, led by G. Gordon Liddy, scattered pills around the office to make it look like a junkie was responsible.

The police assured Dr. Fielding that the break-in was made in search of drugs, even though he found Ellsberg's records removed from their folder. An innocent black man, Elmer Davis, was arrested, convicted and sent to prison, while Liddy remained silent. Mae corresponded with Davis, and after he finished serving Liddy's time, he ended up living with Mae.

It was a romance made in Conspiracy Heaven.

STEVE EARLE: STICKING TO HIS PRINCIPLES

"What part of recovery don't you fucking understand?"

That's the rhetorical question Steve Earle asked free-lance journalist Mitch Myers, who was assigned by *High Times* to write a piece on him. Earle had been a junkie for nearly a quarter-century, half of his life. Booze, coke, heroin, methadone, methamphetamine, crack, cough syrup—you name it, he drank, smoked, snorted and mainlined it. In the process, he temporarily destroyed his career as a ground-breaking singer-songwriter, not to mention his function as a dedicated political activist.

Earle also ruined friendships and marriages alike. He was a fool for lust in the guise of love, and has been married six times (twice to the same woman). Hard drugs so severely affected his health that his life almost became six weddings and a funeral. So, although Myers went into great detail about the expanded direction of *High Times*, it's understandable that Earle—who has even given up cigarettes and coffee—might not want to be associated with a magazine that has been so strongly identified with marijuana.

"But," observes Myers, "he still sings 'Copperhead Road,' which is about, among other things, growing weed."

Born on January 16, 1955 at Fort Monroe Army Hospital in Virginia—the same year that both McDonald's and Disneyland opened—Earle was a military brat, raised in Texas, first in El Paso and then in San Antonio. He saw Elvis Presley on TV when he was 3 years old and the Beatles when he was 9, he got his first guitar when he was 12 and smoked his first joint when he was 13, he began performing solo at local coffeehouses and tripping on LSD when he was 14 and he moved to Nashville when he was 19. He would become a musical hybrid, with one foot in country blues and the other in rock'n'roll, going on tour and playing the bar circuit, developing a cult following along the way on his extended and extremely bumpy journey to commercial success.

In a biography published in England, *Hardcore Troubadour: The Life and Near Death of Steve Earle*, Lauren St. John wrote:

"Watching the tree-lined interstates of Tennessee give way to the wide open spaces of Texas, Steve found himself humming songs from *Born in the USA*, the album that had recently catapulted [Bruce] Springsteen into the mainstream. Experiencing Springsteen live and listening to the album had had a profound effect on him. 'I was intrigued by the fact that Springsteen opened the album with "Born in the USA," that it was really a theme and an overture, and he opened the show with it.' Inspired, Steve wrote 'Guitar Town' on the drive home, specifically intending it to be the opening song of his album."

And, similar to Springsteen, it was the *Guitar Town* album which catapulted Earle into the mainstream in 1986.

Ironically, though, according to Bill Bennett, a respected rock promoter, "I used to argue with him and at the end I'd say, 'Why am I arguing with you, you're a junkie.' And he'd yell, 'Well, I wrote *Guitar Town* on junk, so fuck you!'"

When I was assigned by *High Times* to write a piece on Steve Earle, I was *not* informed that, only a week before, he had refused to cooperate with exactly such a project. And so, on a crisp October afternoon in New York City, blissfully unaware of that turndown, I bought a little tape recorder and headed for the combination CMJ 2003 Music Marathon and Do It Yourself Convention at the Hilton Hotel, where Earle would appear on stage, not with his guitar, but as a speaker.

Chicago Sun-Times critic Jim Derogatis, referring to the Atkins diet, is teasing him: "Everybody thinks you're on drugs again since you lost weight."

Earle responds, "No one that saw me when I was on drugs thinks I'm on drugs when they see me now."

"Are you sick of people asking how can you eat all that red meat and be healthy?"

"No. I used to spend $300 a day on cocaine, not sweating meat."

Amos Poe's musical documentary about Steve Earle, *Just an American Boy*, has played in theaters and is available on DVD. A soundtrack double-album from the film has been released by Artemis Records, with all of Earle's best known songs, some alone and others with his band, the Dukes.

"The [documentary] happened," he says, "because Danny Goldberg [head of Artemis] realized that I was talking to some people that I don't normally talk to in the normal promotional cycle of a record, and he thought that we should document that. Amos made the 'Transcendental Blues' video and the 'Jerusalem' video, so when someone proposes a documentary film, for me that means 3 to 6 months with a camera up my ass. It was Amos who I know and I like him, so at least I knew *whose* camera was up my ass. It was easier to sit through when we screened it than I thought it would be. It was somewhat less uncomfortable than a hot poker in one of my eyes."

Just as, in 1962, Lenny Bruce, in his most audacious satirical critique, perceived reality from Holocaust orchestrator Adolf Eichmann's point of view, so, 40 years later, did Steve Earle, in his most controversial song, "John Walker's Blues" on the *Jerusalem* CD, empathize with John Walker Lindh, the American Taliban captured in Afghanistan, wondering why Allah's master plan had U.S. troops "dragging me back with my head in a sack to the land of the infidel," and observing, "If my daddy could see me now, chains around my feet, he don't understand that sometimes a man has got to fight for what he believes." The chorus included eerie Arabic chanting.

Earle maintains that it's his "most poignant album, most proud moment of my career. I got a one-star review from the *New York Post*. I pissed off all the people I was trying to piss off, and everybody that I respect got it, so every bit of shit I got was like I expected to get from the quarters I expected to get it from.

"I worried more about my family early on, just because they worried about me, because their politics is part of the climate in this country. It's a climate of fear, and it's designed to shut us up and keep us from asking questions. And it's absolutely nothing short of that. Taking it any less seriously than that is jerking off.

That's what it is, the new blacklist. It's the new censorship, and it's very, very serious business to me.

"I worried about offending John Walker Lindh's parents, I worried about doing anything to endanger his case, and the closest I came to not doing it was taking that into consideration, and the reason I was sort of predisposed to think that way, I do a lot of work around Modesto [where Lindh's family lives], and I learned a long time ago that I'd never bring an end to the death penalty in this country if I was insensitive to the feelings of victims' families.

"I wrote this song mainly because I have a son exactly the same age as John Walker Lindh—I got a kid, he's 21—and it's scary when your kid gets to be old enough that they don't stay where you put 'em, and the first thing that I related to was, 'My God, he's got parents and they must be sick,' and so I was reasonably sure nobody else was gonna write this song. I never got any negative feedback, and I was in a position where I break-out would've, and I always sort of very hopefully took that as positive feedback. If I *did* hear anything from *him*, I probably wouldn't tell you, but I haven't. If I did, I'd probably lie. Because I think it was the right thing to do.

"The very first person killed in this country by an abysmal situation in the wake of 9/11 wasn't even Muslim, he was a Sikh who was killed because rednecks *thought* he was a Muslim, and that was what made me aware of an awful lot of what 'Jerusalem' was about. I always hope I learn something when I make any kind of art, and that's the whole point of it to me, and what I learned was how ignorant I am of Islam, how ignorant *we* are of Islam, and I can't think of anything more dangerous right now than being ignorant of Islam."

Earle points out the contrast between "the age of Hillary Duff and Clay Aiken and the age of Bob Dylan and MC5 and performers associated with politics. There was a lot of pop music that was just pop music, and rock 'n' roll that was just rock 'n' roll, that's *totally* okay, there's not anything wrong about that. The whole body of my work—I didn't marry *every*body I wrote a song about—I just didn't learn to write songs any other way. It's just never occurred to me to exclude issues and what's going on around me politically.

"My main area of activism is the death penalty, but I'm turning down death penalty stuff right now, because to me the priority right now is stop the war, but I don't think you can stop the war as long as Bush is president, so the priority with the election coming up is to get Bush out of office, *then* stop the war, and then everybody gets back on to their own field of activism.

"We've gotta elect somebody that can beat Bush. We are stuck with this two-party system. I do think a third-party run right now is unrealistic. The war unfortunately became the way that Bush could be beaten, and he wasn't vulnerable until recently. I knew we were getting somewhere when I walked into a truckstop and saw all those farting Bush dolls. That wasn't possible six months ago, but it's a dilemma. It's really important that you find out everything you can, you're gonna have to make those decisions."

During the questions-from-the-audience portion of Earle's presentation, I approach the microphone in the aisle: "First I just wanna mention that not only is there a George W. Bush action figure, there's also an Ann Coulter doll—you pull the string and it spews venom." Earle laughs and I continue. "Since you and I are both on the same label—Artemis Records, run by Danny Goldberg—and this is a Do It Yourself Convention, yet you're on a label that released *Who Let the Dogs Out*—"

"Which allows him to put out records by me and you, which is okay, I'm okay with that, definitely—"

"I'm happy to be subsidized—"

"Absolutely," he says, "that's what it's all about—"

"But I think it wouldn't be the same if it wasn't Danny Goldberg. As [radio personality] Don Imus said, 'He's not like the other thugs in the industry.' So I'm just wondering about that, because he is essentially one of us and is sort of like a missing link—working with him has been for me the same feeling I would have if I was *really* doing it myself, and I was just wondering if it's been the same for you."

"Without the pain in the ass. The way I came to Danny was, I had a label—an imprint, E-Squared at Warner—I made a bluegrass record and *that* pissed people off even worse than 'John Walker's Blues' did, so I ended up leaving and I went to Artemis. I was still operating an imprint, and what I discovered was that in this climate, having a record label was sort of like going in a pickup truck, everybody kept calling me to help them move because everybody I knew was out of a record deal, and it got to be kind of anti-art. I did it for five years, and so I know—I mean we ran one side of E-Squared as a free-standing independent record label and it was distributed through Warner—we basically misappropriated what was supposed to be our operating budget for Warner and used it to make records. At the end of it nobody arrested us, and so it turned out really good.

"But recording for Artemis—the reason I support it as much as I do is, it is commerce but it's set up completely differently than every other record label that I know of that has anywhere close to its resources, and the vision was from the beginning that there would never, ever be a public stock offer, because as soon as you start doing that, then you're beholden to your stockholders, and I think we may have learned by now it's a really, really bad way—it just doesn't give you enough time to develop any kind of art when you have to answer to a stockholder every three months. So that's the main thing, and that was what Danny wanted to do, and it's been tough. We all, every one of us artists, owe a lot to Danny hanging in there and to Warren Zevon, God bless him, 'cause it's still going, and we'll see how it turns out."

(The legendery Zevon had died of inoperable lung cancer the previous month, after Artemis Records released his final, heartbreaking, farewell album, *The Wind*.)

I ask Earle about his upcoming appearance on the Fox News Network (which has beer sponsors), with the conservative and cantankerous Bill O'Reilly. "I'm just gonna go," he replies, "until I get him to say 'Shut up!'"

"That means three minutes."

Earle had to catch a train to New Jersey. Although this was the first time we met, we knew of each other's work, and as he was leaving, we shook hands. "It's an honor," he said.

"That's mutual. Listen, I'm writing a piece about you. How can I contact you if I have any questions?"

He hurriedly gave me his e-mail address and departed. But, after learning about his adverse attitude toward *High Times*, I sent an e-mail asking him to reconsider, and never heard back. I was disappointed, though I understood his silence. In fact, ironically enough, Earle's adamantly sticking to his principles became the inextricable core element of this story. Besides, he had already *publicly* discussed the areas which interested me, so I've published those quotes here without violating any journalistic ethic.

And, what the hell, Eric Alterman wrote a whole *biography* of Bruce Springsteen without ever communicating with *him*. On the other hand, Dave Marsh, editor of *Rock & Rap Confidential*, wrote a book about Springsteen, and their friendship was enhanced in the process. Marsh told me that on one occasion, he was in Los Angeles interviewing Springsteen, and at the end of the session, each said he'd brought a record for the other. It turned out that both of them had brought Steve Earle's *Guitar Town*. The cycle was now complete.

In the course of my research, I learned that Earle had once credited Dave Marsh with saving his life. I asked Marsh about this, and he replied:

"Here's the only thing I can think of that it pertains to. Do you know the story about Steve punching out an off-duty Dallas cop? This was backstage, I think it was New Year's Eve, and I know that the cop, working as security at Steve's show, had somehow manhandled Steve's dad. This became an 'assaulting a police officer' felony. Steve refused to plea bargain, which meant he was taking a big chance on going down for serious prison time, especially since nobody outside Dallas was paying any attention to it at all.

"I think it was Teresa Ensenat, wife number 4-B or something like that, but then a girlfriend (and the A&R person who discovered Guns 'n Roses, if that's relevant), who told me about what had happened, what was about to happen. I wound up writing about the case at some length in the *Village Voice*, and got the prosecutor to make some admissions that were harmful to the state's case (if I remember right). Anyway, the big problem in the case was that Steve really wasn't going to plead guilty to anything whatsoever, because he just felt so strongly that he hadn't done anything wrong. It took a lot of persuading by a lot of people that this was a very bad idea, but one way or another, the case was settled. I expect the cop was after a civil judgment, but don't think he ever got one.

"Other than that, it'd have to be something way third-hand that I wrote or said somewhere that he saw. I *worried* about Steve, just as an artist I respect and a person I'd met a bunch of times and really liked, but we weren't in contact very often, never have been, and it seems like he dropped off a lot of radar once he got seriously into the crack. If I'm right about what he means, the oddest part of it is that I always was afraid that maybe it was wrong to keep him out of prison. The stubbornness and self-righteousness he displayed is part and parcel of addiction. Maybe, it's occurred to me a few times since, he'd have been better off doing a bit, would have gotten cleaned up sooner.

"This of course is near-terminally stupid, since drugs are way available in every prison in the country; it's part of how the prisons are managed, just like rape is another part. In the somewhat gentler jail in which Steve began getting sober, he was incarcerated for a much shorter time and probably with slightly less dangerous company. Really, the reward for his survival is everybody's—all those songs that we get to share. The first time I heard 'Fort Worth Blues,' I wrote Steve a letter and apologized for not being there for him more and better, and I meant it. He made a very generous reply. I think we're friends. I know I'm a fan and thank the universe frequently that he's still around."

In November 2003, Earle was a guest on *The O'Reilly Factor*. During their encounter, Bill O'Reilly didn't tell him to shut up. He began by asking Earle to define himself politically.

Earle: "I am an unapologetic lefty. . . ."

O'Reilly: "*Tell Us the Truth*—your three-week concert tour of U.S. clubs—so what are you going to tell us? What's the truth here, Mr. Earle?"

Earle: "*Tell Us the Truth* is about media consolidation and other factors around media in this country and how they affect the quality of our—you know, in terms of the music business, what I do for a living and the quality of information that we receive."

O'Reilly: "Can you be more specific? I mean what are you objecting to?"

Earle: "I object to television news and radio news, and even print media to some extent, that makes decisions on what we hear and in what order we hear it in, based on commerce rather than what might be the most important information that we need to make the decisions as citizens. I think the media directly affects the outcome of our elections. When it gets to the point where we have a media climate that participates in accusing people that speak out against these policies of being unpatriotic and unAmerican, I think that's dangerous."

O'Reilly: "Well, I agree with you. I think anybody who's sincere should be able to speak out and should be heard—which is why we are happy you came on *The Factor* tonight, Mr. Earle. Good luck with your concert tour."

O'Reilly said that John Walker Lindh "was tried and convicted of treason." Earle said that wasn't true; Lindh pleaded guilty to supplying services to the Taliban government and carrying explosives in commission of a felony. O'Reilly's misstatement was edited out.

In December 2003 at the Berkeley Community Theater, Wavy Gravy—countercultural clown, social activist and ex-Ben & Jerry's ice-cream flavor—emceed a concert which he had organized as a benefit to celebrate the 25th anniversary of Seva (the Sanskrit word meaning "divine work" or "service to God"), featuring performers Bonnie Raitt, Jackson Browne, Buffy Sainte-Marie, the Dead, Hamza el Din—and Steve Earle.

The concert raised $250,000 for Seva, an organization which has been supporting projects and hospitals that have given back sight to more than two million blind persons through low cost or free surgery in developing countries around the world, plus community self-development programs that have helped thousands of indigenous peoples to drink clean water, read, write and deliver healthier babies, as well as promoting diabetes prevention for Native Americans.

Inspired by the event, Earle said, "None of us are without hope—otherwise you wouldn't be here tonight." He was obviously speaking to himself as well as to the audience.

When introducing his song "Christmas in Washington (Come Back, Woody Guthrie)," he has always paid passionate tribute to his heroes—like Joan Baez, Abbie Hoffman, former Illinois Governor George Ryan (for his courageous stance against capital punishment, not for his alleged tax fraud), Vermont Senator Patrick Leahy (for defying Attorney General John Ashcroft over the fascistic Patriot Act)—but this time Earle included Wavy Gravy and Seva's executive director, Dr. Larry Brilliant. Later, in private, he told them that he wanted to visit Seva sites such as Chiapas, Nepal and Tibet.

"I'm in recovery," he explained, "and part of recovery is that you gotta do service. This will be my service."

And that's a part of recovery I *absolutely* fucking understand.

THE IRONIC ORDEAL OF DR. L.

There's a byproduct of the war on drugs—a side effect, if you will—a war against doctors who prescribe painkillers, putting a chill on legitimate pain treatment by physicians who fear prosecution.

The Justice Department is particularly concerned with Vicodin, Dilaudid and—America's most abused pain pill—OxyContin. Just ask Rush Limbaugh and Courtney Love. There are even doctors' offices now with signs on the wall, warning, "Don't ask for OxyContin" and "No OxyContin prescribed here."

Dr. Ronald Myers, president of the American Pain Institute, stated, "Such is the climate of fear across the medical community that for every doctor who has his license yanked by the DEA, there are a hundred doctors scared to prescribe proper pain medication for fear of going to prison."

A major protest at the National Mall in April 2004 was organized by the National Pain Patients Coalition, to bring attention to what some experts regard as the number one health issue in the nation—the undertreatment of chronic pain—in the hope that state leglislators will pass bills guaranteeing patients' rights to alleviate their suffering.

San Francisco attorney Patrick Hallinan said that honest doctors all over the country are being targeted by the DEA under the supposition that their patients were violating the law without the doctor's knowledge by selling their prescriptions on the street, and that the agents are using the same tactics against them that are used against narcotics dealers.

"There isn't any doubt," he added, "that these prosecutions are increasing under the Bush administration. It is like busting a car dealer because somebody runs off the road and kills somebody."

The campaign began under Janet Reno and has increased in intensity under John Ashcroft—storming clinics in SWAT-style gear and ransacking doctors' offices.

Here's a case history of a family physician I know. He practices in a small town and calls himself "a country doctor." I'll call him Dr. L. I first met him at the height of the Anthrax scare, right after envelopes containing Anthrax had been sent to ABC and NBC. Tom Brokaw ended the evening news by saying, "Thank God for Cipro," referring to the antibiotic that would counteract the effects of Anthrax if not the hysteria. Before I could even tell Dr. L. my medical emergency—an attack of diverticulosis causing severe stomach pain—he said, "I suppose you want a prescription for Cipro." He had already gotten several requests for the drug that week.

I explained the purpose of my visit, but he acted as though I was faking it in order to obtain a painkiller. When he determined that my condition was real, he prescribed antibiotics and a painkiller. Ultimately we became friends, and I learned the reason for his suspicious approach.

Dr. L. was once convicted for what he sardonically describes as "the heinous crime of prescribing tylenol codeine for the treatment of migraine syndrome in a couple of ladies." They turned out to be undercover operatives for the Medical Board of California.

"This story is not unique," he told me. "It is being repeated across the United States every day. Our country seems to be slipping into a fascist regime with dictatorial, uncontrolled coercive state power."

Over a period of several days, the two women, who were wired, visited Dr. L's office, complaining of symptoms that were consistent with migraine headaches. After listening to their history, he gave each of them 30 tylenol codeine tablets until he could obtain their previous records. He even called one of the physicians who had been listed in the intake form—a doctor in Oshkosh, Wisconsin—but an elderly telephone operator told him she had lived in that town for 70 years and had never heard of such a doctor.

Some weeks later, there was a melodramatic search warrant served by agents with drawn guns. They were from the DEA, BNA (a state agency comparable to the DEA) and the local police. This is a common practice of ass-covering, so that no single agency can be blamed if anything goes wrong.

The raid had a terrible effect on the economic health of Dr. L's family practice, a standard mix of obstetrics, pediatrics and internal medicine. A story was planted in the local media—via press releases from those government agencies—stating that he was a drug-dealing doctor and would lose his license. He was shunned by colleagues.

"Several weeks later," he says, "I was arrested at my office while many startled patients watched in utter disbelief as their doctor was handcuffed and led away. The arresting officers would not let me take off my clinic coat or stethoscope—this picture was worth more with them on. I was booked and subsequently released on bail."

His trial didn't come up until six years later. After ten days in court, he was found guilty, sentenced to six months in jail, fined more than $11,000, and required to perform 200 hours of community service. The case went to the Court of Appeals, and later to the California Supreme Court, where, on the last day of the session, a hearing was denied.

He was now in debt for legal fees of over $300,000. Moreover, In order to serve his sentence, he had to close his office. And, based on the felony convictions—at a hearing which he could not attend because he was in custody—his medical license was revoked.

An additional appeal resulted in a decision against the prosecutor, accusing him of lying, deceit, skullduggery, prevarication, you name it, and another hearing was ordered to be held by the Medical Board. Dr. L was placed on five years probation. But his nightmare continued.

"Subsequently," he says, "Medicare, Medi-Cal and Champus certifications were revoked. In addition, my name was added to the nefarious National Practitioners Data Bank. Thus, no HMO would consider me for employment, no malpractice carrier would insure me, and I was even ineligible for hire by a state prison because of my felonious status.

"Physicians are the number one target for prosecution by the DEA and the 50 states operating in tandem. This prosecutorial targeting of physicians which definitely includes entrapment and selective prosecution, has come about, I believe, because of an erroneous and nefarious assumption that our prescriptions are sold on the street to satisfy the needs of addicts. This fallacious exercise in logic is called 'diversion' and the general claim had been made by the DEA that physicians bear the blame for the failed war on drugs.

"This circular illogic and self-fulfilling prophecy is used as a pretext for promoting the greatly undeserved Bad Doctor Syndrome. There are unlimited funds available for such government investigations. Often they are triggered by a complaint a local pharmacist registers with the Pharmacy Board about a physician he believes uses too many drugs for the relief of pain."

Conversely, a California jury recently awarded $1.5 million to the family of an 85-year-old man whose doctor *failed* to treat him adequately for pain for a few days as he lay dying of lung cancer. That verdict was only the third in American history for the *undertreatment* of pain, and the first against a doctor. It was also the first time a jury awarded such a verdict under elder abuse laws instead of a medical negligence lawsuit.

Kathryn Tucker, director of legal affairs for Compassion in Dying Federation, pointed out that this case could serve as the catalyst for better pain management by the medical profession and educate the public that it should take action when these needs are ignored. Nor is there any shortage of potential lawsuits. A study published in the *Journal of the American Medical Association* found that 40 percent of nursing home patients with acute or chronic pain are not getting pain treatment that brings relief.

Dr. L shakes his head as he contemplates the overwhelming irony.

"I spent six months in jail," he observes, "while now one gets a malpractice lawsuit for inappropriate relief of pain. What a most interesting and contravening juxtaposition in such a few years. I do not really think that we have a system of justice—merely a system of laws."

Recently, Dr. L's medical license was reinstated, and his family practice clinic can now be diagnosed as vigorously healthy.

Postscript: Dr. Tad Lonergan was killed in a car accident on July 4, 2005.

AN INTERVIEW WITH
ROBERT ANTON WILSON

Bob Wilson's books include *The Illuminatus! Trilogy* (with Robert Shea); the *Cosmic Trigger* trilogy, *The New Inquisition*, the *Schrodinger's Cat* trilogy, *Prometheus Rising*, *The Walls Came Tumbling Down*, *Wilhelm Reich in Hell*, *Natural Law, Sex, Drugs & Magick* and *Everything is Under Control: An Encyclopedia of Conspiracy Theories*.

He is also the subject of a feature-length documentary movie by Lance Bauscher, *Maybe Logic: The Lives and Ideas of Robert Anton Wilson*, featuring 23 different Bobs, Tom Robbins, R.U. Sirius, George Carlin and myself. For more information, go to maybelogic.com. Wilson continues to explore his consciousness and communicate his ideas and causes, with passion, wit, imagination and insight. This interview was conducted by the electronic magic of e-mail.

Q. You've written 34 books with the aid of pot. Could you describe that process?

A. It's rather obsessive-compulsive, I think. I write the first draft straight, then rewrite stoned, then rewrite straight again, then rewrite stoned again, and so on, until I'm absolutely delighted with every sentence, or irate editors start reminding me about deadlines—whichever comes first. Hemingway and Raymond Chandler had similar compulsions but used the wrong drug, booze, and they both attempted suicide. Papa succeeded but poor Ray didn't and just looked like a sloppy alcoholic. (He tried to shoot himself in the head and missed.) Faulkner also had obsessive components and died by falling off a horse, drunk. I don't think booze is a very safe drug for us obsessive-compulsives. Almost as bad as becoming known as a Sage. By the way, Congress should impeach Dubya and impound [then drug czar] Asa Hutchinson.

Q. The piss police read High Times. *What would you like to tell them?*

A. "You are all equally blessed, equally empty, equally coming Buddhas." But some of them are such assholes it will take a long time to get from there to here.

Q. Columnist Clarence Page recently wrote about the DEA raiding "a legitimate health co-operative [WAMM, the Wo/Men's Alliance for Medical Marijuana] that was treating more than 200 patients, some of them terminally ill, in Santa Cruz. Snatching medicine out of the hands of seriously ill patients sounds like terrorism to me. In this case it was federally sponsored and taxpayer-financed." Tell me about your own relationship with WAMM.

A. I thought you'd never ask. Long before I needed WAMM, Valerie Coral, the founder, came regularly to my *Finnegan's Wake* reading/rapping group, and I considered her incredibly bright. As I learned about her WAMM activities, distributing pot to terminal cancer and AIDS patients, sitting with them, giving love and support during the death process, I decided she was also a saint. I never thought I would become another WAMM patient. My post-polio syndrome had been a minor nuisance until then; suddenly two years ago it flared up into blazing pain. My doctor recommended marijuana and named WAMM as the safest and most legal source. By then, I think I was on the edge of suicide; the pain had become like a permanent abcessed tooth in the leg. Nobody can or should endure that. Thanks to Valerie and WAMM, I never have that kind of torture for more than an hour these days. I pop one of their pain pills and I'm up and back at the iMac in, well, if not an hour, then at most two hours. By the way, Congress should impeach Dubya and impound Asa Hutchinson. Or did I say that already?

Q. I think you did.

A. Well, it bears repeating.

Q. When the City Council staged a public giveaway of medical marijuana, a DEA agent asked, "What kind of message are city officials sending to the youth of Santa Cruz?" How would you answer him?

A. "The powers not delegated to the United States by the Constitution, nor prohibited by it to the States, are reserved to the States respectively, or to the people." I didn't invent that; I found it in the back of my dictionary, in a dusty old historical document called "U.S. Constitution," which Dubya seemingly has never heard of, but it's supposed to be the rules of our government. I wish more people would look at that document, because it has a lot of other radical ideas that seem worth thinking about. Look it up before the Bush Crime Family forces dictionary publishers to remove it. Congress should impeach Dubya and impound Asa Hutchinson. Or does this begin to sound like an echo chamber?

Q. How does all that tie in with your book, TSOG? *First, what does TSOG mean, and how do you pronounce it?*

A. TSOG means Tsarist Occupation Government and I pronounce it TSOG, so it sounds like a monster in a Lovecraft story. The book presents the evidence that ever since the CIA-Nazi-Tsarist alliance of the 1940s, the Tsarists have taken over as the "brains" of the Control System and America has become a Tsarist nation, with the Constitution only known to those who peek in the back of their dictionaries, like I did. Hell, we even have an official Tsar and he has the alleged "right"—or at least the power—to come between my doctor and me, and decide how much excruciating pain I should suffer before dying. What next? Is he going to rule on controversial questions in physics and astronomy? In mathematical set theory? In biology? Believe me, there's no Tsar mentioned in the Constitution. Personal doctor/patient matters are left to the individuals. You see, this was supposed to be a free country, not a Tsarist despotism.

Q. *You were brought up as a Catholic and became a Marxist when you were 16. What disillusioned you about each of those belief systems?*

A. Their rigidity. All rigid Belief Systems (B.S.) censor and warp the processes of perception, thought and even empathy. They literally make people behave like badly-wired robots. Philip K. Dick noticed this too, and worried a lot about the possible robots among us. Some people think he was crazy, but I've never met anybody with rigid beliefs who seemed fully human to me. Phil got it right: a lot of them do act like robots. Especially in government offices and churches. Gort, Dubya barada nikto, dig?

Q. *What was the purpose of what you call the Christian conspiracy?*

A. Well, I regard the Bill of Rights as the result of a conspiracy by the intellectual freemasons of the Enlightenment Era. It's always had a precarious existence because of the rival Christian conspiracy to restore the dark ages—Inquisitions, witch-hunts and all. With the Tsarist take-over, the Christians appear to have won. Not a single clause in the Bill of Rights hasn't gotten either diluted or totally reversed.

Q. *Why are you so skeptical about organized skepticism?*

A. Like I keep saying, rigid Belief Systems frighten me and make me think of robots, or "humanoids"—some kinda creepy mechanism like that. Organized skepticism in the U.S. today contains no true skeptics in the philosophical sense. They seem like just another gang of dogmatic fanatics at war with all the other gangs of dogmatic fanatics, and, of course, with us model agnostics also. Look at the Committee for Scientific Investigation of Claims of the Paranormal. They never do any Scientific Investigation at all, at all. Why? My guess is that, like the Inquisitors who refused to look through Galileo's telescope, they have a deep fear that such research might upset their dogmas.

Q. *What's the basis of your obsession with Hannibal Lecter?*

A. Hannibal Lecter, M.D., please. In the books, he seems one of the greatest creations in literature to me. I admire Thomas Harris more than any novelist since James Joyce. Everything about Dr. Lecter is likeable and even admirable except that one Nasty Habit [cannibalism], but that habit's so intolerable, even to libertarians, we can never forget *it* even when we find him most likeable and most admirable. A paradox like that can inspire Ph.D. candidates for 1,000 years. I mean, how can you resist a psychiatrist who tells a lesbian patient, as Hannibal did once, "There's nothing wrong with being weird. You have no idea how weird I am"—and really means it? In the films, of course, Dr. Lecter also has the stupendous contribution of intelligence and eerie charm only Anthony Hopkins can project. By the way, God bless Valerie Coral and God *damn* Asa Hutchinson.

Q. *I thought you don't believe in God?*

A. I have no "beliefs," only probabilities; but I was not speaking literally there. A poetic flourish, as it were.

Q. *I know you don't believe in life after death, but I'm intrigued by the notion that, during 42 years of marriage, you and Arlen imprinted each other's nervous systems. Could you elaborate on that?*

A. I don't "believe" in spiritualism, but that does not keep me from suspecting an unbreakable link between those who have loved deeply. To avoid sounding esoteric, let me put it in nitty-gritty terms. I literally cannot look at a movie on TV without knowing what she'd say about it. For instance, if a film starts out well and ends up a mess, I can virtually "hear" her saying, "Well, they had one story conference too many. . . ."

Q, *Would you relate the tale of Arlen and the encyclopedias?*

A. She liked to collect old encyclopedias from second-hand bookstores, and at one point we had eight of them. When I wrote my first historical novel—back in 1980, before I was online—I used them often as a research tool. For instance, I learned that the Bastille was either 90 feet high or 100 feet or 120 feet. This led me to formulate Wilson's 22nd Law: "Certitude belongs exclusively to those who only look in one encyclopedia."

Q. *How has the Internet changed your life?*

A. It has felt like a neurological quantum jump. Not only does the word-processing software make my compulsive rewriting a lot easier than if I still had to cut my words on rocks or use a typewriter or retreat to similar barbarism, but the e-mail function provides most of my social life since I became "disabled." I do most of my research on the World Wide Web, get my answer in minutes and don't have to hunt laboriously through my library for hours. It has improved my life a thousand ways. I also have a notion that Internet will eventually replace government.

Q. How do you discern between conspiracy and coincidence?

A. The way Mr. and Mrs. Godzilla make love: very carefully.

Q. A dinner party was scheduled for March 31, 1981, the day after an assassination attempt on Ronald Reagan, which, if successful, would have elevated Vice President and former CIA chief George Bush to the presidency. The dinner was immediately cancelled. It would have been held at the home of Neil Bush, and a guest was to be Scott Hinckley, brother of the would-be killer. Hinckley's father and Bush were friends and fellow oil industrialists. A PR firm issued a statement: "This horrible coincidence has been devastating to the Bush Family. Our condolences go out to all involved. And we hope to get the matter behind us as soon as possible." Congressman Larry MacDonald was the only legislator who demanded an investigation, but his plane crashed. Whattaya think—coincidence or conspiracy?

A. To me, it looks at first glance like coincidence by about 75 percent probability. I mean, who would be dumb enough to use an assassin with such obvious links to his employers? But then again, the Bush Crime Family seem to think they can get away with anything, from S&L fraud to stealing an election in the clear light of day with the whole world watching. They must have an even lower opinion of the intelligence of the American people than I do. Maybe I should change the probability down to about 50 percent. I guess this does deserve further investigation, by somebody who doesn't fly in airplanes.

Q. Ishmael Reed said, "The history of civilization is the history of warfare between secret societies." Do you agree?

A. Yes and no. I would say there is no history, singular; only histories, plural. The warfare between secret societies is a history, one that both Ishmael and I have explored. There also exists a history of class war, a history of war (or competition) between gene pools, a history of primate/canine relations, etc., ad infinitum. None of them contradicts the others, except in the heads of aristotelian logicians, or Ideologists. They each supplement all the others.

Q. You and I have something in common. Lyndon LaRouche has revealed the truth about each of us: You're really the secret leader of the Illuminati; and I was brainwashed at the Tavistock Institute in England. Do you think he actually believes such things, or is he consciously creating fiction, just as the FBI's counterintelligence program did?

A. I still don't understand some of my computer's innards and you expect me to explain a bizarre contraption like the brain of Lyndon LaRouche? I can only hazard that he seems more a case for a bile specialist than a psychiatrist.

Q. *What was LaRouche's factoid about the Queen of England?*

A. He said Liz sent Aldous Huxley and Alan Watts over here to destroy us with Oriental religions and drugs, so England could become the top Super-Power again. If you took Liz and England out and put Fu Manchu and the Third World in her place, it would make a great matinee thriller. I think Dubya lives in that film with Mickey and Goofy and Osama bin Laden and Darth Vader.

Q. *What's the most bizarre conspiracy theory you've come across?*

A. A group called Christians Awake claims Ronald Reagan was a Gay Freemason and that he filled the government and courts with other Gay Freemasons. I suppose they let Clarence Thomas in as a concession to the Gay Prince Hal Lodge.

Q. *And what would be the least known conspiracy theory—I mean, that you know of?*

A. The Church of Positive Accord believes—and I think they make a damned good case—that the God of the Bible is corporeal, not spiritual. In udder woids, he eats and shits just like you and me. And, contrary to my 1959 heresies, he definitely has a penis. He even has boogers: they proclaimed that in an interview with [SubGenius Church reverend] Ivan Stang. They point out that all "spiritual" ideas of God derive from Greek philosophy, not the Bible, and claim that gaseous Greek god has been promoted by a conspiracy of intellectuals. Just re-read the Bible with that grid and it makes sense, in a Stone Age sort of way. He walks, He talks, He's a serial killer, and in the sequel He even knocks up a teen-age chick.

Q. *Your readers can't always discern—when you write about the Illuminati, for example—whether you're sharing information or satirizing reality. Does it make any difference?*

A. To quote Madonna, "I'm only kidding—not." Add my Celtic sense of humor to Niels Bohr's model agnosticism and out comes my neo-surrealist novels and "post-modern" criticism.

Q. *I've had many occurrences of satirical prophecy, where something I invented turned out to become reality. Has that happened with you?*

A. Well, in *Illuminatus* (published 1975), terrorists attack the Pentagon and only succeed in blowing a hole in one of the five sides. Sound familiar? Also, in *Schrodinger's Cat* (published 1981), terrorists blow up Wall Street. I don't regard either of those "hits" as precognition or even "intuition," just common sense. It seemed obvious to me that the TSOG could not run amok around the planet, invading and bombing damned near everybody, without somebody firing back eventually.

Q. Here's a confession. In my article on the conspiracy convention in High Times, *I did a reverse of satirical prophecy. I had once asked Mae Brussell, the queen of conspiracy researchers, why the conspirators didn't kill her, and she explained that agents always work on a need-to-know basis, but they would read her work and show up wherever she spoke, in order to get a peek at the big picture, because, she said, it was "a safety valve for them on how far things are going." I asked, "Are you saying that the intelligence community has allowed you to function precisely because* you *know more than any of* them?" *And she replied, "Exactly." Well, in my* High Times *satire ("Murder At the Conspiracy Convention"), I put those words into the mouth of somewhat fraudulent conspiracy researcher David Icke. Anyway, my question is, do you think the conspirators allow* you *to live because you know too much?*

A. I doubt it. I don't think they've ever heard of me. They don't read books.

Q. The original meaning of conspiracy was "to breathe together." What's your personal definition of conspiracy?

A. When me and me friends gits together to advance our common interests, that's an affinity group. When any crowd I don't like does it, that's a goddam conspiracy.

Q. After my High Times *column on the Prophets Conference, in which I referred to you as "the irreverent bad boy at this oh-so-polite conference," why were you disinvited from speaking at future Prophets Conferences?*

A. A lot of my fans think I got booted for lack of respect for His Royal Fraudulency George II. I take that as an assertion beyond proof or disproof. The managers said it was for finding a Joycean epiphany in a Spike Lee movie. I take that as an assertion beyond even comprehension.

Q. I'd like to hear about your—perhaps psychotic?—experience with higher consciousness and the resulting epiphany.

A. I have had not one but many seeming encounters with seemingly nonhuman intelligences. The first was a Christmas tree that loved me—loved me more than my parents or my wife or my kids, or even my dog. I was on peyote at the time. With and without other drugs—for instance by Cabala—I have seemingly contacted a medieval Irish bard, an ancient Chinese alchemist, an extraterrestrial from the Sirius system, and a giant white rabbit called the pook or pookah from County Kerry. I finally accepted that if you already have a multi-model ontology going into the shamanic world, you're going to come out with multi-model results. As Wilson's Fourth Law sez, "With sufficient research you will find evidence to support your theory." So I settled on the magick rabbit as the model nobody could take literally, not even myself. The real shocker came when I discovered that my grandmother's people, the O'Lachlanns, came from Kerry and allegedly have a clan pookah who protects us from becoming English by adding periodic doses of weirdness to our lives.

Q. *The dedication in my book,* Murder At the Conspiracy Convention and Other American Absurdities, *reads: "This one is for Robert Anton Wilson—guerrilla ontologist, part-time post-modernist, Damned Old Crank, my weirdest friend and favorite philosopher." Since these are all terms you've used to label yourself, would you explain what each one means?*

A. Well, I picked up "guerrilla ontology" from the Physics/Consciousness Research Group when I was a member back in the 1970s. Physicists more usually call it "model agnosticism," and it consists of never regarding any model or map of Universe with total 100 percent belief or total 100 percent denial. Following Korzybski, I put things in probabilities, not absolutes. I give most of modern physics over 90 percent probability, the Loch Ness Monster around 50 percent probability and anything the State Department says under 5 percent probability. As Bucky Fuller used to say, "Universe is nonsimultaneously apprehended"—nobody can apprehend it all at once—so we have no guarantee that today's best model will fit what we may discover tomorrow. My only originality lies in applying this zetetic attitude outside the hardest of the hard sciences, physics, to softer sciences and then to non-sciences like politics, ideology, jury verdicts and, of course, conspiracy theory. Also, I have a strong aversion, almost an allergy, to Belief Systems, or B.S.—a convenient abbreviation I owe to David Jay Brown. A neurolinguistic diet high in B.S. and low in instrumental data eventually produces Permanent Brain Damage, a lurching gait, blindness and hairy palms like a werewolf.

Then I started calling myself a post-modernist after that label got pinned on me in two different books, one on my sociological works and one on my science-fiction. Then I read some of the post-modernists and decided they were only agnostic about other people's dogmas, not their own. So then I switched to Damned Old Crank, which seems to suit my case better than either of the previous labels. Besides, once my hair turned snowy white, some people wanted to promote me to a Sage, and I had to block that. It's more dangerous to a writer than booze. By the way, Congress should impeach Dubya and impound Asa Hutchinson.

Q. What's your reaction to the recent mid-term elections?

A. Profound boredom. I don't give a hoot whether the thieves and cut-throats in power call themselves Republicans or Democrats. If they want power over you and me—the power to use violence against us—they should be put in nut-houses and heavily sedated until a cure for this condition is found. Like all other marauders and predators.

Q. Since you believe that the universe is indifferent, why are you an optimist?

A. It may have genetic origins—some of us bounce up again no matter what we get hit with—but as far as I can rationalize it, nobody knows the future, so choosing between pessimism and optimism depends on temperament as much as probabilities. Psychologist John Barefoot has studied this extensively and con-cludes that optimists live about 20 percent longer than pessimists. When the outcome remains unknown, why should I make the bet that keeps me miser-able and shortens my life? I prefer the gamble that keeps me high, happy, and cre-ative, and also increases lifespan. It's like the advantage of pot over aspirin. Pot not only kills pain better, but the high boosts the immune system. High and happy moods prolong life, miserable and masochistic moods shorten it.

Q. Recently, when I spoke at a college campus, a student asked what I wanted my epitaph to be. I replied, "Wait, I'm not finished." What do you want your epi-taph to be?

A. I have ordained in my will that my body will get cremated and the ashes thrown in Asa Hutchinson's face. The executor of my will should then shout one word only: "Gotcha!"

SCOOP, HOLLY AND ME

My friend Scoop Nisker manages to maintain his balance between current events and the infinite void. As a commentator on KFOG radio in San Fran-cisco, his slogan is, "If you don't like the news, go out and make some of your own."

He's also a practicing Buddhist, and his other slogan is, "Stay high, but keep your priorities straight."

Scoop, the sit-down meditator, and I, the stand-up comic, have been co-leaders of humor workshops at Esalen and other New Age resorts. The first one was a five-day workshop at Hollyhock, on Cortes Island off British Columbia. On the final day, Scoop suggested that the group remove all their clothing and wade into the ocean, returning to the shore covered with seaweed. As we watched their naked bodies following that instruction, I muttered, "We mustn't let this power get into the wrong hands."

Scoop once persuaded me to attend a ten-day meditation retreat where I would have to survive without any of my usual media distractions. I was afraid at first, but decided to go only in order to *confront* my fear. Then my daughter Holly called. She was now seventeen. She wanted to go to college in San Francisco and live with me again. So—keeping my priorities straight—I immediately canceled out of the Buddhist retreat. That whole experience would only have been polluted by my irresponsibility in not being home to help Holly with her re-entry.

One afternoon, Holly and I were waiting at a bus stop, on our way to a movie, and there was a luscious teenage girl waiting for the bus.

"Ooh, yummy," I whispered.

"Daddy, she's *my* age."

Her words echoed around in my cranial cavity. Lust for teenagers permeates our culture. I had slept with four 17-year-olds in my life, but now I felt myself caught between the lines of dialogue in *Stripes*, where Bill Murray mentions getting "wildly fucked by teenage girls," and *Tempest*, where John Cassavetes says, "If you touch my daughter, I'll kill you."

When Holly got involved with a new boyfriend, they cooked spaghetti in my kitchen, and they threw a few strands up at the ceiling, where they stuck, thereby passing the gourmet chef test. She spent a lot of time at his place, and my moment of truth arrived, not in a bullfight ring, but in the form of a question from Holly. She wanted to know if her boyfriend could spend the night at our house. I pretended to be nonchalant. I prided myself on being a permissive parent. Holly and I had agreed that I wouldn't tell her what to do unless it involved health, safety, or the rights of others. And now she was calling my bluff.

"Okay, sure," I said, "but tell him that he can't smoke cigarettes in the house."

At least I felt justified in asserting *some* parental authority. When I was Holly's age, I would be in my bed wondering if my parents did *it* in their bed. Now I was in bed knowing that my daughter *was* doing it in her bed. Holly was no longer my little girl saying, "Daddy, would you scratch my back?"

Holly didn't accompany us when Scoop and I went to cover an anti-nuclear-power demonstration at the Diablo Canyon site in California. We reserved a motel room for that night. During the day, we became friendly with a couple of female protesters and invited them to use their sleeping bags on our floor. At one point, Scoop was about to take a shower, and asked, "Anybody want to join me?" And one of the women decided to join him. Later, Scoop and I found ourselves in the double bed, while the two women were in their sleeping bags on the floor.

I finally broke the long, awkward silence: "I feel like I'm on a Polish double date."

Scoop is now the editor of a Buddhist journal, *Inquiring Mind*. In the May 2004 issue, he writes: "It's time for a mythological revolution. Not only do we need some regime change in world governments, we also need a new spiritual pantheon. We have lived long enough with the old stories: the *mishugas* of warring desert tribes; the personified sky gods who judge and punish; the idea that we aren't tied to materiality, to atoms or to the elements; and the notion that our true identity has some life beyond the one we are now living. Isn't it time to be more in the present? Isn't it time to come back home?

"Our current mythology is not only out-of-date, it has become dysfunctional. It has stripped us off the Earth and placed the divine somewhere else. Our major religions have come to regard Earth as little more than a training camp, a place where we come to learn some special lessons, get rid of some karma, or get saved by some messiah or another. The general hope is that once we're done here, we can go off to a better place, where we truly belong, and be in a better life, forever and ever!"

Meanwhile, whenever I find myself looking lustfully at a teenager, I still automatically hear Holly's voice saying, "Daddy, she's *my* age!"

BODY PARTS

BOOBS IN THE NOOZ

They're all over the Internet, from "Tender Teenage Tits" to "Mammoth Mammaries," from "Busty Amateurs" to "Big Breasted Porn Stars." My personal favorite: "Touch Our Beautiful Titties." In recent months, boobs and the bras that cover them have been bobbing up in the media.

The *New England Journal of Medicine* reported that the sexual excitement men feel when they're staring at female breasts gets the heart pumping and improves circulation—ten minutes of ogling is equivalent to a half-hour of aerobics workout—thus reducing the risk of heart attacks (though, of course, simultaneously increasing the number of strokes).

In Colombia, a trio of young women preyed on men by smearing their breasts with a powerful drug and luring the victims into licking them, which made the men lose all will power, while the women proceeded to depart with their wallets and cars.

Because Attorney General John Ashcroft didn't like being photographed in front of a 12-foot statue representing the Spirit of Justice—a woman with arms raised and one breast exposed—the Justice Department spent $8,000 on blue drapes to hide her.

During a Kansas City performance with his band, the Accelerators, actor Bruce Willis fired up the crowd by urging females in the audiences to throw their bras up on stage. He then took off his own T-shirt and adorned himself with a black bra that had been thrown on stage, prancing around with it for the rest of the concert.

A cruise ship with 2,000 nudists aboard stopped in New Orleans for the Mardi Gras celebration, contributing mightily to the large number of women who flashed their breasts, in exchange for which costumed revelers on the passing parade floats tossed down garish strings of party beads.

A new Swedish soft drink that reportedly increases the size of a woman's breasts was headed for sale in American bars, night clubs and health-food stores. The gold-colored liquid is called *Wunder Titte* (German for "Wonderful Breasts").

The male stars of *Friends* did a double-take when Jennifer Aniston, Lisa Kudrow and Courteney Cox all arrived with unduly well-endowed bosoms. The three women kept a straight face until Kudrow burst out laughing, and they admitted that they were all wearing the new air bras.

A reader wrote to an advice columnist for the (Durham, N.C.) *Herald Sun*: "You recently told a concerned grandmother that her 16-year-old grandson's breast enlargement might be due to marijuana. I can only wonder what *you* were smoking! Contrary to government propaganda, marijuana has not been linked to breast development in anybody."

England's ministry of defense has admitted to footing the bill for a dozen breast-augmentation surgeries. The $36,000 operations are performed in military hospitals to boost the morale of female soldiers.

Brava, a non-surgical breast enlarger in the form of a computerized bra, is now obtainable for $2,500. A woman must wear it for ten hours a day for ten weeks. An alarm sounds if the wearer moves the wrong way and breaks the vacuum seal. Two huge plastic domes supposedly induce cell growth by suctioning the breast tissue.

Breaking a long-standing magazine-industry taboo, *Teen Vogue* and *Seventeen* have accepted ads for Bloussant breast-enhancement pills.

Two women were killed by a bolt of lightning in London's Hyde Park when their underwired bras acted as conductors. "A pure act of God," said the coroner, recording a verdict of "death by misadventure."

A man wrote to Ann Landers to share his method of avoiding sleeping on his back in order to prevent snoring. He wears one of his wife's old bras backward, with a baseball sewn in each cup to ensure discomfort.

A Michigan woman was cutting the grass when a 1-1/2-inch nail shot out from under the lawn mower and punctured her right breast; fortunately her Maidenform padded "liquid curved" bra broke the speed of the nail and it stopped short of her heart.

The Superbra contains easily accessible compartments for a .38 caliber handgun and a can of pepper spray. The Techno Bra incorporates a built-in heart monitor and cell phone—police are instantly notified of unexpected spikes in the heart rate, although the cause of such an adrenaline rush is not communicated.

Nipple warmers in the form of possum-fur bra inserts are now available. Also on the market: Body Perks—erect silicone nipples ($20 a set)—that are tucked inside a bra to simulate a bra-less look. More than 1,000 pairs were sold at a South Dakota motorcycle rally.

The *British Journal of Plastic Surgery* reports that 40 percent of men in their 30s and 40s have trouble removing bras, and some have suffered serious injuries, such as the 27-year-old who suffered major ligament damage and fractured one of his fingers when he got his hand caught in the straps of his girlfriend's bra.

Finally, in a functional mode, a couple of items about breast-feeding:

Comedy Central's *The Man Show* featured a woman standing on the sidewalk ostensibly nursing a baby, but she was actually using a hidden device to squirt long streams of milk onto passing strangers whose reactions ranged from humor to anger.

And Tess Hennessy, the founder of Citizens Against Breast-Feeding, proclaimed: "This primitive ritual has continued to be a violation of babies' civil rights, an unlawful, incestuous relationship with mother that leads to a child's moral decay." However, the 600-member organization does not really exist—it's just a good old-fashioned hoax—and Tess Hennessy is actually professional prankster Alan Abel.

DOLLY PARTON'S TITS

When the Grateful Dead received a gold record, Jerry Garcia noticed that it had more tracks than their actual album. He peeled off the label, only to discover that the award was actually a gold-plated Dolly Parton record. As a stand-up comic, I mentioned that, and after the show a woman in the audience thanked me for not making an obvious joke about the size of Dolly Parton's bosom.

Her name had become a national generic reference. Upon hearing the words "Dolly Parton," a contestant on *The New $25,000 Pyramid* blurted out her instant association—"Big busted woman." Burt Reynolds, Dolly's main squeeze, couldn't resist telling Johnny Carson, "Her breasts have their own zip code."

Even Ronald Reagan loved to indulge in dirty jokes. Following his attempted assassination, he told doctors at George Washington Hospital the story of a gynecologist who found a tea bag during a routine examination and asked his patient about it. "My God," she exclaimed, "then what did I put in the hot water?"

Nor was I immune from sharing raunchy humor in those decadent early 1980s.

At the Village Gate in New York: "There's definite sexism in the movie *E.T.* I mean, how do we know E.T. is male? Because the little boy says, 'I'm keeping him'—a blatant male chauvinist assumption. I've seen *E.T.*, and there's no penis. Even if there were, it would be human chauvinism to think it was a penis. How do we know it's not just a spare battery holder for E.T.'s finger with the red light?"

At the Improv in Los Angeles: "They did a test on Canadian mice and discovered that, when male mice smoked marijuana, they grew female breasts. The same phenomenon has been found with humans. Men who smoke marijuana have actualy been growing female breasts. That's the bad news. The good news is that it's cutting down on sexual harassment in the office."

At a Radical Humor Festival: "The Hyde Amendment, which was upheld by the Supreme Court, means that poor women can't get an abortion paid for by Medicaid. Fortunately, there's the Big Sister Abortion Clinic. They introduced a teenage girl who was pregnant and unmarried, but couldn't afford an abortion, to her Big Sister, a wealthy woman who was married, had a successful career, did social work, had three kids of her own, but had never undergone an abortion and felt unfulfilled as an emancipated woman because the issue was *choice*, and she just wanted to exercise her choice. The Clinic arranged for a fetal transplant, where the fetus was transplanted from the womb of the poor teenage girl to the womb of the wealthy woman. This was a perfectly safe operation, it was legal, and it was paid for by Medicaid. The teenage girl didn't have to bear an unwanted baby, and the wealthy woman got an abortion as soon as the scar from the fetal transplant healed."

The next day, my performance was analyzed by an unofficial women's caucus. One critic complained, "In sniping at the Hyde Amendment, Krassner was taking potshots at middle class women—they became his victims, his real target—and we all laughed. For me, that's one of the scariest aspects of comedy."

But, what caused the biggest stir was my reference to the use of turkey basters by single mothers-to-be who were attempting to impregnate themselves via artificial insemination. A lesbian comic explained, "You have to understand, some women still have a hang-up about penetration."

I must have been suffering from Delayed Punchline Syndrome, because it wasn't until I was flying back home, meditating on the notion that freedom of absurdity transcends gender difference, that I finally responded to her, in absentia: "Yeah, but *you* have to understand, some men still feel threatened by turkey basters."

Now, two decades later, we return to Dolly Parton, performing at a 4th of July celebration, televised from the nation's capital. She is wearing red-white-and-blue, starred-and-striped shorts and halter, with an Uncle Sam top hat. After singing "Nine to Five" with patriotic fervor, she has a few words for the soldiers in Iraq. "I have a couple of secret weapons myself," she says, cupping the air surrounding her watermelon-sized breasts. "I call them Shock and Awe." Then she added, "And if there are any goodie-goodies who are offended by that, I don't give a Shiite."

A friend of mine who had recently been released from prison told me what had changed the most in Washington, D.C. during his ten-year absence: "The amount of inspections and clearances are incredible. It applies to every building I go into. Yesterday I attended the Dolly Parton concert on the Capitol Lawn and saw cops with machine guns standing nearby. Unbelievable."

That's funny, I didn't notice *them* on my TV screen.

The Great Foreskin Conspiracy

There are those spiritual gurus who claim that an individual soul chooses the specific parents of the fetus it will occupy. I have no such recollection, but even if I did decide to be born, I was circumcised against my will. I used to joke about having my foreskin reattached, but there's actually a book, *The Joy of Uncircumcising*, and an organization with just such a purpose, the National Organization of Restoring Men (NORM), with 21 chapters in the United States, and five in other countries.

Virtually all of the disembodied cocks busily fucking and getting blown on Web porn sites these days appear to be circumcised, but that may be changing. Although the United States is the only country that continues to circumcise the majority of its newborns for non-religious reasons, as parents have become more educated about the surgery, the circumcision rate has fallen to 57 percent.

Paul Fleiss has been publicly identified as Heidi's father and Madonna's pediatrician, but he also supports a controversial cause perhaps less well known than his daughter or his client. He has been a militant campaigner against circumcision for 26 of the 36 years that he has been practicing, and he's written a treatise, *The Function of the Foreskin*.

In a talk at the (now gone) Midnight Special Bookstore in Santa Monica, Dr.

Fleiss said, "The foreskin is there to keep the end of the penis warm and clean and moist. There are thousands of nerve endings in that little bit of foreskin you're cutting off. Those of us who have been circumcised were mutilated. We've lost a very important function of our body."

Marilyn Milos, a registered nurse who opposes circumcision as a violation of human rights, was fired from Marin General Hospital after showing parents a video of circumcision. She now heads the National Organization of Circumcision Information Resource Centers, headquartered in San Anselmo, California.

Milos recalls with horror: "To see a part of this baby's penis being cut off— without an anesthetic—was devastating. But even more shocking was the doctor's comment, barely audible several octaves below the piercing screams of the baby, 'There's no medical reason for doing this.'"

Ten states have dropped Medicaid funding for circumcision, and other states are considering such action. The American Academy of Pediatrics first acknowledged that there was no medical justification for routine circumcision in 1971, and reaffirmed in 1999 that it does not recommend routine circumcision. The American Medical Association concurred in 2000, calling routine circumcision "non-therapeutic."

Doctors were not very happy about North Dakota District Judge Cynthia Rothe-Seeger, who ruled that a baby who is circumcised can sue his doctor when he is an adult. Suing parents is the next logical step. Meanwhile, the same decision that made doctors unhappy made lawyers very happy. J. Steven Svoboda, executive director of Attorneys for the Rights of the Child, stated:

"This is the latest in a series of warnings to doctors who still circumcise. Proceed at your peril, because even if you get parental consent and do a standard job of the circumcision, the child can still grow up and sue you for taking away part of his penis. Doctors ignore a lot of medical literature, and they ignore the screams of the babies, but they listen when they hear the word 'malpractice.' As a lawyer willing to sue, I've never had a doctor not listen to me."

Take the case of Josiah Flatt, who was circumcised soon after he was born in 1997. Two years later, his parents sued the doctor and the hospital. They didn't claim that the circumcision was botched. Nor did they deny that Josiah's mother had consented to the surgery in writing. Rather, their complaint was that the doctor had failed to tell them about the pain, complications and consequences of circumcision. The main harm they sought compensation for was "diminished sexual sensation injury."

The hospital's lawyers insisted, "This lawsuit is an attempt to abolish circumcision in North Dakota of newborn males with healthy foreskin. Plaintiffs want to change public policy so that only a competent male once he reaches adulthood, and not his parent, should be able to consent to circumcision." Only three in 1,000 men who were not circumcised at birth choose to have the procedure as an adult.

In February 2003, the case finally went to trial. A jury of nine decided against the plaintiff because the mother signed the consent form.

Circumcision is quite a profitable business. About 1.2 million newborns are circumcised in the United States every year, at a cost of $150-$270 million. Moreover, human foreskins are in great demand for a number of commercial enterprises, and the marketing of purloined baby foreskins is a multi-million-dollar-a-year industry. But that's another whole story, and there's no more space, so I'm going to have to cut this off right here.

THE WAR AGAINST PLEASURE

This country was founded by pioneers with a lust for freedom and by puritans with a disdain for pleasure. These opposing characteristics have evolved along with everything else, and the problem is those individuals who are still burdened by that certain streak of anti-pleasure keep trying to impose laws upon the pro-pleasure individuals.

Take, for example, the attempt in Mississippi that would have made it a crime for a man who is sexually aroused, although fully clothed, to appear in public. Violators could face up to a year in prison and a $2,000 fine. Public indecency would have been redefined to include "the showing of covered male genitals in a discernibly turgid state." In other words, if hard-ons are outlawed, only outlaws will have hard-ons.

"Talk about hitting below the belt," complained the press secretary of the Libertarian Party. "Are phallic felonies really so frequent in Mississippi that the state needs a Private Parts Police to patrol men's underwear?"

The bill was intended to regulate the behavior of patrons at strip clubs. But recently, in Las Vegas, county commissioners—eager to *prevent* men from getting erections—adopted an ordinance that strictly limits which parts of a dancer's body can touch a patron, and that outlaws putting tip money behind a dancer's G-string.

Commissioner Yvonne Atkinson Gates originally wanted to require a 6-foot separation between patron and dancer, but she supported the final draft, which allows the dancer to slide down a patron's leg as long as she doesn't touch his groin or his feet. What about the big toe, though?

Then there was the law passed in Alabama that banned the sale of vibrators and other sex toys. The punishment for violating that statute in the privacy of your own home was a $10,000 fine and one year of hard labor. A lawsuit to overturn it was unsuccessful. It had been filed by a group of women, including the owner of an adult shop, a salesperson for the Saucy Ladies line of sexual aids and novelties, and a woman who used a doctor-recommended vibrator to overcome sexual dysfunction.

In July 2004, Sherri Williams of the Pleasures store chain had her acquittal for the sale of non-prescribed vibrators overturned by the 11th Circuit Court of Appeals, though two Alabama juries had found in her favor.

According to historian Rachel Maines in her book, *The Technology of Orgasm: "Hysteria," the Vibrator, and Women's Sexual Satisfaction*, the vibrator was originally developed to perfect and automate a function that doctors had long performed for their female patients—the relief of physical, emotional and sexual tension through external pelvic massage, culminating in orgasm.

"Most of them did it because they felt it was their duty," said Dr. Maines. "It wasn't sexual at all."

Just as Mattel's Nimbus 2000 broomstick, as seen in the movie *Harry Potter*, wasn't sexual, even though it has a vibrating feature (powered by three AA batteries). Remember, kids are supposed to ride this toy broomstick by putting it between their legs. And so, making the rounds of the Internet was Amazon.com's Web page, including these customer comments:

"This toy was #1 on my daughter's Christmas list. So what the heck, I figured it would be good for imaginative play. It wasn't until after she opened her gift and started playing with it that I realized the toy *vibrates* when they put it between their legs to fly. Come on—what were the creators of this toy thinking? She'll keep playing with the Nimbus 2000, but with the batteries removed."

And, "My 12-year-old daughter is a big Harry Potter fan, and loved the part with the Nimbus 2000, so I decided to buy her this toy. I was afraid she would think it was too babyish, but she *loves* this toy. Even my daughter's friends enjoy playing with this fun toy. I was surprised at how long they can just sit in her room and play with this magic broomstick!"

Anyway, the Alabama law prohibited "any device designed or marketed as useful primarily for the stimulation of human genital organs." In the Court of Appeals, the state's attorney general defended the statute, arguing that "a ban on the sale of sexual devices and related orgasm-stimulating paraphernalia is rationally related to a legitimate interest in discouraging prurient interests in autonomous sex," and that "there is no constitutional right to purchase a product to use in pursuit of having an orgasm."

Ironically, five months earlier, the FDA had approved a device specifically designed to help women achieve sexual satisfaction, marking the first time that the federal government has licensed an aid for women with sexual dysfunction. The Eros, which uses the same basic principle as Viagra to promote sexual arousal—stimulating blood flow to the genital area—is a battery-operated vacuum attached to a suction cup that fits over the clitoris. The device, available only by prescription, costs $359. However, fingers, tongues and dicks are all free—and still legal.

The anti-pleasure syndrome applies to the desire to get stoned as well as the urge to relieve horniness. Thus, it was considered a form of progress when scientists announced that by chemically blocking the brain's cannabinoid receptors, which respond to a key compound in marijauna, the high caused by the weed is squelched. Dr. Marilyn Huestis, the lead government researcher, said that the findings help point the way toward a possible treatment for people addicted to marijuana.

"It's certainly an issue that is still a little controversial," she admitted, "of whether marijuana can cause addiction."

And the battle goes on. As in a chess game, the opponents try to outwit each other. What's coming, a pill that makes every flavor of ice cream taste like wallpaper paste? But, while George Carlin rhetorically asks—"Why are there no recreational drugs in suppository form?"—teenage girls are *actually* experimenting with tampons dipped in vodka as a way of getting intoxicated without their parents detecting booze on their breath.

Score one for the forces of pro-pleasure.

MISSING FROM THE VAGINA MONOLOGUES

In September 1968, I covered the protest at the Miss America Pageant in Atlantic City. There were a few hundred women there. On the boardwalk, demonstrators were holding a special ceremony. Icons of male oppression were being thrown into a trash barrel—cosmetics, a girdle, a copy of *Playboy*, a pair of high-heeled shoes, a pink brassiere—all with the intent of setting the whole mix on fire. But there was an ordinance forbidding you to burn *anything* on the boadwalk, and the police were standing right there to enforce it. So there was no fire, but that didn't matter. The image of a burning bra became a symbol inextricably associated with women's liberation.

The goal of that movement was equality with men, but who could have guessed that now—when equality still doesn't exist on golf courses, salary checks, and corporate boards—at least women would have their very own disease, sexual dysfunction, to match men's erectile dysfunction. But it's a disease that was invented by the pharmaceutical companies in order to market the female equivalent of Viagra. A turning point came in 1999 when the *Journal of the American Medical Association* published an article claiming that "43 percent of all women over 28 experience sexual dysfunction." It was a faultily arrived at statistic, but what the hell, it sells pills.

Here are some other recent bits of cooz in the nooz:

☞ Betty Dodson, known as "The Mother of Masturbation," is an artist as well as a female sexuality activist. She produces erotic drawings and "pussy portraits." And a woman who goes by the name "J" creates her own colorful but non-exlicit vulva paintings. She explains the process: "Lying on my back and using brushes of different sizes, I apply the paint around my shaved vagina and onto my inner thighs in whatever pattern and colors strike me. Once I get the paint on the way I like it, I lift my legs up and spread them open as wide as I can. Then I press the canvas panel against my vagina and the painted area around it, transferring the paint to the canvas." She sold these paintings on e-Bay until they were banned.

☞ If the word "queef" was ever mentioned on *Jeopardy*, the correct answer would be, "What is a cunt fart?" I may be jaded, but I was slightly stunned when Howard Stern had a queefer actually peforming songs on his radio show. On the televised version, the sight of her musical vagina was blocked out. But customers of adult entertainment now have access to uncensored queefing. Already there is a collector's item, under the title, "Amber, the Queefing Lesbian." She is 23 years old, and has had the ability to fart tunes with her labia since she was a young teen, but after years of anonymity she has finally brought her unique talent to video. She has trained her vagina lips to play everything from classics like the "Blue Danube" waltz to rock anthems like "We Will Rock You." With musicals *Moulin Rouge*, *Chicago* and *De-Lovely* becoming blockbuster hits, it was only a matter of time before queefing would come into its own.

☞ At the Laser Vaginal Rejuvenation Center in Beverly Hills, a woman could have a board-certified gynecologist re-sculpt and rejuvenate—that is, tighten—her vagina, in only one hour, supposedly resulting in better sex. The same procedure is ordinarily used to relieve urinary incontinence—leaking from the bladder during coughing, exercise and fucking. Some women request "designer laser vaginoplasty," a remodeling of the labia. This a purely cosmetic operation, for aesthetic purposes, nothing practical like, say, enabling the labia to produce a wider range of musical notes. In fact, there can be a loss of sensation in the labia after such surgery. The doctor also does "hymen reconstruction." In other words, ladies, you can become a virgin again. As if. But why would you even *want* to?

☞ Extra Large Underpads for the Protection of Bedding and Furniture are also intended for urinary incontinence, but some female ejaculators use them for the purpose of preventing their sexual gushers from soaking their sheets. A lesbian writer confessed in the *Village Voice* that "the woman who taught me how to ejaculate is now my girlfriend. She's made me a squirtaholic, and I've gotten a little obsessed with how many times I can make her squirt, how much I can make her squirt, and how far I can make her squirt. Our personal best: four feet, from the middle of a hotel-room bed to the TV screen on the dresser." And did she remember to call Room Service for a package of Extra Large Underpads?

☞ At Northwestern University, the medical staff conducted a study to determine which kind of pornography women found to be sexually arousing. Women between the ages of 20 and 40 were paid $30 to watch audio-visual erotica and answer surveys for an hour and a half. A 4-inch probe would be placed in a woman's vagina while she viewed several different types of porn. The researchers found that female arousal was at the same levels for images of male-female couples, lesbians, and gay men. They liked it *all*. Unless, of course, the women were actually aroused by those 4-inch probes.

Brain Damage Control

Swimming in the Dead Pool

When Ken Kesey's son, Jed, was killed in an accident—the van carrying his wrestling team had skidded off a cliff—I immediately flew to Oregon. "I feel like every cell in my body is exploding," Kesey said as we embraced. A few days later, several friends were sitting around the dining-room table, and someone mentioned that the Dead Kennedys were on tour.

"I wonder if Ted Kennedy is gonna go see 'em," I said.

Kesey, standing in the kitchen, said, "That's not funny."

"You're right, I apologize. It's not very abstract right now."

"It's *never* abstract."

I recalled that little dialogue as I began to explore The Game, now in its 34th year, the longest-running dead pool in America, currently with 125 players. Before January 1st, everyone submits 68 names of people who might die that year. (Dr. Death, Game co-founder, liked to work on a legal pad—34 lines, two columns, 68 names.) Points are awarded according to the age of each dead person—anybody in their 50s is worth five points; 60s, four; 70s, three.

Each participant gets one wild card per year, worth five points no matter how old the deceased. Gamesters generally pick one-pointers for their wild card to get four extra points. Last year, most picked Bob Hope. When he died, one Gamester said, "My father was shot during World War II. While recuperating in England, Mr. Hope came up to his bedside and stuffed a half-dozen golf balls into his mouth. It cheered my old man up."

Deaths become official when mentioned in the *New York Times* or any two major newspapers. One player "is extremely frustrated," I was told. "He has Idi Amin, who is on life support in a Saudi hospital. Now there have been death threats, and armed guards have been posted." Since the listees are all on various rungs on the ladder of celebrityhood, the Game is understandably rife with abstraction.

"After all, the dead pool has probably been around since the phenomenon of fame itself," write Gelfand and Wilkinson in *Dead Pool*. "It has certainly been around as long as gallows humor has. In the heyday of hard-boiled journalism (the *Front Page* days of the 1930s), reporters who covered a country ravaged by organized crime and engaged in a world war found respite in the dark humor of the dead pool. . . . Even before the Internet, the dead pool was slowly emerging from the shadows of our culture."

As with dead pools, ranging from business offices to Howard Stern's radio show, that book is a guide to profiting from money bets. But members of The Game play solely for the fun of it. Whoever has the most points at the end of the year wins—"bragging rights only"—slightly ironic since Gamesters (lawyers, ad people, educators, psychology professsors, lobbyists, writers, everyday working folks) all play under aliases like Frozen Stiff, Fade to Black, Worm Feast, Decomposers, 2 Dead Crew, Johnny B. Dead, Wm. Randolph Hearse, Daisy Pusher, Silk Shroud, Necrophiliac Pimp, Legion of Doom, Gang Green, Habeas Corpse, Die-Uretic, Shovelin' Off, Blunt Instrument, Rig R. Mortis, Flatliners, Unplugged, Toe Tag, Clean Underwear and Gratefully Dead.

One couple, the Moorebids, insist, "We play for honor, not bragging rights. It has to do with honoring who you get the hit on."

Another player told me, "I compare playing The Game to my day job, science. We do a lot of data collection and data analysis, play our hunches. Our reward is not financial, but peer recognition. One selects some names to acknowledge the person. Other names are selected because earning you points is their last opportunity to do something productive and honorable in their otherwise useless life. My most missed hit was Spiggy [Nixon's disgraced vice president, Spiro] Agnew; I was distressed at missing him."

Each Gamester pays $10 to Pontius, official coordinator and editor, to keep score and report the hits. There are players in over thirty states (23 in New York), plus one each in Quito, Kuwait, England and Australia. You can become a Gamester only by being recommended by another Gamester. They're mostly baby boomers, attracted by a whimsical, informative style of reporting.

Forty-nine Gamesters "hit" Buddy Ebsen. Obituaries mentioned that after ten days of filming *The Wizard of Oz*, Ebsen fell ill because of the aluminum make-up on his skin, and was replaced as the Tin Man by Jack Haley. (One player wondered, "Did Jack Haley add something to the aluminum make-up at the *Wizard* set?") On the other hand, there have been "solo's" on the unexpected demise of Princess Diana and JFK, Jr.

"A solo I am proud of," one Gamester told me, "is the hit on Christian Nelson, who invented the Klondike Bar."

"Yes, it's sick," admitted one player, "but c'mon, *it's just a game!* The Game is a light-hearted way of spitting in death's eye . . . your opportunity to pick a Generation-X rock star who OD's on heroin, a geriatric blue-hair who finally kicks the bucket, a fascist totalitarian in the Mid-East who is assassinated. I'm not doing great this year because I invested too heavily in Hamas, but I'm still in the top ten. The IDF [Israel Defense Forces] is doing its job, I just guessed wrong. Last year I scored on Khattab, a Chechnian rebel leader who was killed by a letter he opened that was poisoned. Our first poison-pen-letter death."

Isn't it somewhat ghoulish?

"Ghoulish?" a participant responded. "No more so than fantasy baseball. We can get up in the morning, and either pick up the newspaper or turn on the Internet to see if we scored, every day. It's like baseball stats, you want to move up in the standings of the veterans. The reason we Gamesters play, I would say it's about *style*. Style involves who you pick. Some concentrate on music, some on politics, some on sports."

As for social significance, one player explained that "the pastime has been going on for more than 400 years, so I don't think it's reflective of any given time or society. Every Gamester comes with their own perspective. The Game is irreverent, even a bit shocking, and some take pleasure in that. It's a poke to the ribs that lie beneath stuffed shirts, a tweak of bluenoses. The Game is a competition—challenging, engaging and energizing. The Game heightens awareness and helps us to recognize our kinship with those whose deaths we note. The Game is a way of sharing and staying in touch with friends, whether near or far. It gives people a reason to call and correspond."

Pontius' predecessor, Ghostwriter, thanked many folks in his farewell message, including "Persephone, who enabled me to say, 'Yes,' when a friend here in Central New York said, 'Do you know a good adoption lawyer in Arkansas?' It was my greatest cameo role, my finest hour as a networker, and I couldn't have done it without The Game and this wise, wonderful woman."

The Game's listserv e-mails are titled "It's a Hit!" They can be poignant, respectful, even sentimental: "July 4th—A score of swaying Gamesters were heard singing 'I Can't Get Enough of Your Love, Babe' as each collected a five note from velvety-voiced singer Barry White. . . ."

Or they can sound like a warhorse race: "July 22nd—Mosul, Iraq. Qusay and Uday, the brutal and powerful sons of former Iraqi dictator Saddam Hussein, were ambushed by Special Forces and the 101st Airborne that resulted in a deadly four-hour firefight. Enjoying the best day of his career was Tomb Essence who had a 14-point Daily Double. . . ."

But The Game giveth and The Game taketh away: "August 21st—British and American armed forces in Iraq announced today that they had arrested Ali Hasan al-Majid, aka Chemical Ali. Back in April 2003, the British armed forces announced they had killed him. Tomb Essence celebrated then, but is crying like a baby now. . . ."

Animals have also been "scored," from Morris the Cat to Dolly the cloned sheep to Keiko the killer whale. Choices can get personal, though. A player told me, "I purposely left off a good friend [former *New York Post* editor Jerry Nachman] who I knew was dying, and one of our game mates refused to list a friend's [famous] mother who she knew was dying. Sometimes we just don't want to 'cash in' on our friends' pain. How un-American of us."

Gamesters have scored on all the Kennedys as well as Lorraine Petersen, the model on the Sunmaid Raisins box. But, under the title "It's *Not* a Hit!" came this e-mail: "August 9th—The entire Game failed to list dancer and actor Gregory Hines, 57." In The Game's 2001 Hit List, under the subhead, "Other Notable Deaths That No One Picked," included was "Ken Kesey, 11/12/01, author, *One Flew Over the Cuckoo's Nest.*"

I had a visceral reaction. This was not abstract.

"I never could decide if leaving Kesey off my list was the right thing to do," a Gamester told me. "The Merry Pranksters obviously inspired my *non de plume*, the Bury Pranksters."

BEHIND THE INFAMOUS
TWINKIE DEFENSE

On November 27, 1978, former cop Dan White cold-bloodedly killed San Francisco mayor George Moscone and supervisor Harvey Milk. To commemorate the 25th anniversary of that historical event, I was invited to be on a panel at the University of San Francisco with two other reporters who also covered the trial.

White had resigned from the Board of Supervisors because he couldn't support his pregnant wife on a salary of $9,600 a year. But he'd been the swing vote on the Board, representing downtown real estate interests and the conservative

Police Officers Association. With a promise of financial backing, White told Moscone he wanted his job back.

"Sure," Moscone said, "a man has the right to change his mind."

However, there was opposition to White's return, led by Milk, the first openly gay elected official in the country. He had cut off his ponytail and put on a suit so he could work within the system, but he refused to hide his sexual preference. Now he warned pragmatic Moscone that giving homophobic White his seat back would be seen as an antigay move in the homosexual community. Even a mayor who wants to run for reelection had the right to change his mind.

On a Monday morning, after a brief conversation with Moscone, White shot him twice in the body, then two more times in the head, execution-style, as he lay on the floor. The Marlboro cigarette in his hand would still be burning when the paramedics arrived. White walked hurriedly across a long corridor to an area where the supervisor's offices were. His name was already removed from the door of his office, but he still had a key. He went inside and reloaded his gun.

Milk was in his office. White walked in and said, "Can I talk to you for a minute, Harvey?" White followed Milk into his inner office, then fired three shots into his body, and while Milk was prone on the floor, White fired two more shots into his head. He later turned himself in to the police. Moscone's body was buried. Milk's was cremated. His ashes were placed in a box wrapped in *Doonesbury* strips, and scattered at sea. They had been mixed with the contents of two packets of grape Kool-Aid and formed a purple patch upon the Pacific.

A day before the trial began, Assistant D.A. Tom Norman was standing in an elevator at the Hall of Justice. He heard a voice behind him speak: "Tom Norman, you're a motherfucker for prosecuting Dan White." He turned around, saw several police inspectors, and faced the door again. These were his drinking buddies, and now they were mad at him. "I didn't know who said it," he confided to a courtroom artist, "and I didn't want to know."

In a surprise move, White's defense team presented a biochemical explanation of his behavior, blaming it on compulsive gobbling down of sugar-filled junk-food. This was a purely accidental tactic. Dale Metcalf, a former member of Ken Kesey's Merry Pranksters who was now a lawyer, contacted me during the trial. He told me that he happened to be playing chess with Steven Scherr, one of Dan White's defense attorneys. Health-conscious Metcalf had just read *Orthomolecular Nutrition* by Abram Hoffer. He questioned Scherr about White's diet and learned that while under stress White would consume candy bars and soft drinks. Metcalf recommended the book to Scherr, even suggesting the author as an expert witness. In the book, Hoffer revealed a personal vendetta against doughnuts, and White had once eaten five in a row.

Flash ahead to November 23, 2003, when an article titled "Myth of the 'Twinkie Defense'" in the *San Francisco Chronicle* stated: "During the trial, no one but well-known satirist Paul Krassner—who may have coined the phrase 'Twinkie defense'—played up that angle. His trial stories appeared in the *San Francisco Bay Guardian*. 'I don't think Twinkies were ever mentioned in testimony,' said chief defense attorney Douglas Schmidt, who recalls 'HoHos and Ding Dongs,' but no Twinkies."

The fact is, psychiatrist Martin Blinder testified that, on the night before the murders, while White was "getting depressed about the fact he would not be reappointed, he just sat there in front of the TV set, bingeing on Twinkies." Now Blinder complains, "If I found a cure for cancer, they'd still say I was the guy who invented the 'The Twinkie defense.'"

The *Chronicle* article also quoted Steven Scherr about the Twinkie defense: "'It drives me crazy,' said co-counsel Scherr, who suspects the simplistic explanation provides cover for those who want to minimize and trivialize what happened. If he ever strangles one of the people who says 'Twinkie defense' to him, Scherr said, it won't be because he's just eaten a Twinkie."

Scherr was sitting in the audience at the campus theater where the panel discussion was taking place. When he was introduced from the stage, I couldn't resist saying to him on my microphone, "Care for a Twinkie?"

Schmidt and Scherr appear to have forgotten another psychiatrist, who testified, "If not for the aggravating fact of junk food, the homicides might not have taken place." Schmidt's closing argument became almost an apologetic parody of his own defense. He told the jury that Dan White did not have to be "slobbering at the mouth" to be subject to diminished capacity. Nor, he said, was this simply a case of "Eat a Twinkie and go crazy."

A representative of the ITT-owned Continental Baking Company asserted that the notion that overdosing on the cream-filled goodies could lead to murderous behavior was "poppycock" and "crap"—apparently two of the artificial ingredients in Twinkies, along with sodium pyrophosphate and yellow dye—while another spokesperson for ITT couldn't believe "that a rational jury paid serious attention to that issue." Nevertheless, some jurors did. Observed one: "It sounded like Dan White had hypoglycemia."

What should have been a slam-dunk verdict—guilty of first degree murder—

had morphed into the lesser crime of involuntary manslaughter. Instead of capital punishment or a life term, White was sentenced to less than eight years, with time off for good behavior, ultimately on the basis of the Twinkie defense, in the guise of "diminished capacity."

While White was serving time, the *San Francisco Chronicle* published this correction: "In an article about Dan White's prison life, Chronicle writer Warren Hinckle reported that a friend of White expressed the former supervisor's displeasure with an article in the *San Francisco Bay Guardian* which made reference to the size of White's sexual organ. The *Chronicle* has since learned that the *Bay Guardian* did not publish any such article and we apologize for the error." Actually, it was 10 feet long, 3 feet 6 inches high, 3 feet 8 inches wide, and weighed more than a ton. No, not White's penis; I'm referring to the world's largest Twinkie, unveiled in Boston in 1981.

The "Twinkie defense" now appears in law dictionaries, in sociology textbooks, in college exams, and in over 2800 references on the Google search engine. Sirhan Sirhan told the *Los Angeles Times*: "If [White] had a valid diminished capacity defense because he was eating too many Twinkies, I sure had a better one [for assassinating Robert Kennedy] because of too many Tom Collinses, plus the deep feeling about my homeland that affected my conduct."

In January 1984, White was released from prison. In October 1985, he committed suicide via carbon monoxide poisoning in his garage. He taped a note to the windshield of his car, reading: "I'm sorry for all the pain and trouble I've caused." He had served a little more than five years for committing a double political assassination. The estimated shelf life of a Twinkie is seven years. That's two years longer than he spent behind bars, and a Twinkie which had remained in his cupboard would still be edible.

THE RISE OF SIRHAN SIRHAN IN THE SCIENTOLOGY HIERARCHY

The FBI has labeled me "a raving, unconfined nut." I prefer to think of myself as an investigative satirist. Irreverence is my only sacred cow. When I was writing the script for a fake *Doonesbury* strip, that slogan would grace the cover of *The Realist*, even though the masthead stated, "Fact Checker: None," I verified with a source in Mafia circles that Frank Sinatra had once delivered a suitcase full of money to Lucky Luciano in Havana after he was deported.

Recently I met a 25-year-old woman who told me about "The Parts Left Out of the Kennedy Book," not knowing that I had written it. She believed that the act of "necrophilia" had actually occurred. What I had originally intended as a metaphorical truth has become, in her mind, a literal truth. Thanks to current realities, that piece of satire is now a credible urban myth. When I moved from New York to San Francisco in 1971, I wanted to publish something in the 13th anniversary issue that would top "The Parts Left Out of the Kennedy Book." I had observed a disturbing element being imposed upon the counterculture—various groups all trying to rip off the search for deeper consciousness—and I felt challenged to write a satirical piece about this phenomenon.

Scientology was one of the scariest of these organizations, if only because its recruiters were such aggressive zombies. Carrying their behavior to its logical conclusion, they could become programmed assassins. I chose Sirhan Sirhan— in prison for killing presidential candidate Robert Kennedy—as a credible allegory, since Sirhan was already known to have an interest in mysticism and self-improvement, from the secrets of the Rosicrucians to Madame Helena Blavatsky's Theosophy.

In a list of upcoming features for the anniversary issue, I included "The Rise of Sirhan Sirhan in the Scientology Hierarchy." Then I began do my research. I even developed a source (Deep E-Meter) within the Scientology organization. The goal of Scientology was to become a Clear—that is, a *complete* zombie—moving up to higher and higher levels by means of auditing sessions with an E-Meter, essentially a lie detector. John Godwin wrote in *Occult America* that the E-Meter "made lying difficult for the impressionable."

I decided to try one at the San Francisco Center. The stares of the Scientology practitioners seemed to be tactical, their smiles unfelt. In confronting their guilts and fears through the medium of a machine, they had become machine-like themselves, and they responded like automatons. I took hold of the E-Meter's tin cans, one in each hand.

"Wow," I said, "I just felt a surge of energy go pulsating through me."

"Paul," my auditor replied, "they're not even attached yet."

"Well, such is the power of auto-suggestion."

There was no charge for the personality test by which prospective Scientologists screened themselves into "the world of the totally free." It consisted of 200 questions on topics ranging from fingernail-biting to jealousy.

In *World Medicine*, David Delvin reported that when *his* answers were processed, he was told, "You've got quite a bit of agitation and you're moderately dispersed, but we can help you to standard tech. . . . So, you see, it's all *very* scientific—thanks to the fact that our founder is a man of science himself."

Dr. Delvin confessed, "I hadn't the heart to tell him that his super-scientific system had failed to detect the fact that I had marked the 'Don't know' column against all 200 questions in the test."

Founder L. Ron Hubbard's original thesis in his book *Dianetics* (which became a bestseller because Scientologists had infiltrated the *New York Times* and learned which bookstores the *Times* based its list on) was that traumatic shock occurs not only during early childhood, but also during the pre-natal stage.

In *Neurotica* magazine, G. Legman took off on that concept with his own cult, Epizootics, "demonstrating the basic cause of all neurosis in father's tight-fitting jockstrap."

Not to be outdone by parody, Hubbard in 1952 turned Dianetics into Scientology, which traced trauma back to *previous* lives—not necessarily incarnations that were spent on this planet, either. In fact, Scientologists were forbidden to see the movie *2001* in order to avoid "heavy and unnecessary restimulation."

By what? When Hal the computer says, "Unclear"?

In 1955, Hubbard incorporated Scientology as a religion, based in Washington, D.C. This would enable its ministers to gain entry into hospitals and prisons, not to mention getting tax exemption. He issued the *Professional Auditors Bulletin*, a handbook for luring prospects into the Scientology fold.

One example was the "illness research" method, taking out a newspaper ad, such as: "Polio victims—a charitable organization investigating polio desires to examine several victims of the after-effects of this illness. Phone [telephone number]." Hubbard explained, "The interesting hooker in this ad is that anyone suffering from a lasting illness is suffering from it so as to attract attention and bring about an examination of it. These people will go on being examined endlessly."

Another example, under the subhead "Exploiting," was the "casualty contact" method, "requiring little capital and being highly ambulatory." All it needed was "good filing and a good personal appearance." Hubbard elaborated:

"Every day in the daily papers, one discovers people who have been victimized one way or the other by life. One takes every daily paper he can get his hands on and cuts from it every story whereby he might have a pre-Clear. As speedily as possible, he makes a personal call on the bereaved or injured person. He should represent himself to the person or the person's family as a minister whose compassion was compelled by the newspaper story concerning the person. The goal is to move the customer from group processing to individual attention at a fee."

In 1962, Hubbard wrote to President John F. Kennedy, claiming that his letter was as important as the one Albert Einstein had sent to President Franklin D. Roosevelt about the atomic bomb. Hubbard insisted that "Scientology is very easy for the government to put into effect," and that "Scientology could decide the space race or the next war in the hands of America." Kennedy didn't respond— the bloody fool, daring not to answer a question he hadn't even been asked.

The E-Meter was presented as a panacea that could cure such "psychosomatic" problems as arthritis, cancer, polio, ulcers, the common cold, and atomic radiation burns. In October 1962, the Food and Drug Administration was investigating Scientology, so Hubbard wrote that the E-Meter is "a valid religious instrument, used in Confessionals, and is in no way diagnostic and does not treat." Nevertheless, in January 1963, the FDA raided Scientology headquarters, seizing 100 E-Meters. Scientology claimed that this violated their freedom of religion, and Hubbard wrote to President Kennedy again. He wanted to meet with him so that they could "come to some amicable answers on religious matters." Again, no response.

Then Hubbard wrote to Attorney General Robert Kennedy, "even though you are of a different faith," asking for protection of the Scientology religion. Bobby didn't respond, either. And there it was—my satirical angle—Hubbard's motivation for programming Sirhan Sirhan to kill Bobby Kennedy would be *revenge*. Hmmmmm. Had I accidentally stumbled into a real conspiracy when I thought I was merely making one up?

In Scientology, Kennedy could have been declared an "Enemy," subject to "Fair Game," a penalty described in a Hubbard Policy Letter whereby an Enemy "[m]ay be deprived of property or injured by any means by any Scientologist. May be tricked, sued or lied to or destroyed."

In October 1968, four months after the assassination of Senator Kennedy, Fair Game was "repealed," due to adverse publicity. "The practice of declaring people Fair Game will cease," Hubbard stated in a Policy Letter. "Fair Game may not appear on any Ethics Order. It causes bad public relations."

While Sirhan Sirhan found himself awaiting trial, he was given several psychological tests. In one of these, he couldn't provide a simple yes-or-no response to only two specific statements: "At one or more times in my life, I felt that someone was making me do things by hypnotizing me." And, "Someone has been trying to influence my mind."

During the trial, psychiatrist Bernard Diamond used post-hypnotic suggestion to program Sirhan into climbing the bars of his cell. But there were two different accounts of that experiment.

In *Psychology Today*, Dr. Diamond stated: "He went over toward the guards and climbed the bars like a monkey. I asked him why. He answered in that cool way he affected, 'I am getting exercise.' Then I played the tape to prove to him that he had been under hypnosis to do just that. But he denied it and complained that I was bugging him."

However, in his book *RFK Must Die*, Robert Kaiser—who was also there—wrote: "Sirhan had no idea what he was doing up on the top of the bars. When he finally discovered that climbing was not his own idea, but Dr. Diamond's, he was struck with the plausibility of the idea that perhaps he had been programmed by someone else, in like manner, to kill Kennedy. . . ."

When Scientology was kicked out of Australia, the official inquiry concluded: "It is only in name that there is any difference between authoritative hypnosis and most of the techniques of Scientology. Many Scientology techniques are in fact hypnosis techniques, and Hubbard has not changed their nature by changing their names."

At a Scientology meeting in Chicago, someone asked, "I understand that Scientology has been banned in England and Australia. Why was this done?" The reply: "Cool! I'm glad you asked that. You see, the kind of person who attacks Scientology is frightened of anything that offers real enlightenment to mankind. In Australia, the man who attacked Scientology was a so-called psychiatrist who was performing lobotomies with ice picks."

Even L. Ron Hubbard admitted the need for a "canceller," which was a contract with a patient stating that whatever the auditor said would not be literally interpreted by the patient or used in any way. So, immediately before patients were permitted to open their eyes at the end of a session, they were supposed to be told, "In the future, when I utter the word *Cancelled*, everything which I have said to you while you are in a therapy session will be cancelled and will have no force with you. Any suggestion I have made to you will be without force when I say the word *Cancelled*. Do you understand?"

When the word was used, it was not further amplified. Just that single word, *Cancelled*, would be uttered. Hubbard warned, "The canceller is vital. It prevents accidental positive suggestion. The patient may be suggestible or even in a permanent light hypnotic trance." Moreover, in his book *The Job*, William S. Burroughs stated: "Hubbard has refused to publish his advanced discoveries. There is every indication that the discoveries of Scientology are being used by the CIA and other official agencies."

Ironically, using the Freedom of Information Act, Scientology obtained secret CIA documents which proposed mind-control experiments where hypnotized subjects would have an uncontrollable impulse to "commit a nuisance" on Groundhog Day on the steps of City Hall, in order to find out whether an unwilling subject could be quickly hypnotized, then be made to undergo amnesia by "durable and useful post-hypnotic suggestion." The CIA also collaborated with the U.S. Army's "special operations division" in bacteriological and chemical "open air" tests in the streets and subway tunnels of New York City.

My ultimate fictional connection between Sirhan and Scientology was inadvertently suggested by Burroughs in *Evergreen* magazine: "Take a black militant and put him on the E-Meter. Tell him to mock up a nigger-killing Southern sheriff chuckling over the notches in his gun. The needle falls off the dial. He mocks up the sheriff again. The needle falls off the dial. Again, again, again, for two hours if need be. No matter how long it takes, the time will come when he mocks up the sheriff and there is no read on the E-Meter.

"He is looking at this creature calmly with slow heartbeat and normal blood pressure and *seeing it for what it is*. He has *as-is*ed [Sheriff] Big Jim Clark. *As-ising does not* mean acceptance, submission, or resignation. On the contrary, when he can look at Big Jim with no reaction, he is infinitely better equipped to deal with the external manifestation, as a calm man fights better than an angry one. If you can't bring yourself to see the target, you can't hit it. When the needle reads *off* you are *off target*."

I began to work on "The Rise of Sirhan Sirhan in the Scientology Hierarchy," based on the actual case history of a friend who had been on the crew of Hubbard's Sea Org, a paramilitary fleet of ships. Crew members wore maritime uniforms and had to sign an unusual contract:

"I do hereby agree to enter into employment wth the Sea Organization and, being of sound mind, do fully realize and agree to abide by its purpose, which is to get Ethics in on this Planet and the Universe and, fully and without reservation, subscribe to the discipline, mores and conditions of this group and pledge to abide by them. Therefore, I contract myself to the Sea Organization for the next billion years."

Give or take a few centuries. Anyway, my friend decided to leave Scientology, but he had surrendered his passport and, remaining true to his experience but simply changing his name, I wrote:

"When Sirhan tried to get his passport back, he was required to stand in a corner, handcuffed, not allowed to speak to anyone, and given food only on someone's whim. Sirhan finally recanted, admitted that he didn't really want his passport returned, and he was forgiven. Hubbard apparently didn't bother to check the weather before pushing off. The ship sailed into a storm. Sirhan was at the helm. He couldn't stay on course, and Hubbard yelled at him. Sirhan shouted back—'Here, take the fuckin' wheel yourself!'—and he walked away. Hubbard threw a temper tantrum and began to cry.

"Sirhan was nervous. He was afraid he would be declared a 'Suppressive Person,' with whom no Scientologists were allowed to associate. He could be 'restrained or imprisoned.' Moreover, the 'homes, properties, places and abodes of Suppressives are all beyond any protection.' When Sirhan considered how he had acted toward Hubbard, he realized that he might even be guilty of Treason: 'May be turned over to civil authorities. Full background to be explored for purposes of prosecution.'

"But Sirhan was declared guilty neither of being a Suppressive Person nor of Treason. Rather, for punishment, he was forbidden to bathe or brush his teeth for the entire two-month cruise. When he got caught using soap and toothpaste, he was transferred to another job in London. He spent seven days a week, from 7 a.m. to midnight, at a salary of ten pounds per week, dictating 200 letters a day, urging dropouts to re-enroll in Scientology. Like all Scientologists, he received periodic security checks while he was working his way through the advanced courses. These were conducted by an Ethics Officer with an E-Meter. There were 150 questions. Here are some samples:

"Have you ever mistrusted your E-Meter? Do you think selling auditing is really a swindle? Have you ever written, then destroyed critical messages to L. Ron Hubbard? Have you ever had any unkind thoughts about L. Ron Hubbard? Have you ever had sex with any other student or staff member? Have you ever used Dianetics or Scientology to force sex on someone? Have you ever raped anyone? Have you ever been raped? Have you ever been involved in an abortion? Do you have any bastards? Have you ever been sexually unfaithful?

"Have you ever practiced homosexuality? Have you ever practiced sodomy? Have you ever had intercourse with a member of your family? Have you practiced sex with children? Have you ever used hypnotism to practice sex with children? Have you ever practiced cannibalism? Have you ever slept with a member of a race of another color? Have you ever practiced sex with animals? Have you ever killed or crippled animals for pleasure? Have you ever had anything to do with pornography? Have you ever masturbated?

"Have you ever lived or worked under an assumed name? Have you ever been a newspaper reporter? Have you ever blackmailed anybody? Have you ever been blackmailed? Have you ever embezzled money? Have you ever forged a signature, check or document? Have you ever hit and run with a car? Have you ever murdered anyone? Have you ever hidden a body? Have you ever attempted suicide? Have you ever peddled dope? Have you ever been in prison? Do you think there's anything wrong with invading a pre-Clear's privacy? Have you permitted a pre-Clear to have secrets from you?

"Have you ever used hypnotism to procure sex or money? Have you ever been a prostitute? Have you ever taken money for giving anyone sexual intercourse? Have you ever had anything to do with Communism or been a Communist? Are you in communication with someone who understands more about Scientology than does L. Ron Hubbard? Do you know of any secret plans against Scientology? Have you ever coughed during Scientology lectures? Have you ever done anything your mother would be ashamed to find out? Do you have a secret you're afraid I'll find out? What unkind thoughts have you thought while I was doing this check?

"And—Sirhan's favorite—'Have you ever tried to act normal?'

"All that information could certainly be utilized as a source of blackmail. Hubbard had based Scientology's secret file system on that used by Nazi spy chief Richard Gehlen. The Ethics exam includes the following disclaimer which an auditor is supposed to read aloud:

"'While we cannot guarantee you that matters revealed in this check will be held forever secret, we can promise you faithfully that no part of it nor any answer you make here will be given to the police or state. No Scientologist will ever bear witness against you in court by reason of answers to this security check.'

"However, one auditor swears that he has often seen pre-Clears' files with information circled, along with notations like, 'We can use this.' Indeed, one man had confessed to skimming $25,000 a year from his business, but when he attempted to quit Scientology and get back $40,000 worth of future auditing he'd signed for after getting little sleep for four days, he was told that if he pursued his claim, they would reveal his tax-cheating to the Internal Revenue Service.

"Nevertheless, Sirhan wrote to a friend, 'Scientology works.' He was back with the Sea Org. 'I was put through some processes called *Power* and the darn things helped me get rid of so much tension, so much unreality, that I am still gaining from it. The funny thing is that I don't know why it is helping, and I guess that the more I study, the more I will find out about this technology that gets results. I am a month away from reaching the Clear level, and there are now six levels above that, and two more to come after that.

"'It is all so incredible, but I am finding out who I am, where I fit in, what a group is, and most of all that I can go through something very, very difficult without running away or leaving it. I am on to something that will make me *me* and that is what I have always wanted. But I am not the master of my fate any longer until I'm out of this scene, which is getting more cloak and dagger every day. I am growing through the restrictions I and this ship have placed on me.'

"Scientology's secret files held an awful lot of extremely intimate details about Sirhan's life, things he had admitted over the years in order to get 'a clean needle' reading on the E-Meter, and they could certainly get people to do all *sorts* of things for fear of being exposed, but he wasn't concerned about that. . . ."

Then, in the course of my research, a strange thing happened. I learned of the *actual* involvement of Charles Manson with Scientology. In fact, there had been an E-Meter at the Spahn Ranch where his "family" stayed. Suddenly, I no longer had any reason to use Sirhan Sirhan as my protagonist. Reality will transcend allegory every time.

Manson was abandoned by his mother and lived in various institutions since he was 8 years old. He learned early how to survive in captivity. When he was 14, he got arrested for stealing bread and was jailed. He was supposed to go to reform school, but instead went to Boys Town in Nebraska. He ran away from Boys Town and got arrested again, beginning his life-long career as a prison inmate and meeting organized crime figures who became his role models. He tossed horseshoes with Frank Costello, hung out with Frankie Carbo, and learned how to play the guitar from Alvin "Creepy" Karpas.

Eventually, he was introduced to Scientology by fellow prisoners while he was at McNeil Island Penitentiary. He needed less deconditioning than his cellmates, who had spent more time in the outside world. One of his teachers said that, with Scientology, Charlie's ability to psych people out quickly was intensified so that he could zero in on their weaknesses and fears immediately. Thus, one more method was now stored in his manipulation tool-chest.

When Manson was released in 1967, he went to the Scientology Center in San Francisco. "Little Paul" Watkins, who accompanied him there, told me, "Charlie said to them, 'I'm Clear'—what do I do now?' But they expected him to sweep the floor. Shit, he had done *that* in prison."

In Los Angeles, he went to the Scientology Celebrity Center. Now this was more like it. Here he could mingle with the elite. I managed to obtain a copy of the original log entry: "7/31/68, new name, Charlie Manson, Devt., No address, In for processing = Ethics = Type III." The receptionist—who, by Type III, meant "psychotic"—sent him to the Ethics office, but he never showed up.

At the Spahn Ranch, Manson eclectically combined his version of Scientology auditing with post-hypnotic techniques he had learned in prison, with geographical isolation and subliminal motivation, with singalong sessions and encounter games, with LSD and mescaline, with transactional analysis and brainwashing rituals, with verbal probing and the sexual longevity that he had practiced upon himself for all those years in the privacy of his cell.

Ultimately, in August 1969, he sent members of his well-progammed family off to slay actress Sharon Tate and her unborn baby, hairstylist and dealer to the stars Jay Sebring, would-be screenwriter Voytek Frykowski and his girlfriend, coffee heiress Abigail Folger. The next night, Manson accompanied them to kill supermarket mogul Leno LaBianca and his wife.

In 1971, my old friend, Ed Sanders, founder of the Fugs—the missing link between rock and punk—was covering the Manson trial for the *L.A. Free Press* and working on a book, *The Family*, about the case. I wrote to him for permisson to print any material that might be omitted from his book because the publisher considered it in bad taste or too controversial. Otherwise, I told him, I would have to make up those missing sections myself.

Sanders put a notice in the middle of one of his reports: "Oh, yes, before we ooze onward, I am not, nor shall I be, the author of any future article in *The Realist* titled 'The Parts I Left Out of the Manson Story, by Ed Sanders.'" He assured me that this was "a joke," but also, understandably, it was a safeguard.

I had known Ed for ten years. He was always on the crest of nonviolent political protest and outrageous cultural expression, such as *Fuck You: A Magazine of the Arts*. In 1961, he got arrested with others for trying to swim aboard the *Polaris* nuclear submarine. The next year he published a parody catalog listing actual relics, such as Allen Ginsberg's cold-cream jar containing one pubic hair. He sent the catalogs to universities and sold the items at outlandish prices. But now his courage and determination had taken a different path, and I flew to New York to pore through his Manson files. Sanders was a data addict, and his research notes were written in the form of quatrains. He had become an investigative poet.

When I returned to San Francisco, a young man with a child on his shoulders came to my house and rang the bell. I opened the door, and he served me with a subpoena. The Church of Scientology was accusing me of libel and conspiracy, simply for having *announced the title* of an upcoming article, "The Rise of Sirhan Sirhan in the Scientology Hierarchy"—which, ironically, I no longer planned to publish. They were suing me for three-quarters of a million dollars. I published their complaint in *The Realist*:

"[This] was published for the purpose of exposing plaintiff to public hatred, contempt, ridicule, obliquy, and did cause it to be shunned and avoided, intended to injure plaintiff in the further proselytizing of the religion of Scientology and to heap embarrassment and humiliation upon it through the distribution of the aforesaid statement throughout the State of California, the United States of America and the world at large. . . . "[The statement] was intended to be understood by the general public and readers, and was so understood by them, charging, asserting and imputing that the plaintiff is not involved in a religious movement, but rather some form of unlawful or unethical activity and that the plaintiff employs criminal methods in furthering its religion. . . .

"As a direct and proximate result of the foregoing, plaintiff has suffered pecuniary loss in that many members, prospective members and persons in the general public have not made or have decreased the amount of their fixed contributions, offerings and donations to plaintiff because of the defamatory statement. . . . Plaintiff does not know at this time the exact amount of the pecuniary loss resultng from the foregoing, and plaintiff prays to leave to amend this allegation and insert the true amount of the loss when the same becomes known to it. . . .

"Defendants have conspired between themselves and with other established religions, medical and political organizations and persons presently unknown to plaintiff. By subtle covert and pernicious techniques involving unscrupulous manipulation of all public communication media, defendants and their co-conspirators have conspired to deny plaintiff its right to exercise religious beliefs on an equal basis with the established religious organizations of this country. These conspirators have utilized what has now become their modus operandi of hiring strangers to write libelous documents for them and then trying to hide behind them. Publication of said statement and the proposed article is one act in furtherance of that conspiracy.

"Said conspirators and diverse other parties, members of the established social, religious and economic society of America today, have a conspiratorial party line whereby they harass, ridicule, defame and malign any new organizations, religious, social or economic, regardless of their merits, when it appears that they are about to become a threat to the established orders, source of funds or membership. Said conspirators thereby seriously protect their established order and economic well-being for their own selfish, economic, social and ideological reasons and thereby prevent dissemination of new ideas and freedom of speech. . . ."

By publishing their complaint, I allowed Scientology to reveal more about itself than anything I could have imagined about Sirhan. My attorney, James Wolpman, filed a petition to remove the suit to a federal court because of the constitutional question it raised concerning freedom of the press. It reached the interrogatories stage, with questions such as, "Have you ever spoken with or received communication from Sirhan Sirhan, his immediate family or his duly authorized agents or attorneys?" I refused to answer, on the grounds that it was privileged information.

Scientology eventually offered to settle out of court for $5,000, but I refused. Then they said they would drop the suit if I would publish an article in *The Realist* by Chick Corea, a jazz musician and Scientologist, but that wasn't quite the way I made my editorial decisions, and I refused again. Scientology finally dropped their lawsuit altogether. However, their records show that they had other plans for me. Under the heading "Operation Dynamite"—their jargon for a frame-up—a memo read:

"Got CSW from SFO to *not* do this on Krassner. I disagree and will pass my comments on to DG I US as to why this should be done. SFO has the idea that Krassner is totally handled and will not attack us again. My feelings are that in PT, he has not got enough financial backing to get out *The Realist* or other publications and when that occurs, will attack again, maybe more covertly but attack, nonetheless."

Later on, I flew to Kansas City to participate in a symposium at the University of Missouri, where I would link up with Ken Kesey. He had written to me from Mexico about this event with Henry Kissinger, B.F. Skinner and Buckminster Fuller. I, in turn, was supposed to contact Ed Sanders, who proceeded to compose a song about Kissinger. However, the Student Activities Office had sent Kesey a copy of the previous year's program. This year's program was honoring the memory of Robert F. Kennedy. So Sanders had to compose another song:

> *If Robert Kennedy still were alive*
> *Things would be different today*
> *Richard Nixon would still be on Wall Street*
> *Selling Pepsi in Taiwan . . .*

The war would be over today
And J. Edgar Hoover would be watching gangster movies
In an old folks home. . . .

Before singing it at the university, he announced, "In the course of my research in Los Angeles, it became evident that Robert Kennedy was killed by a *group* of people including Sirhan Sirhan." In *The Family*, he had written, in reference to the Process Church of the Final Judgment, to which Manson had ties: "It is possible that the Process had a baleful influence on Sirhan Sirhan, since Sirhan is known, in the spring of '68, to have frequented clubs in Hollywood in occult pursuits. He has talked several times subsequent to Robert Kennedy's death about an occult group from London which he knew about and which he really wanted to go to London to see."

Since the London-based Process Church had been an offshoot of Scientology, this looked like it could be a case of satirical prophecy. I was tempted to return to my original premise involving Sirhan, but it was too late. I had already become obsessed with my Manson research. I was gathering piece after piece of a mind-boggling jigsaw puzzle, without having any model to pattern it after. It was clear that members of the Manson family had actually but unknowingly served as a hit-squad for a drug ring. Furthermore, conspiracy researcher Mae Brussell put me in contact with Preston Guillory, a former deputy sheriff, who told me:

"We had been briefed for a few weeks prior to the actual raiding of Spahn Ranch. We had a sheaf of memos on Manson, that they had automatic weapons at the ranch, that citizens had complained about hearing machine-guns fired at night, that firemen from the local fire station had been accosted by armed members of Manson's band and told to get out of the area, all sorts of complaints like this.

"We had been advised to put anything relating to Manson on a memo submitted to the station, because they were suposedly gathering information for the raid we were going to make. Deputies at the station of course started asking, 'Why aren't we going to make the raid sooner?' I mean, Manson's a parole violator, machine-guns have been heard, we know there's narcotics and we know there's booze. He's living at the Spahn Ranch with a bunch of minor girls in complete violation of his parole.

"Deputies at the station quite frankly became very annoyed that no action was being taken about Manson. My contention is this—the reason Manson was left on the street was because our department thought that he was going to attack the Black Panthers. We were getting intelligence briefings that Manson was anti-black and he had supposedly killed a Black Panther, the body of which could not be found, and the department thought that he was going to launch an attack on the Black Panthers. . . ."

And so it was that racism in the Sheriff's Department had turned law enforcers into unintentional collaborators in a mass murder.

After the panel at the University of Missouri, Ed Sanders and I went to the cafeteria for lunch. Ed ordered a full vegetarian meal and then couldn't eat any of it. I had never seen him so shaken. It was because the Process people had been hassling him. He said he was having trouble sleeping. Occasionally he mumbled things to himself as though they were marginal notes describing the state of his depression.

I recalled that, in the summer of 1968, while the Yippies were planning a Festival of Life at the Democratic National Convention in Chicago, some zealots from the Process cult visited me in New York. They were hyper-anxious to meet Tim Leary and kept pestering me for his phone number. The Process, founded by Scientology dropouts, first came to the U.S. from London in 1967. Members were called "mind benders" and proclaimed their "dedication to the elimination of the grey forces."

In January 1968, they became the Process Church of the Final Judgment, a New Orleans-based religious corporation. They claimed to be in direct contact with both Jesus and Lucifer, and had wanted to be called the Church of the Process of Unification of Christ and Satan, but local officials presumably objected to their taking the name of Satan in vain.

The Process struck me as a group of occult provocateurs, using radical Christianity as a front. They were adamantly interested in Yippie politics. They boasted to me of various rallies which their *vibrations alone* had transformed into riots. They implied that there was some kind of connection between the assassination of Bobby Kennedy and their mere presence on the scene. On the evening that Kennedy was killed at the Ambassador Hotel, he had been to a dinner party in Malibu with Roman Polanski and Sharon Tate.

Bernard Fensterwald, head of the Committee to Investigate Assassinations, told me that Sirhan Sirhan had some involvement with the Process. Peter Chang, the district attorney of Santa Cruz, showed me a letter from a Los Angeles police official to the chief of police in San Jose, warning him that the Process had infiltrated biker gangs and hippie communes.

And Ed Sanders wrote in *Win* magazine:

"[W]ord came out of Los Angeles of a current FBI investigation of the RFK murder, the investigation growing, as the source put it, out of 'the Manson case.' Word came from another source, this one in the halls of Government itself, that several police and investigatory jurisdictions have information regarding other murders that may have been connected to the Robert Kennedy shooting; murders that occurred after RFK's.

"A disturbing fact in this regard is that one agency in the Federal Bureaucracy (not the FBI) has stopped a multi-county investigation by its own officers that would have probed into such matters as the social and religious activities of Sirhan Sirhan in early '68, and into the allegations regarding RFK-connected murders."

In 1972, Paulette Cooper, author of *The Scandal of Scientology*, put me in touch with Lee Cole, a former Scientologist who was now working with the Process Church. I contacted him and flew to Chicago. Cole met me at the airport with a couple of huge men whose demeanor was somewhat frightening. They drove me to a motel, where I checked in, paying cash in advance.

Cole arranged for a meeting with Sherman Skolnick, a local conspiracy researcher. He was in a wheelchair. Two men, one with a metal hook in place of his hand, carried him up the back stairway to my motel room. Cole kept peeking out the window for suspicious-looking cars. The scene was becoming more surrealistic every moment.

Early the next morning, the phone rang. It was Skolnick: "Paul, I'm sorry to wake you, but you're in extreme danger." I was naked, but with my free hand I immediately started putting my socks on. "That fellow from last night, Lee Cole, he's CIA." My heart was pounding. I got dressed faster than I had ever gotten dressed in my life, packed my stuff and ran down the back steps of the motel without even checking out. At another motel, I called Cole. He denied being with the CIA. We made an appointment to visit the Process headqarters.

"And this time," I said, giving my best imitation of Clint Eastwood bravado, "you can leave those *goons* of yours at home."

The Process men were dressed all in black, with large silver crosses hanging from their necks. They called each other "Brother" and they had German shepherds that seemed to be menacing. The Brothers tried to convince me that Scientology, not the Process, was responsible for creating Charles Manson. But what else could I have expected?

Lee Cole's role was to provide information on Scientology to the Process. To prove that he wasn't with the CIA, he told *me* stuff about Scientology. For example, he described their plan to kidnap former boxing champion Joe Louis from a mental hospital, so that Scientology could get the credit for curing him. Back in San Francisco, I asked journalist Roland Jacopetti to check that one out, and he discovered that Scientology actually *did* have such a plan, although it had been aborted.

Not that belonging to the CIA and Scientology were mutually exclusive—infiltration is often a two-way street—but I called up Sherman Skolnick in Chicago, and he apologized for scaring me the way he did.

"You know us conspiracy researchers," he chuckled. "We're paranoid."

In January 2003, Sirhan Sirhan lost a Supreme Court appeal, part of his effort to get a new trial in the 1968 assassination of Senator Robert Kennedy. The justices refused without comment to consider whether Sirhan's case could be impartially reviewed by some California courts. Sirhan claims that his lawyer at the trial in Los Angeles was working with the government to win his conviction.

On that same day, Attorney General John Ashcroft endorsed giving religious organizations government money for social services, which many critics contend would be a blatant violation of the constitutional principle of separation of church and state. Of course, the Church of Scientology, which has high hopes for inclusion in this ripoff of taxpayer funds, is trying very hard to act normal.

CAMPAIGN IN THE ASS AND OTHER UNFORGIVING MINUTES

SCHWARZENEGGER AND STEWART

Starring in the role of governor of California, Arnold Schwarzenegger called the legislators who weren't going to vote for his proposed budget "girlie men." Although he was attempting to rabble-rouse the crowd, he unthinkingly insulted women, gays and metrosexuals alike. On *Larry King Live*, Bill Maher referred to accusations of sexism and homophobia as "fake outrage."

There had been a sort of precedent.

Two days after the terrorist attacks on 9/11, Ann Coulter—former Justice

Department attorney and Senate aide, now a professional reactionary and Step-ford pundit—wrote in *National Review Online*, "We should invade their countries, kill their leaders and convert them to Christianity." The Web site refused to run her syndicated follow-up column, because it included a reference to "suspicious-looking swarthy males."

Coulter publicly dissed *National Review*, which had received "a lot of complaints" from sponsors and readers, so her column was dropped, and the magazine dumped her as a contributing editor. After she was fired, she went on *Politically Incorrect with Bill Maher*, accusing *National Review* of censorship and calling the editors "just girlie boys."

Incidentally, in October 2001, Coulter and I both played pundit on the same TV panel (about the assassination of Robert Kennedy, on the short-lived series, *The Conspiracy Zone*). During a commercial break, I suggested that the labels "conservative" and "liberal" have become obsolescent, and I asked what she thought might be appropriate substitutes. A lightning bolt shattered the bulb hovering above her head.

"Americans and cowards," she said.

"Yikes," I said.

But the question remains, how do you separate the girlie boys from the girlie men?

And the answer is: With a shoehorn.

———

Fox News has a weekly program called *Newswatch*, which presents a group of journalists discussing various controversies in the media. On Saturday, panelist Jane Hall revealed her growing skepticism of Martha Stewart because "she compared herself to Nelson Mandela." Actually, Stewart had *contrasted* herself to him, indicating that a measly five months was a pittance as opposed to the twenty-seven years that Mandela was imprisoned. Hall's false statement was not contradicted by fellow panelists James Pinkerton, Cal Thomas and Neal Gabler, nor by moderator Eric Burns.

When Stewart revealed to Barbara Walters on *20/20* that she was going to research Danbury, which might be her involuntary home for five months, I contacted my own source within the penal system. This is how he responded:

"Boy o' boy, Martha Stewart sure fucked up getting the judge to recommend to the B.O.P. [Bureau of Prisons] that she be sent to FCI [Federal Correctional Institution] Danbury. FCI's are medium security facilities. There are two mediums for women in the U.S., no maximums. Danbury is where they send the bad girls. All the scooter tramps, Latina gang-bangers and otherwise crazy, whacked-out broads too vicious to place in camps. Danbury will be a particularly nasty experience for her. I wonder if she's ever contemplated being raped by a woman."

Although the possibility of prison rape isn't intrinsically funny, the late-night TV talk-show hosts—desensitized by their own need to be topical—will undoubtedly include such cheap shots in their monologues. But the mere possibility of prison rape deserves *real* outrage.

DEFYING CONVENTIONS

My name is Rumpleforeskin, and I approve this message. I defy conventions for a living, and last week I defied the Democrats' convention. Here are some highlights:

Teresa Heinz Kerry began by saying, "Onjay and I avehay iftyfay-eight ositionspay." She paused in her speech several times to walk out into the audience and pull delegates' thumbs out of their mouths.

A 12-year-old girl, who was outsourced from Bombay, representing Kids For Curry, stated, "When the vice president publicly said the F-word to a senator, I realized *that's* why we have the First Amendment in this great nation."

In the press tent, a fistfight broke out between Tom Brokaw and Ted Koppel over whether the word "media" was singular or plural. "Is too," Brokaw shouted. "Are not," intoned Koppel. Fox network presented a montage of Al Sharpton saying "Slap my donkey" over and over. And CNN experts critiqued Dennis Kuchinich while he was speaking but with the sound turned off.

A scandal developed when it was revealed that Elizabeth Edwards inisisted on being paid $100,000 in cash as a reward for product placement if she would mention Wendy's fast-food chain in the context of family values.

John Edwards displayed signs of Tourette's Syndrome as he frequently interrupted his own speech with uncontrollable outbursts: "Bush!" "Cheney!" "Ashcroft!" He seemed to waiting for someone named Hope to arrive, but she was delayed somewhere in Boston gridlock. Edwards kept reassuring the crowd, and explained that if Hope never arrived, then for the 2008 convention, he would be sure to invite Help to be on the way.

A psychic was on hand to predict how many manipulative applause lines each speaker would indulge in. As for entertainment, Michael Moore sang a reggae version of "Won't Get Fooled Again," followed by a trio—Whoopi Goldberg, Linda Ronstadt and Ann Coulter—who performed a stunning rendition of "You Can't Always Get What You Want."

In the streets, a sequel to the infamous Stanford experiments was taking place in a makeshift concentration camp. About a dozen protesters played the part of prisoners being tested by actual guards to determine the precise point at which abuse becomes torture. This study concluded that such a determination is totally subjective, depending on whether you are a prisoner or a guard.

The real heroes of this convention were those plain folks from across the country—walking back and forth behind TV correspondents reporting from the convention floor—smiling at the cameras and saying into their cell phones, "Can you see me now? God bless America. Can you see me now?"

Oh, yes, John Kerry's speech was brief and to the point: "I have decided to decline your generous nomination," he roared above a standing ovation, "because I want to spend more time with my family."

Backstage, Teresa was absolutely furious.

"Oveshay it!" she shouted at Kerry. "Oveshay it!"

THE PRICE OF WATER

I was in Boulder, Colorado for a few days, and on the plane coming back, I was reading in the The Onion an answer by humorist Andy Borowitz to the question, "What is funny?" Excerpt: "Even one word can be funny. I remember the first time I saw a McDonald's Express. I thought, now there's a concept: a McDonald's, only faster. Obviously, the McDonald's Corporation believes that there are people out there saying, 'Gosh, I'd love to go to McDonald's, but who has the time?'"

I was reminded of another single-funny-word observation by satirist Harry Shearer. Commenting on George Bush's "linguistic oddity," he said, "When Bush is reassuring us that the good news outweighs the bad, he only says, 'We're making good progress.' Now, me, I'm of the cast of mind that I immediately wonder, 'What's *bad* progress?' What would that be? I thought progress is good. I was raised an American; progress is good."

Well, not only can one word be funny, a single *letter* can make a difference. The previous week, I had written in the *New York Press*: "[John] Edwards kept reassuring the crowd [at the Democrats' convention], and explained that if Hope ever arrived, then for the 2008 convention he would be sure to invite Help to be on the way."

While I was in Boulder, *Press* research editor Lionel Beehner sent an e-mail, checking to make sure that I had intended to write "ever" rather than "never." Since I was away and couldn't respond, he used his judgment and decided to begin the word with an "n." I thought that made my point funnier and stronger, inasmuch as when Edwards kept repeating, "Hope is on the way," he was starting from less than zero.

But something *between* letters can also alter your perception, such as the distinct design of an arrow between the E and the X in the FedEx logo. Even the way people respond to humor can shift your focus. When Jon Stewart laughs, he covers his mouth; when Dennis Miller laughs, he covers his eye.

A concept—in this case, the concept of security—can be tragic on one side of a coin and absurd on the other. In Boulder, I was invited to a gathering where a delegate for John Kerry was describing his experience at the convention. He had to have his credentials checked every morning, because there had been attempted counterfeiting.

His bottle of water would have to be confiscated. He indicated that the cap was still sealed, but that made no difference. He asked, "How about if I drink from it?" The guard said, "Go ahead." The delegate drank some water from the bottle. Nevertheless, the guard then tossed it into a bin filled to the brim with bottles of water. Inside the convention, they were selling water for nearly $3 a bottle. Just like at a rock festival.

"Same thing happened to me," says Harry Shearer. "I drank the whole thing. The only difference is, my bottle was spring water, what they were selling inside the Fleet Center was Aquafina—Pepsi's mineralized tap water."

MARTIAL MUSIC

On this 35th anniversary of Woodstock, everyone who was there has their own specific memories and associations. The '60s were over. Negroes had become blacks. Girls had become women. Hippies had become freaks. Richard Alpert would become Ram Dass. Hugh Romney would become Wavy Gravy.

There was the music and the mud. There was the dope and the dancing. There was the free food and the free love. There were the Port-o-Potties and the politics. Most of all, there was a sense of community. The political contingent was encamped in a red and white striped tent called Movement City. In the afternoon, Yippies were churning out flyers proclaiming that the festival should be free, and at night they were busy unscrewing the chain link fences.

While The Who was performing, Abbie Hoffman, tripping on acid, climbed up on the stage with the intention of informing the audience that John Sinclair (manager of the band MC5 and chairman of the White Panthers) was serving ten years in prison for possession of two joints—that this was really the politics behind the event—but before he could get his message out, Pete Townshend—also tripping, having been dosed backstage—transformed his guitar into a tennis racket and smashed Abbie in the head with a swift backhand.

My yellow leather fringe jacket, which I had been wearing for the first time, was stolen from the Movement City tent. But I found myself dealing with a much more significant kind of paranoia. I had been informed by a reliable source that a think tank, the Rand Corporation in Santa Monica, California, was contracted by the Nixon administration to determine how Americans might react to a cancellation of the election in 1972 because of "internal civil unrest" in response to the Vietnam war. Investigative journalist Ron Rosenbaum was able to determine that I was the fourth person down from a leaker in the White House.

Feeling like the Ancient Mariner waving his filthy albatross in front of anybody who would listen, I did my best to spread the word, regardless of the possibility that I was being used to float a trial balloon. I worked my way up from the underground papers to the reporters in the press tent at Woodstock. I blabbed about it at campus appearances and in alternative radio interviews. Ultimately the story filtered up into the mainstream media.

When Attorney General John Mitchell announced that whoever had started this rumor should be "punished," I sent him a letter confessing my sin, but I never heard back. Meanwhile, the Rand Corporation concluded that the average American citizen would not stand for a cancellation of the election. Now, 35 years later, that same possibility has been floated *publicly* by the Bush administration, a trial balloon propelled by the arrogance of power but pricked by the polls. Oh well, there's always the possibility of declaring martial law.

SEPTEMBER SURPRISE

Here's the Rumpleforeskin Report, dropping the other convention shoe—with some highlights of the Republicans' turn at producing the traditional campaign infomercial extravaganza.

The tag-team mud-wrestling match between the Kerry sisters and the Bush twins was a sure way to attract the much coveted youth vote.

The Swift Boat race along the Hudson River provided a breath of fresh air that sounded more like listening to Nixon speak.

When John McCain referred to a "disingenuous filmmaker," Quentin Tarantino stood up and took a bow in his own living room.

Alan Keyes castrated himself in order to prevent "selfish hedonism."

Tim Russett, host of NBC's *Meet the Press*, revealed that he is actually the missing Quaid brother.

As demonstrators chanted—"No more Bush! No more Bush!"—Whoopi Goldberg assumed it was a shout-out for bikini-waxing special-interest groups.

Every time that the marching protesters yelled out, "Whose streets?" there was a chorus of New York City police responding, "Our streets!"

This event also served as the political equivalent of *American Idol*, where presidential wannabes such as Rudy Giuliani, John McCain, George Pataki and Arnold Schwarzenegger auditioned as future candidates.

Schwarzenegger goosed Laura Bush, then she tried to grab his balls in retaliation, but she couldn't find them due to his heavy use of steroids.

While talking about the state of the American economy, Cheney suddenly broke into a popular country song, "Take This Job and Go Fuck Yourself."

But the biggest surprise during those four days was the introduction of George W. Bush by Osama bin Laden himself, wearing an orange jump suit, handcuffed behind his back and feet shackled to each other. The audience alternated between cheering and booing the bedraggled figure for a full eight minutes. Bin Laden's capture had been a superbly kept secret for five suspenseful weeks.

"Unaccustomed as I am to public speaking," he began, "I am honored to launch the re-election of your President Bush. That may seem strange to you, so let me assure you that my presence at Madison Square Garden has absolutely nothing to do with any kind of plea bargain. First of all, I happen to *agree* with the message of this convention that the world is a better place without that inhumane infidel, Saddam Hussein. Moreover, I very much appreciated the $43 million that your government gave to the Taliban four months before September 11, 2001. Certainly, I wish to express my eternal gratitude to Allah for providing the best possible recruiter for al Qaeda, and I am speaking here of Mr. Bush. . . ."

Meanwhile, waiting in the wings to walk out onto the specially built circular stage, Bush was plucking the petals of a daisy and muttering, ". . . gonna win . . . not gonna win . . . gonna win . . ."

FLUNKING OUT

What if there were no Electoral College? There would be no red and blue states. There would be no battleground states that could go either way. There would not have been an American invasion of Iraq, Al Gore would now be running for re-election, and the Democrats would be warning that a vote for Ralph Nader is a vote for John McCain. In the 2000 election, there were 50,999,897 votes for Gore, as opposed to 50,456,002 votes for George Bush. In Florida, Bush won by just 537 votes.

Last week, among the articles in the media about the Electoral College, there was one in *USA Today* and another in *TheSpoof.com*. Below are excerpts from each. Which story is from which publication? I report, you decide.

1. "Even as President Bush accepted the Republican nomination Thursday and the final chapter of the campaign began, strategists in both camps were preparing for an unprecedented situation when it ends. An Electoral College tie. Shifts in electoral votes and the realities of an evenly divided nation mean there is a credible case that the final tally in Bush vs. Kerry could be 269-269—an outcome that would throw the election to the House of Representatives. . . .

"The Constitution outlines what follows in case of a tie, which has happened only once, in 1800. The newly elected House of Representatives chooses the president from the top three finishers; each state has one vote. The newly elected Senate chooses the vice president; each senator has a vote. . . . This time, the process presumably would favor Bush. Republicans control 30 of the 50 state delegations in the House; the GOP almost certainly will keep control in the November elections. Republicans now have 51 seats. But if Democrats regain an edge in the Senate—which is conceivable—the choice for vice president could get interesting. A George W. Bush-John Edwards administration?"

2. "All 538 electors of the U.S. Electoral College unamimously vetoed a permanent recess of the U.S. Electoral College and ban on all Electoral College methods of carrying out national elections today. Earlier this month the landslide referendum on ending the system led to support for a bill in Congress. The executive branch then subsequently signed that bill. The Electoral College's actions taken to undo the ban come as a major setback to thousands of politicians and mllions of citizens who campaigned in favor of a ban. . . . Detractors purportedly include up to 75 percent of the United States population."

The Electoral College system was originally designed in part to cater to slavery and to the disenfrancisement of women. A few months ago, I sent the following letter to Hillary Rodham Clinton: "I write a column for the weekly *New York*

Press, and I have a question for you. I recall that when you were elected to the Senate, in the wake of the debacle in Florida that led to Bush being in the White House, you promised to do your best to get rid of the Electoral College system. Were you able to get anything going along those lines? If so, what transpired? And if not, what were the obstacles? I would very much appreciate hearing from you."

I have yet to receive a reply.

Hillary Clinton was able to fly into the senate on the wings of Rudy Giuliani's prostate cancer. If Bush wins in November, then it would be karmic irony in the 2008 presidential election if Clinton wins the popular vote but the Electoral College goes for Giuliani.

SECRET STORM

I had told Abbie Hoffman how Lenny Bruce once printed the word FUCK on his forehead with strips of paper towel in a courthouse lavatory to discourage photographers from taking his picture. During the 1968 Democratic National Convention in Chicago, Abbie was arrested while we were eating breakfast, ostensibly for having the word FUCK written in lipstick on his forehead, but really just to get him off the streets. He might have gotten away with it if only he hadn't tipped his hat to the police who were assigned to follow us.

"The duty of a revolutionist," Abbie informed the cops, "is to finish breakfast."

———

In 1969, a few years after my first marriage broke up, I had a two-night stand with Jada Rowland. She was an actress, on TV every afternoon in *Secret Storm*. I fell in love with Jada, but I hated soap operas. They were the ultimate creation of a value system that was the antithesis of my own. Their main function was to program viewers into becoming greater consumers by manipulating them to identify with the lives of other people who didn't even exist. One viewer even sent a letter warning Jada that her "husband" was seeing another woman. Still, within that corrupt context, Jada maintained a sense of integrity. Once, the script called for her to put down her young daughter by referring sarcastically to her imagination, and Jada refused to say the line.

Richard Avedon had invited me to be included in a collection of his photos of countercultural people. I accepted on the condition that Jada and I could pose together, and we would choose the pose. What we had in mind was a take-off on the *Two Virgins* album cover, where John Lennon and Yoko Ono stood nude, holding hands.

We would be standing naked, too, smiling with our arms around each other. Jada would also be holding a patriotic cup with stars and stripes, and there would be arrows pointing to her breasts and crotch, and I would be holding a small American flag. Oh, yes, and I would have an erection. If *Two Virgins* was about anatomy, this would be about physiology. Jada was willing to risk losing her $1,000-a-week job to participate just for the fun of it.

"I think it was my idea," she recalls, "to do a take-off on Lennon/Ono. I was on one of my rants, objecting to the fact that the penis could never be seen erect and that there was a certain hypocrisy in their pretended 'innocence' as it seemed to me that they must have known that everyone just wanted to see the tits of the girl who stole the Beatle away."

I had ingested a capsule of THC powder before the photo session. Jada and I were now standing before the camera, and the only thing missing was my hard-on. I had heard that THC was actually an elephant tranquilizer. I would soon find out if that was true.

Avedon asked what music we wanted to listen to during the session. I asked for the Beatles' "Hey Jude," but he didn't have it, so instead he played my second choice, Bob Dylan singing "Lay, Lady, Lay."

Jada and I began to kiss.

"This is obscene," she whispered.

"No," I whispered back, "it's very pure. But you're right, it *is* kind of goal-oriented."

As she remembers it, "What was 'obscene' in my view was that I wasn't in love or in lust with you, so giving way to your request that I kiss you so you could get a hard-on seemed obscene. I felt both uneasily guilty, as I became aware that I was taking advantage of your fondness for me in order to be photographed by Avedon, and quite uncomfortable that you were taking advantage of the situation in order to kiss me. Those were the only 'obscenities' in my eyes."

We continued kissing. Dylan was now asking the musical question, "Why wait any longer for the world to begin?" My penis rose to the occasion, and the crew cheered us on.

I signed a release, assuming that the photo would never be seen because the publishing of an erection was so taboo then. However, in 1999—three decades later—my bluff was called. Avedon and Diane Arbus published a $75 book of photos, *The Sixties*.

A *Los Angeles Times* review said that I looked "sheepish" and "sustained an erection."

Little did they know.

On the back cover of the book, there's a photo of Abbie Hoffman, holding a toy rifle in one hand and giving the finger with the other. He is smiling broadly, sticking his tongue out, and on his forehead the word FUCK is written in lipstick.

A KINDER, GENTLER PAPER

A reporter for the *Los Angeles Times* interviewed me for an article she was writing on humor about the presidential candidates. As an example, I said that "I perceive John Kerry as being like an arranged marriage. I could learn to like him. He'll certainly be a good provider. And at least he's better than that wife-beater in the White House."

But here's how the *Times* ended up publishing it: ". . . better than [what we have now] in the White House." If I may paraphrase Dan Rather, "I have documents that have been authenticated by our experts which *prove* that George W. Bush has beaten Laura, or my name isn't Roger Mudd."

This was all before there was any news about Kitty Kelley's book on the Bush multi-generational mafia, *The Family* (also the title of Ed Sanders' book about Charles Manson and *his* brainwashed followers). She writes that someone expressed fear that Bush was abusing Laura. To think that my metaphorical joke might possibly be an actual occurrence is overshadowed in absurdity only by an anonymous editor's irrational censorship of my punchline in an article about humor.

Hey, it was a *metaphor*! Now I understand how political-party turncoat Zell Miller must have felt when he wished he could challenge Chris Matthews to a duel because Matthews took literally Miller's metaphor about the military use of spitballs as a weapon.

Meanwhile, the *Sunday Los Angeles Times Book Review* assigned me to write an essay based on *From the Lower East Side to Hollywood: Jews in American Popular Culture* by Paul Buhle. My piece included a long paragraph of mini-dialogues I've had with countercultural icons about various aspects of Jewishness. For example, I said to Ken Kesey, "I don't believe that Jews are the chosen people, or that people are the chosen species."

He responded, "I don't believe that people are the chosen species, but I believe that Jews are—or were—the chosen people. [But] when the train that pulled into the station 2,000 years ago didn't look like My Son, the Messiah, but like a beatnik in sandals and Day-Glo yarmulke, well the train waited around a while for the chosen to hop on board, then pulled on out. A few hobos hanging out in the yard—lazy yids and hustling *goyim*, mostly—slipped into the boxcar."

On the Thursday before publication, my editor sent me an e-mail: "I'm not sure why this is happening now, rather than yesterday, but now my dear colleagues on the copy desk are doublechecking if it's OK to print 'yid' in the paper, even in a quote."

I argued that if they took out "lazy yids," they'd have to take out "hustling *goyim*" too, and just put in an ellipsis to replace the whole phrase. Not only did "yid" stay in, but they also left in this quote from the book: "The most famous or notorious Jewish story of the *Ed Sullivan Show* was the firing of Jackie Mason for acting 'too kikey' on camera." However, if Sullivan had called Mason a wife-beater . . .

I always thought that the reason Mason got fired was because he had given Sullivan the finger on camera. I once wrote an article for the *Los Angeles Times*, in which I mentioned a guest on a TV show who "gave the finger" to the host, but that was changed to "gestured toward."

"The *Times*," I was told, "is a family newspaper."

FIRE DAN RATHER

A few years ago, at the 135th anniversary of *The Nation*, I was on a panel of satirists, along with Al Franken, Jim Hightower and Michael Moore. The event was held at the posh University Club in New York. I wore jeans, a red Bread & Roses T-shirt and a tuxedo jacket, but the gatekeeper informed me that I didn't meet their dress code.

"But I'm an entertainer," I explained, "and this is my costume."

He instructed me to go around the corner, through the employees' entrance, past the kitchen and up the elevator, directly into the ballroom where the $600-a-plate dinner was taking place. Liberal celebrities were milling around, including Phil Donahue, Harry Belafonte, Nora Ephron, Jules Feiffer and, sitting at a $1,000-a-plate table, Dan Rather.

He has excellent posture, which he maintains even when he laughs.

"Mr. Rather," I said from the dais, "you ended your broadcast the other night by saying, 'If you like the CBS News, be sure to tell your neighbors,' and I just wanted to take this opportunity to tell you personally that I went around recommending your newscast to all my neighbors, but they kept chasing me away because they mistook me for a census taker."

Rather had previously been ending his nightly newcast with one word—"Courage"—which is exactly what he needs now as he waits to see whether he'll be booted off the CBS island in this real-life reality show.

More than three decades ago, George W. Bush ignored a direct order to take a flight physical while serving in the National Guard. Several Guard officials could not recall another pilot who skipped his mandatory medical examination.

"There were cases where they'd be a few weeks late because their regular jobs might get them in a bind," said Jerry Marcontell, a Houston physician who spent ten years as the flight surgeon for Bush's air wing, "but I don't remember anyone missing a physical for months at a time. Certainly not a year."

One rumor floating around has it that Bush wanted to avoid having his use of cocaine revealed during the course of a routine medical exam.

In any case, the documents upon which Rather based his story were apparently forged, and conservative media vultures were anxious to borrow Donald Trump from NBC just to spit out those two little words that Trump would like to copyright: "You're fired."

The irony is that, just hours before air-time, the journalistic thrill of presenting the National Guard scoop on *60 Minutes* pre-empted a half-hour segment that was scheduled for the same program that night; a team of correspondents had spent more than six months investigating the Niger documents fraud, which purported to show Iraqi efforts to purchase uranium, a falsehood Bush included in his 2003 State of the Union speech to justify the invasion of Iraq.

And *that's* why Dan Rather should be fired—for making such a foolish priority the basis of his editorial choice in the first place. Moreover, that pre-empted segment won't be shown at all now, because CBS News says it's too close to the election. Courage, my ass.

SCENE OF THE CRIME

To participate in the 40th anniversary of the Free Speech Movement, I flew to Berkeley, the epicenter of political correctness. This was the week before Columbus Day, so I wasn't surprised to see a sign in a store window announcing that it would be "closed on Monday to celebrate Indigenous Day." Ironically, a slogan that became associated with the FSM—"Don't trust anyone over 30"—would today be considered ageist.

It was coined by Jack Weinberg, a graduate student at UC-Berkeley who, in October 1964, was arrested in Sproul Plaza for handing out leaflets about civil rights, in violation of a campus ban on political activities. The rule prohibited handing out leaflets or collecting money for any off-campus political cause, even advocating Lyndon Johnson or Barry Goldwater for president. For two weeks, the students tried unsuccessfully to negotiate with the administration.

At noontime, Weinberg was placed in a campus-police car, which was spontaneously surrounded by 3,000 students. The vehicle couldn't be driven anywhere, having inadvertently become the centerpiece of 32-hour protest. Several students climbed on top to speak—but first they removed their shoes. The roof was soon dented, though demonstrators would later pay to fix the damages. One of the speakers was a 21-year-old philosophy student, Mario Savio, who two months later would deliver a passionate plea from the steps in front of Sproul Hall, the administration building.

"There is a time," he told an an audience of 4,000, "when the operation of the machine becomes so odious, makes you so sick at heart, that you can't take part, you can't even passively take part, and you've got to put your bodies upon the gears and upon the wheels, upon the levers, upon all the apparatus, and you've got to make it stop. And you've got to indicate to the people who run it, to the people who own it, that unless you're free, the machine willl be prevented from working at all."

Nearly 800 students were inspired to occupy Sproul Hall with a sit-in that would resonate across the country. They were handcuffed and taken away the next day in the largest arrest of students in U.S. history.

But Timothy Leary told me that "Such demonstrations play right onto the game boards of the administration and the police alike. The students could shake up the establishment much more if they would just stay in their rooms and change their nervous systems."

"It's not a case of either-or," I argued. "They can protest *and* explore their 13-billion-cell minds simultaneously."

Indeed, there was a false rumor that, during the mass imprisonment, a Bible which had been soaked in an LSD solution easily made its way into the cells. The students just ate those pages up, getting high on Deuteronomy, tripping out on Exodus.

Now, four decades later, there were 3,000 people gathered around a campus-police car in Sproul Plaza once again, only this time it was *provided* by the campus police. A make-shift ramp led to a wooden platform cushioned by foam

264 ～ PAUL KRASSNER

rubber that organizers placed on top of the car. A photo of Jack Weinberg's face was taped to the rear window.

And, although the San Francisco FBI office had put Mario Savio on the Reserve Index, a secret, unauthorized list of people to be detained, without judicial warrant, in the event of a national emergency (I was on the New York FBI's Reserve Index), in 1997, a year after Savio's death, the steps in front of Sproul Hall were named the "Mario Savio Steps."

I guess those are signs of progress.

KERRY AND THE SEX WORKER

John Kerry didn't know it was the 30th anniversary of the first national Hookers Convention when he told the *New York Times*: "We have to get back to the place we were, where terrorists are not the focus of our lives, but they're a nuisance. As a former law-enforcement person, I know we're never going to end prostitution. We're never going to end illegal gambling. But we're going to reduce it, organized crime, to a level where it isn't on the rise."

Margo St. James, a former prostitute and founder of COYOTE (Call Off Your Old Tired Ethics), had turned the finest trick of her life when she turned prurient interest back on itself to spread the message of the Hookers Convention. Their official poster featured an illustration of a woman fingering her clit, with the slogan, "Our convention is different—we want *everybody* to come!"

The event was held at Glide Memorial Church in San Francisco. In the lobby, T-shirts were on sale, flaunting a slogan, *'74—Year of the Whore!* Reverend Cecil Williams greeted the overflow crowd: "This church is open to everybody. It has always been concerned with people who are misused and oppressed. I am delighted to welcome you."

There was a growing awareness of the linear connections in suffering, which COYOTE had recognized by the range of its actions, from successfully protesting the automatic forced treatment for undiagnosed venereal disease of women arrested for prostitution—their presumably also-infected male customers went untreated—to the hookers' boycott of crewmen off a ship docked in from torture-infested Chile.

Margo was invited to contribute an essay for the *San Francisco Opera 2004-05 Yearbook* to accompany an essay on *La Traviata*. "Today," she wrote, "the St. James Infirmary, a first-of-its-kind occupational health and safety clinic run by sex industry workers for sex industry workers, provides primary health care for all sex workers in San Francisco. Our mission is not to reform sex workers but to reform society."

I asked her to respond to John Kerry's statement.

"Kerry, Jesse Jackson," she said, "they don't seem to realize the institutionalized racism and sexism produced by the prohibitions on drugs and sex work. There was a ten-year study in the Netherlands, 1985-95, where violence against women was reduced by 75 percent when the official stigma was removed by decriminalization. Look who is serving time—the majority are black. It's also the means by which women's wages are kept at 75 percent of wages for men doing the same jobs.

"The drug laws imprison non-violent youth, and allow the seizure of property—many times without an arrest—which is then converted to cash to fund the DEA. The two wars—on whores and drugs—are the foundation for the discrimination against women and minorities, and the justification for violence by the state. Actually, Kerry has probably never been a client or he would know that the prohibitions create the atmosphere for organized crime."

John Kerry should choose his words more carefully. A *real* "nuisance" is a serving of dogshit on the sidewalk.

DUELING IMPRESSIONISTS

Lenny Bruce was scheduled to perform at the Village Theater on the Lower East Side a week after the assassination of President Kennedy. The whole country was still in a state of shock, and the atmosphere in the theater was especially tense that night. The show hadn't begun yet, but the entire audience seemed to be anticipating what Lenny would say about the assassination. Now he walked on stage. He removed the microphone from its stand. When the applause for his entrance subsided, he stood there in silence for a few seconds, milking the tension.

"*Whew*," he finally whistled into the microphone, "Vaughn Meader is *screwed. . . .*"

There was an instant explosion of laughter. And Lenny was right. JFK impressionist Meader had been scheduled for appearances on *Hootenanny* and *To Tell the Truth*, but he was canceled out of both, even though he had planned other material for *Hootenanny* and would not have appeared on *To Tell the Truth* as JFK. Yes, Vaughn Meader was indeed screwed.

Ah, but not David Frye—*he* could do Lyndon Johnson.

In 1960 I was a misfit among misfits attending a comedy workshop at a Times Square rehearsal loft. A group of would-be stand-ups met every week and tried to make each other laugh. There were two performers who did impressions: Vaughn Meader, whose specialty was John Kennedy; and David Frye, whose specialty was Richard Nixon. So it became an attachment beyond ordinary political considerations that motivated Meader and Frye to root respectively for Kennedy and Nixon in the presidential campaign.

When Kennedy won, Meader seized the opportunity. He bagan to comb his hair with a flamboyant pompadour dipping across his forehead. He consciously regressed to the Boston accent he had previously tried so hard to lose. And he made a comedy album, *The First Family*, which broke sales records and turned him into a star. As for David Frye, he would have to depend on his impressions of Kirk Douglas and Robert Mitchum.

After Kennedy's assassination, Meader dropped out of comedy, moved to San Francisco and became a late-blooming flower child. He returned to New York in 1968, and attended a few Yippie meetings. We invited him to play *Bobby* Kennedy at our counter-convention that summer in Chicago. But then, in mid-March, Kennedy announced that he was going to run for president.

On March 31, Meader asked me for a tab of LSD. That evening, President Johnson went on TV and announced that he would not seek re-election. My phone rang immediately. It was Vaughn Meader. In the middle of tripping, he had just seen LBJ, and wasn't sure if this was an acid hallucination or an April Fool's Eve joke. But it was true—LBJ was out of the race.

"*Whew*," Lenny Bruce whistled from the grave, "David Frye is *screwed*. . . ."

Frye's luck returned when Richard Nixon was elected that November. But in August 1974 Nixon became the first president in American history to resign from office.

"*Whew*," Lenny whistled, "David Frye is screwed *again*. . . ."

THE RAPTURE PRESIDENT

I asked David Shaw, media critic for the *Los Angeles Times*, if he knew of any reporter who had asked George W. Bush what that three-dimensional rectangular *thing* was under the back of his jacket during the first debate. Shaw said he didn't know of any.

Then, at a presidential press conference, Mark Slackman posed this question: "Sir, we still haven't heard a plausible explanation for the bulge under your suit in the first debate. Sir, were you being prompted by a hidden transmitter?"

Slackman is, of course, a reporter in the comic strip *Doonesbury*.

Bush gave his answer the next day, on ABC's *Good Morning America*. "I don't know what that is," he said. "I mean, it is—I'm embarrassed to say it's a poorly tailored shirt."

Yeah, right, and Saddam Hussein married Osama bin Laden in Massachusetts and they adopted a Chinese baby.

But Bush wasn't being prompted by his senior adviser, Karen Hughes, whose job it had been to advise him not to refer to terrorists as "folks." No, Bush was being prompted by God Him-or-Herself. You know, God, the One who Bush says he is on a mission from. God, the One who Jerry Falwell says is pro-war. God, the One who told Pat Robertson that Bush would be re-elected, and then Robertson went ahead and defied God's will by revealing that Bush wasn't concerned about American casualties in Iraq.

Bush once proclaimed, "God is not neutral," which is the antithesis of of my own spiritual path, my own peculiar relationship with the universe—based on the notion that God is *totally* neutral—but I've learned that whatever people believe in, works for them.

Barry Lynn, director of Americans United for the Separation of Church and State, believes that the "God supports Bush" theme holds great currency among Bush's base because Bush wants it to. "It is a belief the president encouraged, and that Karl Rove has encouraged," says Lynn. "It is, I think, extremely dangerous for people to believe that God is a Republican or a Democrat or a Naderite or even a Libertarian."

I'm writing this five days before the election. I predict that either there will be a relatively landslide victory for Kerry, indicating that the polls were skewed—bypassing cell phones, Vote or Die campaigns, disillusioned Christians—or the results will be so close that 50,000 Democratic lawyers will end up battling back and forth in the courts with 50,000 Republican lawyers—dragging out, appealing again and again, stalling around—for, oh, say, at least four years, until finally John Edwards, his pompadour prematurely grey, argues the case unsuccessfully before the U.S. Supreme Court, which by then will be packed with Bush's reactionary appointees. Is that the way the world will end, with neither a bang nor a whimper, but with a bloodless bi-partisan *coup*?

SILKEN TWINE

Now that George Bush has been elected to a second term, the arrogance of his administration will undoubtedly increase suffering in this country and around the world. Yet, in the words of William Blake: "Under every grief and pine/ Runs a joy with silken twine." Not to mention Monty Python: "Always look on the bright side of life."

So, in terms of the cultural divide, even though *The Passion of the Christ*—which finally made Jesus more popular than the Beatles—has supposedly defeated *Farhenheit 9/11*, Michael Moore has written "17 reasons not to slit your wrists" for his choir. A few examples:

"Admit it: We like the Bush twins and we don't want them to go away."

"The only age group in which the majority voted for Kerry was young adults (Kerry: 54%, Bush: 44%), proving once again that your parents are always wrong and you should never listen to them."

"Gays, thanks to the ballot measures passed on Tuesday, cannot get married in 11 new states. Thank God. Just think of all those wedding gifts we won't have to buy now."

"It is against the law for George W. Bush to run for president again."

Of course, it wouldn't be illegal for Dick Cheney to run for president. Oops, I take that back. It *would* be illegal. Cheney has already served two terms as president, in the guise of vice-president. Moreover, Karl Rove is no longer the clandestine flasher who pops out from behind a tree in the park. Now he's in the middle of the street and all over TV, opening his raincoat and shouting, "Hey, lady, take a look at this!"

Ironic Times, the satirical online weekly produced by three former writers for *Not Necessarily the News*, has published "Top reasons why Democrats should not commit suicide: Iraq slides into endless, bloody chaos; U.S. standing in world plummets; Economy sinks into another recession; Terrorist attacks; New TV shows stink"—all these "will be blamed on Bush."

That same point was made by syndicated columnist Robert Scheer, who stated that now Bush won't be able to blame Democrats and liberals for whatever happens domestically and abroad.

It's always been my nature to seek blessings in disguise, a real challenge in these insane times, but at least I won't have to watch John Kerry shooting a goose again while wearing a camouflage outfit apparently to fool the geese. If elected, he promised to send 40,000 additional troops to Iraq. As president, it would've been his fate to watch a member of Iraq Veterans Against the War testify before Congress: "How do you ask a man to be the last man to die in Iraq? How do you ask a man to be the last man to die for a mistake?"

At a Republican victory party, a reporter asked an 11-year-old boy why he wanted to be president. "I would like to be president of the United States," he replied, "so that I can lead the country to war." Four more years of trickle-down barbarism.

But, even as I find myself singing that popular '60s favorite, "Eve of Destruction," I remember an old maxim which insists that things need to get worse before they can get better. Some consolation, huh?

Double Agent

Guerrilla: The Taking of Patty Hearst has been playing in movie theaters. I covered her trial for two publications at opposite ends of the cultural spectrum— the *Berkeley Barb* and *Playboy*. Patty was on trial for robbing a bank with her kidnappers. Here's an angle that wasn't in the documentary.

Patty's parents sat in the courtroom, listening to a communique from their princess, abdicating her right to the throne: "I have been given the choice of, one, being released in a safe area or, two, joining the forces of the Symbionese Liberation Army. . . . I have chosen to stay and fight. . . ."

At the end of the tape, SLA leader Donald "Cinque" DeFreeze issued a triple death threat, especially to Colston Westbrook, calling him "a government agent now working for Military Intelligence while giving assistance to the FBI." This communique was originally sent to San Francsco radio station KSAN. News director David McQueen checked with a Justice Department source, who confirmed Westbrook's employment by the CIA.

Researcher Mae Brussell traced his activities from 1962, when he was CIA advisor to the South Korean CIA, through 1969, when he provided logistical support in Vietnam for the CIA's Phoenix Program. His job was the indoctrination of assassination and terrorist cadres. After seven years in Asia, he was brought home in 1970 and assigned to run the Black Cultural Association at Vacaville Prison, where he bacame the control officer for DeFreeze, who had worked as a police informer from 1967 to 1969 for the Public Disorder Intelligence Unit of the Los Angeles Police Department.

If DeFreeze, who conveniently escaped from prison, was actually a double agent, then the SLA was a Frankenstein monster, turning against its creator by becoming in reality what had been orchestrated only as a media image. When he threatened his keepers, he signed the death warrant of the SLA. They were burned alive in a Los Angeles safe-house during a shootout with police. When DeFreeze's charred remains were sent to his family in Cleveland, they couldn't help but notice that he had been decapitated.

Consider the revelations of Wayne Lewis. He claimed to have been an undercover agent for the FBI, a fact verified by FBI director Clarence Kelley. Surfacing at a press conference in Los Angeles, Lewis spewed forth a conveyor belt of conspiratorial charges: DeFreeze was an FBI informer; he was killed not by the SWAT team but by an FBI agent because he had been "uncontrollable"; the FBI then wanted Lewis to infiltrate the SLA; the FBI had undercover agents in other underground guerrilla groups; the FBI knew where Patty Hearst was but let her remain free so it could build up its files of potential subversives.

At one point, the FBI declared itself to have made 27,000 checks into the whereabouts of Patty Hearst. It was simultaneously proclaimed by the FDA that there were 25,000 brands of laxative on the market. That meant one gastrointestinal catharsis for each FBI investigation, with a couple of thousand loose shits remaining for the ghost of J. Edgar Hoover to smear across "No Left Turn" signs. Patty Hearst had become a vehicle for repressive action on the right and wishful thinking on the left.

The prosecutor asked her, "Were you *acting* the part of a bank robber?"

"I was doing exactly what I had to do," she replied. "I just wanted to get *out* of that bank. I was just supposed to be in there to get my picture taken, mostly."

Ulysses Hall testified that after the robbery, he managed to speak on the phone with his former prison mate, DeFreeze, who told him that the SLA didn't trust Patty's decision to join them. Conversely, *she* didn't trust *their* offer of a "choice," since they realized she'd be able to identify them if she went free—and so they made her prove herself by "fronting her off" at the bank with DeFreeze's gun pointed at her head.

In 1969, Charles Bates was Special Agent at the Chicago office of the FBI when police killed Black Panthers Fred Hampton and Mark Clark while they were sleeping. Ex-FBI informer Maria Fischer told the *Chicago Daily News* that then-chief of the FBI's Chicago office Marlon Johnson personally asked her to slip a drug to Hampton; she had infiltrated the Panther Party at the FBI's request a month before. The drug was a tasteless, colorless liquid that would put him to sleep. She refused. Hampton was killed a week later. An autopsy indicated "a near fatal dose" of secobarbital in his system.

In 1971, Bates was transferred to Washington, D.C. According to Watergate burglar James McCord's book, *A Piece of Tape*, on June 21, 1972, White House attorney John Dean checked with acting FBI director L. Patrick Gray as to who was in charge of handling the Watergate investigation. The answer: Charles Bates—the same FBI official who in 1974 would be in charge of handling the SLA investigation and the search for Patty Hearst. When she was arrested, Bates became instantly ubiquitous on radio and TV, boasting of her capture.

In the middle of Patty's trial—on a Saturday afternoon, when reporters and technicians were hoping to be off duty—Bates called a press conference. At 5 o'clock that morning, they had raided the New Dawn collective, the above-ground support group of the Berkeley underground Emiliano Zapata Unit. Was there a search warrant? No, but the FBI had a "consent to search" signed by the owner of the house, who later admitted to being a paid FBI informant. Accompanying a press release about the evidence seized at the raid were photographs still wet with developing fluid. Bates posed with the photos.

Six weeks later, I received a letter by registered mail on Department of Justice stationery, signed by Charles Bates, advising me that I was on an Emiliano Zapata Unit "hit list" seized during a search. The information "is furnished for your personal use and it is requested it be kept confidential. At your discretion, you may desire to contact the local police department responsible for the area of your residence."

But I was more logically a target of the government than of the Emiliano Zapata Unit—unless, of course, they were the same. Was the right wing of the FBI warning me about the left wing of the FBI? Did the handwriting on the wall read *Cointelpro Lives*? Questions about the authenticity of the Zapata Unit had been raised by its first public statement, which included an unprecedented threat of violence against the left. A communique from the central command of the bomb-leaving New World Liberation Front charged that "the pigs led and organized" the Zapata Unit. "We were reasonably sure that it was a set-up from the beginning, and we *never* sent one communique to New Dawn because of our suspicions."

Jacques Rogiers, aboveground courier for the NWLF, told me that the reason I was on their hit list was because I reported that Donald DeFreeze had been a police informer.

"But that was true," I said. "It's a matter of record. Doesn't that make any difference?"

"If the NWLF asked me to kill you," Rogiers replied, "I would."

"Jacques," I said, "I think this puts a slight damper on our relationship."

And I found another place to live.

CHILLING EFFECTS

"The forces of chastity are amassing once again," says sex researcher Alfred Kinsey in the film biography, *Kinsey*.

As if to prove that statement still applies, a couple of days before the movie opened, conservative groups announced plans to protest the glorification of a man they blame for the sexual revolution and, consequently, AIDS. The director of Concerned Women for America's Culture and Family Institute even compared Kinsey to Nazi madman Dr. Josef Mengele.

Which is all fine with me. That's the risk of free speech. Let them picket theaters and hand out leaflets until pigs fly, the cows come home and Hell freezes over, as long as the government isn't involved. Or, for that matter, the *fear* of government interference.

How chilling the effect must be when the latest fine by the FCC against a TV network—a record $1.2 million against Fox for its "sexually suggestive" *Married By America*—resulted from letters of complaint by only three individuals.

Jack Thompson, an attorney in Coral Gables with a reputation as an obsessive crusader against indecency, has filed a dozen complaints with the FCC about the *Howard Stern Show*, most recently concerning "The Howard Stern Amputee Beauty Contest." (I'd give my right arm to see that.) Thompson says that "this was so far over the line that the content constitutes not just 'indecency' but also 'profanity' as that legal term of art is used in such regulatory matters."

And now lawyer Thompson is indulging in quasi-extortion. In a letter to Sumner Redstone, chairman of Viacom, he states that he intends "to bring a civil action arising from the negligent supervision of the Viacom board in its failure to assure that the *Howard Stern Show* not libel people, not incite death threats against people and, most importantly, not air indecent material." But then comes his demand:

"I have only one requirement, and it must be done quickly. Fire Howard Stern. Terminate him now, and I go away. You know you can terminate him right now for his ongoing promotion, on the air, of his upcoming Sirius program. What he did in that regard yesterday on your air is beyond belief. You can dump him right now for that alone. Everyone knows he's been warned not to do that. Pull the trigger. Fire him. That gives you a 2-for-1 deal. You get rid of Stern and you get rid of Jack Thompson. I'll be much more of a pain than Howard Stern ever was. It's my job."

Meanwhile, *Daily Variety* reported, "Here are some late election returns: Local stations are running scared on program content. . . . The scheduled pre-emptions [of *Saving Private Ryan*] come even though most, if not all, of the stations now balking at running *Ryan* have aired it in the past. Pic, which contains more than three dozen utterances of the word 'fuck,' must air in its unedited form, as per ABC's license agreement with DreamWorks."

In 2002, responding to a complaint from censorship advocate Donald Wildmon, the FCC ruled that *Saving Private Ryan* was *not* indecent. But that was before religious fanatics committed the worst of sins—pride—false pride in thinking that they've taken over the country.

Heathens of the world, unite! You have nothing to lose but your faith! Oops, never mind. . . .

SAVE THE TOMATO CHILDREN

Say what you will about Governor Arnold Schwarzenegger, you have to give him credit for signing a bill to forbid necrophilia. Under the new law, sex with a corpse is a felony punishable by up to eight years in prison. Claiming that the act was consensual will not be considered as a legal defense. Necrophiliacs have been getting away with it all this time, but district attorneys will no longer be stymied by the lack of an official ban.

According to Tyler Ochoa, a professor at Santa Clara University of Law who has studied California cases involving allegations of necrophilia, "Prosecutors didn't have anything to charge these people with other than breaking and entering. But if they worked in a mortuary in the first place, prosecutors couldn't even charge them with that."

Of course, there is a whole spectrum of necrophiliacs, ranging from those who are promiscuous, hopping from one casket to another, to those who like to stick with one corpse.

Here, from my "Great Moments in Necrophila" file, is a dispatch from Associated Press:

"The prosecution in the insanity trial of serial killer Jeffrey Dahmer rested its case. Dahmer has confessed to killing and dismembering 17 young males since 1978. A jury must decide if he will be sent to prison or a mental institution. The final prosecution witness, Dr. Park Dietz, a psychiatrist, testified that Dahmer wore condoms when having sex with his dead victims, showing that he could control his urge to have intercourse with corpses."

I smell a public service announcement there: "If Jeffrey Dahmer is sane enough to have safe sex, what about *you?*"

Whether necrophilia is a victimless crime may still be open to debate, but to arrest a sick person for using medical marijuana undoubtedly transforms a victim into a criminal. States' rights—it's not just for racists anymore.

During the Supreme Court discussion of this issue, Justice Stephen Breyer sure sounded like he'd been smoking some pretty powerful stuff himself: "You know, he grows heroin, cocaine, tomatoes that are going to have genomes in them that could, at some point, lead to tomato children that will eventually affect Boston. . . ."

Chief Justice William Renquist, wasn't present. He's undergoing treatment for thyroid cancer. One of the plaintiffs, Angel Raich—who uses marijuana every few hours for a brain tumor, scoliosis and chronic nausea—said she hoped Renquist's chemotherapy "would soften his heart about the issue. I think he would find that cannabis would help him a lot."

However, there was a definite agenda permeating the unhigh court. Justice Antonin Scalia sarcastically stated, "I understand there's whole communes in California planning on using marijuana for medical purposes." Justice David Souter said that an estimated 10 percent of people in America use illegal drugs, and those states with medical marijuana laws might not be able to stop recreational users from taking advantage. Souter added that making an exception for patients could open the door to widespread marijuana use and to fraudulent claims of illness by recreational pot smokers in California and the ten other states that allow medical marijuana. Justice Stephen Breyer said, "Everybody will say 'Mine is medical.'"

If you simply substitute the word "Viagra" for "medical marijuana," then the anti-recreational-use party line echoed by the Three Stooges is clearly revealed as a double standard.

Maybe it's because you can't grow Viagra—or Prozac, or Vioxx—in your window garden.

KERIK'S NANNY

"[S]keptics in city government circles were questioning the very existence of the nanny . . ."—*New York Times*

Somewhere in Mexico:

Q. So, Maria, how does it feel to have people doubt that you exist?

A. I regret it very much. I am alive and tricking.

Q. You mean alive and kicking.

A. No, tricking. When Mr. Bernie suddenly had me flown back home, I had no money, I had to turn tricks.

Q. Didn't he pay you well?

A. Oh, he did, but I spend it all in Atlantic City on my days off.

Q. What were your duties?

A. I take care of his two girls—they are good kids, shouldn't have to hear all this shit, you know, about their father. And I do some housekeeping. That's when the trouble start.

Q. How do you mean?

A. Well, he has this apartment—we call it the ground zero place—and he wants me to clean *that* up too, and get fresh flowers, wine, weed, would you believe that, so he can fool around with not one but *two* mistresses—I even have to buy the condoms—and I'm friendly with his wife, but I have to pretend like I don't know what's going on.

Q. Did you actually meet those mistresses?

A. Just one, Miss Judith, and she tells me, "Maria, if you keep a journal of everything that goes on behind the scenes, my company will publish it, and you will make a *lot* of money."

Q. And did you do that?

A. No, no, I have very much loyalty to Mr. Bernie. Gifts and everything. For my birthday he give me a taser gun. For Christmas his friend Mr. Rudy give me a Green Card.

Q. Did you know about Kerik's involvement with organized crime people?

A. Are you kidding? In our living room, it was just like watching *The Sopranos* without a TV set.

Q. Was there a highlight for you—something that stands out in your memory—during the time you worked in the Kerik household?

A. Yes, it was during the campaign for president. Mr. Bernie was going to be interviewed for the *New York Daily News* and he was really nervous. I mean there was sweat dripping down his face from his bald head and staying in his mustache. He says, "Maria, I gotta come up with a good sound bite." I say, "What's a sound bite?" He says, "That's the thing I wanna say that will be quoted all over the media." I say, "Why don't you make a warning. Like if that guy Kerry wins, then there will be another attack by the terrorists."

Q. So you wanted the Democrats to lose?

A. They don't need me to lose. They are, you know, chickenshit. Mr. Bernie tells that sound bite to the *Daily News*, and then the Democrats still praise him for Homeland Security.

Q. Do you miss living in America?

A. Yes. I really wanted to see *Spanglish*.

T-SHIRT TROUBLES

As a kid, my favorite radio program was ventriloquist Edgar Bergen with his dummies, Charlie McCarthy and Mortimer Snerd. Charlie was the pretentious city slicker, wearing a top hat and monocle. Mortimer was his naive, freckle-faced, buck-toothed country cousin. I realized that there was something bizarre about featuring a ventriloquist on radio, but it didn't matter—they all *sounded* like different personalities.

One time Bergen said, "Charlie, what are you doing?" He replied, "Oh, nothing." Then Mortimer interjected in his goofy, innocent manner, "Well, then how d'ya know when yer finished?" A Zen koan from the mouth of a wooden dummy.

I ate with a Charliie McCarthy teaspoon, and I wore a Charlie McCarthy T-shirt, which I got in trouble for wearing to a public school assembly. You can understand why I'm particularly sensitive to people getting in trouble for wearing a T-shirt, and this has been a banner year for that offense.

The private Cape Cod Academy in Osterville, Massachusetts updated their student handbook, and the new guidelines forbid *all* T-shirts with writing on them. "This very strict new dress code is, quite honestly, ridiculous," complained the student body vice president. "You can't really represent yourself the way you'd like."

During the national Day of Silence, an annual event sponsored by gay rights groups, a high school junior in San Diego was not allowed to wear a T-shirt that read "Homosexuality Is Shameful" and "Our School Embraced What God Has Condemned."

"The school district wants [him] to be politically correct," his attorney said. "We want the school district to be constitutionally correct."

When the father of Nick Berg, who was beheaded in Iraq by Al Qaeda-connected militants, was a guest on *Good Morning America*, he declined to remove his T-shirt that read "Bring the Troops Home Now," so ABC wouldn't show it on the air.

Michelle Goldberg reported in *Salon* that author Irene Dische was covering a George Bush speech for the German paper *Die Zeit*, sitting with artist Art Spiegelman, when police removed them both from the press stands and questioned them about their T-shirts. Spiegelman's said "Pray For a Secular Society"; Dische's featured the word "Bush" and Chinese characters. She convinced police it said, "I love Bush." It actually meant "Shit on Bush and flush him away."

In Franklin County, Washington on Election day, a man reported being turned away from a polling place because he was wearing a T-shirt that said "Vote or Die."

A federal judge ruled in favor of the Williamstown, Vermont public school officials who forced a student to cover up a T-shirt with a variety of images, including cocaine and a martini glass. It referred to George Bush as a lying drunk driver who abused cocaine and marijuana, and called him the "chicken-hawk-in-chief" who was engaged in a "world domination tour."

No doubt I would get in trouble if I were to wear a T-shirt with a picture of Charlie McCarthy labeled "George W. Bush" at his inauguration. That's the problem with suppressing freedom of expression. In the immortal words of Mortimer Snerd, "How d'ya know when yer finished?"

BITE YOUR TONGUE

Of all the movies I've ever seen, *Midnight Express*—which featured images of appalling conditions and brutality in a Turkish prison—was one of the most powerful, and landed Oliver Stone an Academy Award for best screenplay. Now he's gone and apologized for offending Turkey. "It's true I overdramatized the script," Stone told reporters in Istanbul. "But the reality of Turkish prisons at the time was also referred to . . . by various human rights associations." Stone had been afraid of visiting Turkey since the release of the film in 1978, he said, because of the effect it had on the country. "For years, I heard that Turkish people were angry with me, and I didn't feel safe there. The culture ministry gave me a guarantee that I would be safe, so I feel comfortable now."

Midnight Express was adapted from the book by Billy Hayes, an American who was sentenced to 30 years in prison for attempting to smuggle hashish out of Turkey, and eventually escaped. Stone and Hayes also did a week's worth of interviews in Stone's hotel room after he'd read the galleys.

"That was fun," Hayes recalls, "like being in a washing machine on tilt. And while some people find him a bit much, I love Oliver's energy."

I had contacted him to get his reaction to Stone's statement.

"How would you say that the script was overdramatized?"

"My biggest problem with the screenplay and the film was that you didn't see a single good Turk, so the overall impression was that all Turks are like those depicted in the film. And, of course, this is not true. It doesn't take away from the fact that the prison was brutal and the legal system hypocritical, but that can be said of almost any country, particularly, and unfortunately, ours. Prison guards are not necessarily the cream of any society."

"Did your biting the tongue off a fellow prisoner actually occur?"

"The tongue-biting was the filmmaker's way of having the informer get his dramatically just reward. Actually, I tried to bash that sumbitch's head in but the guards stopped me. I don't have a problem with the intent of that scene, but it's so strange now to remember that kind of up close and personal violence."

"What would say was most offensive to the Turks?"

"The most offensive scene for the Turks was Billy's speech in the courtroom calling them all a 'nation of pigs,' etc. In fact, when I spoke to the court, knowing I was having my sentence changed to life, I was trying to hold on to my shredding sanity and wanted to affect these people who were taking my life away but really knew nothing about me as a person. I said something like, 'I've been in your jail four years now and if you sentence me to more prison I can't agree with you, all I can do is forgive you. . . .' It affected them. The judge told me his hands were tied. They all looked upset. Then sentenced me to life, which the kindly judge reduced to 30 years. Thanks. I think. Anyway, Oliver wanted to know how I could forgive people who had just taken my life away. I told him about trying to maintain my balance. He asked how I felt the next morning after sentencing. I told him I was furious. So he wrote that courtroom speech."

"Was there anything that you thought should have been included in the film that was omitted?"

"What was missing from the film was what I found in jail. A sense of self and the trite but true notion of appreciating each moment. I discovered my reason for being, which is simply to love. It took a lot of banging my hard head against the wall, literally and figuratively, to realize this truth. They didn't deal with it in the film but that made the entire experience worth it."

"Tell me about *Midnight Return*."

"It's a follow-up book about the really weird part of my prison experience— returning to the U.S. and becoming a little mini-celebrity, with all that entails. Hope to get it published one of these days."

"Can you give me an example of mini-celebrity weirdness?"

"February 20th and 24th in 1980 I was mentioned in the *Steve Canyon* comic strip. From the bizarre to the surreal. How weird is that?"

"Oh, yeah? Well, I've been mentioned in *Pogo* and *Zippy the Pinhead*. You get used to it. Anyway, now I can start waiting for Oliver Stone to apologize to Greece for *Alexander*."

Michael Dare once interviewed Billy Hayes and a few other protagonists in Stone's biopics about what it's like to have your life rewritten by Oliver Stone. Their stories all involved some sort of wish fulfillment. At one point, Stone said to each one, "Is there anything you wish you had done but didn't?" Hayes said, "I wish I'd ripped that guard's tongue out." Ron Kovic (*Born on the 4th of July*) said, "I wish I'd gone and talked to the parents of the American soldier I accidentally killed." Richard Boyle (*Salvador*) said, "I wish I'd told off the American ambassador to Salvador when I ran into him at a party." Ray Manzarek (*The Doors*) said, "Fuck Oliver Stone." In each case, Stone replied, "You got it," and he put the subject's fantasy in the movie, except for that scene with Manzarek fucking Stone, which didn't make the cut.

FUZZY MATH

Comic strips like *Doonesbury*, *Boondocks* and *La Cucaracha* are expected to be controversial, so it was surprising when *Get Fuzzy*—an ordinarily non-controversial comic strip which features talking animals—dealt with a human character losing a leg in Iraq, a sequence which, coincidentally, ran simultaneously with a *Doonesbury* sequence on that same theme.

Recently, *Get Fuzzy* presented a series of "Rejected *Get Fuzzy* Storylines." One was, "*Get Fuzzy* attempts to outdo the *South Park* episode where they said 'fuck' 162 times by saying 'fuck' 162 [sic] times." To illustrate this rejected storyline, a cat is saying 'Fuck you' over and over. Although each use of the word 'fuck' had been blacked out by artist Darby Conley, the *Los Angeles Times* quietly substituted a year-old *Get Fuzzy*.

In another non-controversial strip, *Zits*, Jeremy, a lazy, would-be rebellious teenager, asks a friend to hold his backpack while he changes into a T-shirt that says "Question Authority." Jeremy explains, "I'm not allowed to wear this at home." His friend responds, "Weak convictions are better than none, I guess."

That same theme popped up in a sometimes controversial strip, *Non Sequitur* by Wiley Miller, venting via his alter-ego, Joe. Little Danae asks him, "Why are you so grumpy lately, Daddy?" Looking up from his newspaper—which has a front-page headline, "Nothing to See Here, Folks, Move Along"—he replies, "I'm just peeved about our wimpy news media. They're nothing but corporate lap dogs now." "Oh, I see," says Danae, "questioning authority isn't just a good thing, it's patriotic!" Her father, now reading another page—headlined "Nothin' Here Either"—replies, "Absolu . . . I mean, it depends on the authority." Danae says, "Too late, Daddy . . . if that's your *real* name."

In another strip, Miller reveals his disgust with how little attention American media were paying to reports of voting irregularities. A waitress with a New England accent is serving coffee to a customer at Offshore Flo's Diner. She asks, "What'r ya readin' theah, Joe?" He replies, "The *Ukrainian Times*." Waitress: "Uh . . . how come?" Now we can see that the headline reads, "Election Fraud!" Joe: "Oh, I'm just curious what an independent press questioning its government looks like." Waitress: "Why don't we have one of those?" Joe: "I think it has something to do with values."

Miller told *Editor & Publisher* that he's upset by "the laziness and lack of guts by our entire 'news' media—both print and electronic. They should all be embarrassed by what happened in the Ukraine. But that would take integrity, wouldn't it? At least they're providing me with material, so maybe I shouldn't complain."

He added that he would've liked to have seen American media "pursue the election results and the many questions surrounding its legitimacy with the same fervor and interest they showed in the all-important story of steroid use by baseball players. But I guess that in itself shows what's really important to corporate wonks posing as editors today."

Ironically, *Non Sequitur* is syndicated to more than 700 newspapers, none of which rejected his Ukranian-election strip.

EXPLOITING FEAR

Six weeks after 9/11, the U.S.A. Patriot Act became law. It had been secretly drafted by the Department of Justice. There was virtually no debate in Congress. Hardly any legislators had more than a few hours to read 342 pages. Now, that document and its ilk are pierced and probed by Walter Brasch in *America's Unpatriotic Acts: The Federal Government's Violation of Constitutional and Civil Rights*.

"Although I expected the Bush administration to be scared of dissent," Brasch told me, "I don't believe that in my 35 years covering government and politics I have seen a presidential administration so fearful of the people that it would deliberately and arrogantly go to the lengths it has to reduce dissenting views— and even potential dissenting views of any kind at any level. I kept running into incident after incident of the president's 'people' restricting the First Amendment rights of the people. Had I focused only upon this, there would have been nothing else in the book."

Many instances of government repression have occurred too late to be included. For example, at the University of Wisconsin, the student health center informed students that under the Patriot Act, the government may obtain their medical records, and patients will never know.

Canada is concerned that information about citizens living in the United States, working for Canadian companies in the U.S. or for U.S. companies directly falls under the Patriot Act. British Columbia privacy commissioner David Loukidelis stated, "Our research and analysis led us to the conclusion that the U.S.A. Patriot Act knows no borders."

The Department of Justice refuses to confirm whether the government can see what you're reading on the Internet without having to show probable cause for a crime, instead using "pen-traps" to garner such information—tools used without the same judicial oversight required for a wiretap—a practice codified in the Patriot Act.

The Justice Department now finds it necessary to have a website defending the Patriot Act. Their public relations campaign intensified before the November election, and apparently Bush has enough votes to continue most of the Act's provisions past the December 2005 deadline.

"I was upset, although not entirely surprised," Brasch told me, "at the number of people who were so overcome by fear after 9/11 that they said they would willingly give up some of their civil liberties in order to be safe. I expected this from those who stood close to the Bush administration. I did not expect to see so much of this from the people who claim to be moderates or liberals.

"I was also upset, although not entirely surprised, with the level of antagonism for dissenting views. While this nation had a long history of dissent, and an equally long history of people suppressing dissent, it seemed that the past three years have left more people willing to hide the First Amendment as a 'necessity' to keep America safe.

"While all administrations in various ways have tried to curtail opposition, there is in this administration an almost morbid fear of the people—or perhaps it is a fear that if truth emerges, the people will not support the adminstration. The frightening part is that this administration actually believes it has a mandate—from God? the people?—to do what it does, and opposition is not in the nation's best interest. Indeed, we have a more modern divine right of kings."

And the faucet of legalized repression continues to drip drip drip. . . .

Nonpartisan Harassment

Chris Warren is a politically conservative stand-up comic. Recently, he was threatened with arrest by the Secret Service if he dared to repeat a joke he told at the Brickwall Comedy Club in Spokane, Washington. I e-mailed him to find out what the joke was.

He replied, "It is not a wise idea for me to write out the joke online at this point," though he gladly told me the punchline. But first the set-up, revealed in this letter from a female MD to the editor of a weekly paper, *The Inlander,* which was seen by a member of the Air National Guard who reported it to the Secret Service. The letter:

"When I go to an adults-only comedy club, I expect to hear adult humor (including off-color jokes, which are half the fun) but did not expect to come out completely irate. The night started with the owner, Chris Warren, getting up and telling a few jokes. His jokes consisted of not one but multiple jokes about rape. One of them started out by him asking if anyone had heard about the woman who married her rapist. His 'punchline'? 'At what point during the rape did she think, 'Hey, this isn't so bad?' When the room was silent, he made a comment that maybe his joke was too dark for the crowd.

"It was not that his humor was too dark but that violent crimes against women are just not funny. Later he made a comment that Hillary Clinton should be raped and assassinated. When again the room was silent, he said, 'OK, maybe we should assassinate her first, then rape her.' This is supposed to be funny? I don't care what your political persuasion is, wishing any person to be raped and put to death is just wrong. Maybe Warren should look at his material and figure out that there are certain subject matters that are never funny no matter how you tell the joke."

And now the punchline about Hillary: "You'd need to shoot her first, then let the body warm up a little bit." Warren told me, "Response was mixed, some howled, some stared. I told the joke several times after that and got lots of laughs. So I was surprised with the visit by the Secret Service. I was asked to tell them the joke, and they both laughed! However, I was then told that if I was to tell the joke again, I would be subject to arrest, charged with a federal crime, that of threatening a 'protectee' of the Secret Service, then put on a terrorist watch list."

In 2003, he was among the first group of comedians to entertain American troops in Iraq. In 2004, he appeared with *The Right Stuff*, a right-wing comedy troupe that performed for delegates at the Republican convention in New York, at the Improv during the presidential debate in Phoenix, and before several dignitaries in Washington, including Ken Mehlman, Bush's campaign manager, now head of the Republican National Committee.

"I was told I would no longer have clearance to do any of these type shows again. No clearance, as they put it, to work for 'Kenny' again. There was no humor in their tone at this point. I was told that they were continuing the investigation and I was asked for personal information—height, weight, Social Security number, home address, phone numbers—information they obviously already had. It seemed like a subtle threat to me."

The intimidation worked. He hasn't told that joke on stage since then, and won't until his lawyer and the ACLU confirm that he's not going to jail over a joke.

Meanwhile, you guys have been a lot of fun—be sure to tip the waitresses.

TWISTED PRIORITIES

A letter to the editor of a local newspaper begins, "It is my belief that most of the people who drowned in the tsunami had never learned to swim, and the death toll would be less than half of what it is if they knew how to swim." The stupidity of that allegation is overshadowed only by the insensitivity. It serves to intensify the anguish, especially if you're the friend of a victim's family.

In my case, it's Luke Scully, the son of Rock Scully, former manager of the Grateful Dead, and stepson of Nicki Scully, a professional healer and spiritual adviser, whom I first met in Egypt in 1978 when the Dead played the Pyramids, and Jerry Garcia gave the band last-minute instructions: "Remember, play in tune." Happier times. . . .

A credit card transaction placed the missing Luke and his girlfriend Angie at a hotel in Phuket, Thailand on Christmas Eve. All I could do was say my atheist prayers for them among 150,000 anonymous others. Questioning the concept of God is one of the byproducts of this inconceivable tragedy. Star Jones said on *The View* that she would have been there if not for God's blessing. Jon Stewart responded on *The Daily Show* that it wasn't God's blessing, it was God's oversight.

Luke and Angie were, in effect, murdered by twisted priorities. *Expressen*, a Swedish newspaper, reported a crisis meeting attended by Thailand's foremost meteorological experts, who decided not to issue a warning about the tsunami an hour before the first massive wave struck, "out of courtesy to the tourist industry." That's the kind of courtesy that can literally kill you. One can only try to understand their perverted version of *Sophie's Choice*.

"We finally decided not to do anything," explained one of the meteorological experts, "because the tourist season was in full swing. The hotels were 100 percent booked full. What if we issued a warning, which would have led to an evacuation, and nothing had happened. What would be the outcome? The tourist industry would be immediately hurt. Our department would not be able to endure a lawsuit."

Ironically, in Thailand alone, where the tourist industry rakes in almost $8 billion a year, more than 5,000 people died at prime beach resorts—about half of them tourists—and anther 4,500 are still missing. Damages to businesses and property will reach into the billions of dollars, losses that will fall mainly on the tourism industry. Executives acknowledged that it would take time for the tourist trade to recover from the haunting images of bodies piled on the beach, as well as hotel rooms damaged.

Tourists weren't the only victims of human decision. An independent listserv, *CLG* (Citizens for Legitimate Government) *News,* reported a Canadian expert's claim that the U.S. Military and the State Department were given advance warning of the tsunami. Although America's Navy base on the island of Diego Garcia in the Indian Ocean was notified, the warning was not passed on to those countries bearing the brunt of the disaster.

"Get some devastation in the back," Senate Majority Leader Bill Frist instructed a photographer taking a picture of him before leaving Sri Lanka.

The only good news is a worldwide outpouring of aid to the survivors of Nature's blind genocide, even though America is simultaneously wasting so many billions on destroying and rebuilding Iraq. But suppose the Indian Ocean tsunami had somehow managed to reach the Persian Gulf and destroy Iraq's coastline. Would a mutual cease-fire then be declared, so that help—food, water, housing, health care, infrastructure rebuilding—could take place without the fatal annoyance of those pesky insurgents? It would, of course, be only a *temporary* cease-fire.

Meanwhile, the Luke and Angie Fund has been founded by their families to create a project for assistance and rehabilitation in Thailand.

SPRINGTIME FOR HARRY

A recent news report triggered a personal association that flashed back to a sharply etched memory. Concerning a British scandal that involved Prince Harry wearing a Nazi uniform with a swastika armband at a costume party, it was the best wardrobe malfunction since Janet Jackson caused a cosmic titter. Harry's insensitive act occurred because he was simply ignorant, or else he thought it was a come-as-you-are party, or maybe he just happened to come upon an ancestor's dusty old uniform in the attic.

As Andrew Gumbel, correspondent for the *Independent* of London, reminds us: "Nobody [in the British monarchy] represented the flirtation with totalitarianism more than Harry's great-grand-uncle, Edward VIII, the ulti-mate black sheep of the family who openly sympathized with the Nazis and might have pushed Britain into an anti-Stalinist alliance with Hitler had it not been for his insistence on marrying the American divorcee—and equally ardent Nazi apologist—Wallis Simpson, an insistence that precipitated his abdication in 1936. . . .

"The reverberations from the abdication crisis are still palpable among today's royals. Three of Prince Philip's sisters married Nazi sympathizers, and the Windsors who succeeded Edward VIII—his brother, George VI, and George's daughter, Elizabeth II—had to live it down, even after the Third Reich's demise. . . . Harry's costume revived unpleasant parallels between the Nazi taste for bloodthirsty imperial adventure and Britain's own leanings in that direc-tion—like using poison gas on the Kurds, shooting independence protesters in India and so on. Britain has long since repented of its imperial sins, but nostal-gia still abounds in certain upper-class circles. . . ."

When my daughter Holly was eleven, her best new friend was Pia Hinckle, whose father Warren had been editor of *Ramparts*, *Scanlan's* and *City* maga-zine. One afternoon, standing on the Hinckles' front porch, Holly was yelling, "Hitler! Hitler!" That was the name of Pia's cat, so named because of a square black patch under its nose, just like the mustache on Adolf Hitler's face.

I asked Holly, "Do you know who Hitler *was*?"

"Didn't he lead the Jews out of Germany?"

"Well, not exactly."

By the time Holly was 17, she had read *The Diary of Anne Frank* and seen *Holocaust* on TV. She had bleached her blond hair platinum, and when the roots grew in, she maintained a two-tone hairdo. Later, she dyed her hair pitch black and kept it in a style that completely covered one eye. She wore a leather jacket with chains hanging from it, and plenty of makeup, including a multicolored lightning streak on one cheek.

She was planning to audition for a new wave band called The Vktms. A lyric in one of their songs went, "Hey, you know I ain't no martyr, but I ain't no Nazi." She also wanted to change her name to Holly Hard-On, but she had the flu so her audition and name change became moot. Ah, yes, but she would've been following in my footsteps. Introducing Rumpleforeskin and his daughter Holly Hard-On. How proud could a father get?

SEX BOMBS

Yet another news report has triggered a personal association that flashes back to a sharply etched memory. This one is about a secret weapon that had been considered by the United States military—a "sex bomb" which would make enemy soldiers irresistible to each other.

Declassified documents reveal that the Pentagon spent six years and $11 million to develop an aphrodisiac chemical weapon in 1994. The gas would have made enemy soldiers sexually irresistible to each other. The weapon's developers said that widespread homosexual behavior among troops would deal a "distasteful but completely non-lethal" blow to morale.

In 1967, in order to build up public interest in an upcoming antiwar demonstration at the Pentagon, Abbie Hoffman invented an imaginary new drug, a sexual equivalent to the police tear gas, Mace. It was christened Lace, supposedly a combination of LSD and DMSO, which, when applied to the skin, would be absorbed into the bloodstream and act as an instantaneous aphrodisiac. Lace was actually Shapiro's Disapper-O from Taiwan. When sprayed, it left a purple stain, then vanished.

A press conference was called at Hoffman's apartment where Lace could be observed in action. I was supposed to be a reporter who got accidentally sprayed with Lace. To my surprise, I would put down my notepad, take off my clothes and start making love with a beautiful redhead who had also gotten accidentally sprayed, along with another *deliberately* sprayed couple, right there on a mattress on the living-room floor, while the journalists took notes.

I was really looking forward to this combination media event and blind date. Even though the sexual revolution was at its height, there was something exciting about knowing in advance that I was guaranteed to get laid—although I felt somewhat guilty about attempting to trick fellow reporters. But there was a scheduling conflict. I was already committed to speak at a literary conference at the University of Iowa on that same day. So instead Abbie asked me to buy some cornmeal there, to be used in encircling the Pentagon as a prelevitation rite.

In Iowa, novelist Robert Stone drove me to a farm.

"I'd like to buy some cornmeal to go."

"Coarse or fine?" the farmer asked. I glanced at Stone for advice.

"Since it's for a magic ritual," he said, "I would definitely recommend coarse."

I flew back to New York with a 13-pound sack of coarse cornmeal properly stored in the overhead rack. Meanwhile, the Lace story was reported in the *New York Post*, the *New York Daily News* and *Time* magazine, as well as the wire services, perpetuating the promise that three gallons of Lace would be brought to Washington, along with a large supply of plastic water pistols, so that Lace could be sprayed on police and the National Guard at the Pentagon demonstration, causing them to make love, not war.

The guy who substituted for me in that accidental sexual encounter with the beautiful redhead at the press conference ended up living with her. Even though I had never met her, I was jealous. Somehow I felt cheated out of a Yippie romance.

CONDOMS R US

I asked Annie Sprinkle, Ph.D.—the former porn star who is now a sexologist— how she felt about the use or non-use of condoms in porn.

"Condoms in porn are *hot*," she said. "They look sexy. Because they simply say, 'I care,' and to care is sexy. I get totally turned off if there is no condom. I happen to like the hot pink, bright blue and sea green ones myself. But it's important that there is plenty of lubrication and that the condom looks real shiny. Otherwise, I worry about the girl's pussy getting irritated."

The *Los Angeles Times Magazine* featured an article on pornography and HIV which quoted Roger Tansey, former executive director of Aid for AIDS, a West Hollywood based nonprofit organization that provides financial assistance for people with HIV. Referring to performers in gay porn, he said that "They all wear condoms. Gay actors and gay viewers don't see unprotected sex as a fantasy. They see it as watching death on the screen."

However, veteran gay rights activist Jim Fouratt told me, "I suggest you treat the quote from gay spokesperson Tansey with a huge grain of salt. Either he is stupid, involved in the gay porn industry, or simply ill informed. Let me just say that in the last several years, a very strong market has evolved for 'barebacking' specific videos and the re-release of gay porn made prior to the use of condoms and other safe sex guidelines. Much of this demand is created by gay media promotion of barebacking as a 'freedom of choice' of consenting adults."

When I was a kid, condoms were called prophylactics, prophylactics were called rubbers, and rubbers were called scumbags. My friends and I would find used scumbags in a vacant lot or an alley between buildings. Once I found a large package of unused prophylactics in my father's sock drawer. It must have held a dozen. There were nine left. Each was tightly rolled, bound by what looked like a miniature cigar band. I selected one, took the band off, and carefully unrolled it.

There was a legend printed right on the condom: "Sold In Drugstores Only For the Prevention of Disease." What hypocrisy! They were sold for the prevention of *pregnancy*, which is a condition, not a disease. The irony is that now condoms do *not* carry that message and they *are* used for the prevention of disease.

However, the national $170-million-a-year abstinence-only so-called sex education program warns that condoms fail to prevent HIV transmission one-third of the time, despite the fact that studies show that properly used condoms are nearly always effective in blocking HIV and other sexually transmitted diseases.

On January 20, 2005, it was reported that the Roman Catholic Church in Spain supports the use of condoms to prevent AIDS. The very next day, that support was retracted faster than a foreskin in heat, with an explanation that the church still believes artificial contraception is immoral, even while a Mexican Catholic bishop joined the Spanish church's original endorsement, stating that the use of condoms to prevent the spread of AIDS should be tolerated as a "lesser evil."

As an adolescent, purchasing condoms was a traumatic experience. I'd buy other stuff to avoid being embarrassed. "I'd like a *Batman* comic book, and this candy bar—[*whispering*] and a pack of prophylactics—and a tube of toothpaste, please." By the late '80s, there were huge *billboards* proclaiming: "If you can't say no, use condoms," but an executive of the Gannett Outdoor Advertising Company confirmed that they held off putting up those signs until after the Pope's visit to America.

The Catholic Church is faced with an interesting dilemma. On one hand, they are opposed to condoms as an artificial method of birth control. On the other hand, they're well aware that condoms can serve as a protection against AIDS. A group of bishops once argued that any educational program that included information about condoms should also stress that they are morally incorrect.

A compromise is possible, of course. They could manufacture theologically correct condoms, with teeny tiny pinprick holes in the reservoir tips, just enough to give all those spermatozoa a fighting chance. That's fair enough. But the problem then is that if the semen can get out, the AIDS virus can get in. So, then, it's back to the Vatican drawing board.

Now, theologically correct condoms would still have those teeny tiny pinprick holes in the reservoir tips, but there would also be little feather repellers with the message, "Wrong Way—Do Not Enter—Severe Tire Damage."

GRAMMYS, SHRAMMYS

I got a phone call from an old friend: "Hey, congratulations!"

"Thanks. For what?"

"You've been nominated for a Grammy Award."

This was a big surprise. My album, *The Zen Bastard Rides Again*, had been released in September 2004 by Artemis Records, without fanfare, advertising, reviews or, for that matter, sales. I checked the nominations for Best Comedy Album. There was Triumph the Insult Comic Dog for *Come Poop With Me*; Jon Stewart and the cast of *The Daily Show* for *The Daily Show With Jon Stewart*; Ellen DeGeneres for *The Funny Thing Is . . .* ; David Sedaris for *Live At Carnegie Hall*; and Al Franken for *The O'Franken Factor Factor—The Very Best of The O'Franken Factor*.

But not me.

I called my friend back, and learned that my nomination was for Best Album Notes. I didn't even know there was such a category. I had been invited by Shawn Amos at the Shout! Factory label to write a 5,000-word essay, "The Ballad of Lenny the Lawyer," accompanying a 6-CD anthology, *Lenny Bruce: Let the Buyer Beware*.

My competition: the album notes for *The Bootleg Series Vol. 6: Bob Dylan Live 1964—Concert At Philharmonic Hall*; Peter, Paul & Mary's *Carry It On*; *The Complete Columbia Recordings of Woody Herman and His Orchestra & Woodchoppers (1945-1947)*; and *No Thanks! The '70s Punk Rebellion*.

I didn't expect to win, but if I did, it would be a tribute to Lenny, not me. Actually, people often mistake me for Paul Kantner. In fact, when I returned from the Cannabis Cup in Amsterdam, a Customs agent looked at my passport and said, "Hey, you guys made some great music." And my luggage wasn't searched. I could've smuggled in several buds of prize-winning marijuana.

I once attended the Academy Awards in a borrowed tuxedo with a co-writer on Fox's short-lived *Wilton North Report*, Paul Slansky, who had an extra ticket. His friend Albert Brooks had been nominated for Best Supporting Actor in *Broadcast News*. The ceremony was boring—indeed, Brooks had explained to his shrink that he smoked pot because "it makes boredom more tolerable"—so, after Brooks didn't win, Slansky and I left, got some take-out Kentucky Fried Chicken, and watched the rest of the Oscars on TV.

Now, for the Grammy Awards in February 2005, I couldn't afford to fly to Los Angeles and stay at a hotel. I considered selling my tickets—somebody was auctioning six tickets on eBay at a minimum bid of $4,000 each—but instead I decided to give my tickets to a couple of friends. It turned out, though, that I'm entitled to just one complimentary ticket. Only members of the Recording Academy are entitled to two comps. A ticket for Nancy would cost $550. What a racket. Nobody goes to the Grammys alone. My friend offered to reimburse me. However, my nominee order form advised: "Tickets transferred or re-sold without permission will be revoked and their bearers deemed trespassers."

At my request, Danny Goldberg, who ran Artemis, asked its publicist to find out the appropriate person I could speak to who could grant me permission to transfer my tickets. She e-mailed me: "I have checked with NARAS and unfortunately, Grammy tickets are not transferable under any circumstances." So I wrote a letter appealing my case to Neil Portnow, president of the Recording Academy. No reply. My friends will not be going to the Grammys, after all.

As for me, I'll just borrow a tux, get some Chinese take-out and watch the show at home.

Postscript: Since the tickets would not be mailed but had to be picked up, I realized that, obviously, every nominee and industry mogul and their paid-for guests would not be picking up their tickets individually. I called the Recording Academy and explained that I didn't live in Los Angeles, so would it be all right if a friend picked up my tickets?

The answer was yes. They would mail me a Ticket Release Authorization form to fill out and fax back. "Your authorized third party," the form stated, "will be required to present (1) A copy of this authorization and (2) Photo identification (driver's license or passport)." There was also a warning: "Please be prepared to show photo identification for entrance to all Grammy Awards events."

Michael Risman made the pick-up, "though they let you know," he told me, "that they do random checking to insure the ticket-holder is the proper party at the gate." Michael and his wife Rebecca are the friends to whom I was giving the tickets. Rebecca worked at Concord Records, which received several nominations for albums featuring Ray Charles, but she had already left the company.

"We did gain admission to the award show and post party," she told me. "We entered the grounds of Staples Center, having the tickets checked a few times at a number of barricades. No one flinched. No one asked for ID. We found our way to the entrance by walking on the red (it was really green) carpet. The Ray Charles 'Genius Loves Company,' my swan song for the company, did very well. The after party was quite a spectacle. One bar was completely made of an ice sculpture about 5 feet high. We've come a long way since the chopped liver molded into a poultry shape."

The album notes for the Woody Herman CD won the Grammy.

As for me, it was an honor just to be defeated.

PROVOCATIVE PROFESSOR

In 1970, the War Resisters League in New York organized a demonstration at City Hall Park. I was asked to emcee and to burn a giant blow-up of a tax form. Later, a CBS correspondent interviewed me on camera.

"You've just burned that replica of a tax form," he said. "Have you paid *your* taxes?"

"Yes," I replied, "and I would like to confess right here on network television that I'm a mass murderer, because so much of the tax money I pay to the government goes to the Pentagon for just that purpose. I pay taxes, and that money has gone for dropping napalm on children in Vietnam."

My answer never got on the air.

Three decades later, following the 9/11 attacks, on a radio interview, I talked about "the mass anguish experienced by shell-shocked America and beyond. So much human suffering, for the sake of the *nation's* karma."

Compared to Ward Churchill, I'm a fucking girlie-man diplomat. When he wrote that the World Trade Center victims were "the equivalent of little Eichmanns"—with the exception of certain politically correct victims—Churchill was saying the same thing as Osama bin Laden when *he* explained the reason for the attacks.

Defending his position, Churchill says, "It should be emphasized that I applied the 'little Eichmanns' characterization only to those described as 'technicians' of the economy. Thus, it was obviously not directed to the children, janitors, food-service workers, firemen and random passersby killed in the 9/11 attack. According to Pentagon logic, they were simply part of the collateral damage. Ugly? Yes. Hurtful? Yes. And that's my point. It's no less ugly, painful or dehuamnizing a description when applied to Iraqis, Palestinians or anyone else. If we ourselves do not want to be treated in this fashion, we must refuse to allow others to be similarly devalued and dehumanized in our name."

He's playing the Oldie But Goldie card—"Do unto others as you would have them do unto you"—which brings up a phone call I got from a friend of 30 years. She attended Bradley University in Peoria, Illinois at the same tiime Ward Churchill did.

"He's a phony radical from way back," she said. "He snitched me out to the police in 1970. He came over to my house one time and—the very first pound of pot that I ever bought—I sold him an ounce. I didn't get arrested, but I had to suffer the wrath of my parents. They just went nuts. It's one of the reasons I moved away from Peoria."

"What do you think was Churchill's motivation?"

"My guess is he's been arrested before, and his fingerprints are probably still in existence. He may have had it expunged. I think obviously they had him on something else. He might've had a felony conviction. And he went around and ratted everybody out. And I wasn't the only one. He was the campus snitch. I'd love for him to be able to say anything he damn well wants. But he's not the authentic article."

ROONEY'S ASS

Attention, ad agencies: Here's a method to receive more attention for a product than you would from a 30-second spot, yet pay not a penny to the TV networks. Simply produce a commercial that's so raunchy you know it will be turned down. Then those same networks will play your commercial—for free—on their news programs. Or if they call your bluff and allow the commercial to be aired, then you can be sure that viewers will bring their eyeballs to the water cooler. It's truly a win-win situation.

It happened with the Super Bowl commercials. For example, the CBS network turned down a commercial which featured Mickey Rooney baring his ass, but it was pixilated on *all* the network news programs. Ironically, I have no idea what product was being advertised. Old asses, maybe.

In fact, the *Washington Post* published this correction: "The TV Column in the Feb. 8 Style section incorrectly described one of the Super Bowl commercials that were scrapped. The ad featured the bare bottom of Mickey Rooney, not Andy Rooney."

All those old asses look alike.

And now, from the ridiculous to the sublime. . . .

I was touched and intrigued by the story of a woman, Sarah Scantlin, who was the victim of a drunken driver in September 1984. The driver served six months in jail for driving under the influence and leaving the scene of an accident. Sarah was 18 years old at the time. Now, after having been in a coma for 20 years, she finally spoke her first words. For years she could only blink her eyes—one blink for "no," two blinks for "yes."

"I am astonished how primal communication is," her father said. "It is a key element of humanity."

Early in February, one of the nurses at the Golden Plains Health Care Center in Hutchinson, Kansas called Sarah's mother, asked her if she was sitting down, told her someone wanted to talk to her and switched the phone to speaker mode.

"Hi, Mom."

"Sarah, is that you?"

"Yes."

"How are you doing?"

"Fine."

Later, her mother asked, "Do you need anything?"

"More make-up."

I was stunned by that answer. Could the concept of "more make-up" been somewhere in her consciousness at the moment she was struck unconscious because she had just won a spot on the Hutchinson Community College drill team and been hired at an upscale clothing store?

The nurses say that Sarah thinks that she's still living in the '80s. She knows what a CD is, and that it plays music, but she has no idea what a DVD is. When her brother asked whether she knew how old she was, she guessed she was 22. When he told her that she was 38 now, she just stared silently back at him.

Most poignant was that, although she began talking in mid-January, she had requested staff members not to tell her parents until Valentine's day. She wanted to surprise them. Sarah is back in Kansas again.

THE FEAR OF FICTION

Maybe it's because Tom Hanks will star in the movie version of Dan Brown's *The Da Vinci Code*—a novel which has already been translated into 44 languages and sold 20 million copies—that senior Vatican official Cardinal Tarcisio Bertone is suddenly telling Catholics not to buy or read the book, because it involves a painting with clues proving Jesus Christ was not the son of God, that he married Mary Magdalene, fathered a family and, for all we know, frequently used Day-Glo condoms as a method of artificial birth control.

Don Novello, who inhabited the character of offbeat priest Guido Sarducci on *Saturday Night Live*, appeared on MSNBC in his clerical costume to comment on this literary phenomenon:

"Starting in 320 A.D., popes have commissioned, preserved and collected works of art, and now this guy comes from nowhere, making a fortune from a book that is based on a painting *we own*. He used our painting for his own benefit. Where was he when we were taking care of it for 500 years—dusting it all that time, and keeping it away from mildew—where was he? And worse, he did it in a *holy* year. Holy years come once every 50 years—we put a lot of money behind planning and promotion—and he comes out with his book *then*. Year 2000 coincidence? He waited until a holy year, he jumped on our wave, *he stole our holy year*. If it's Mary Magdalene instead of St. John, where did St. John go? Did Jesus have to tell him, 'Sorry, there's no room for you in this painting.' So send for the Da Vinci De-Coder Ring right now. . . ."

And now, on top of that theological controversy, there's the case of Terri Schiavo and her right to die. Consider the possibility that last-minute, unprecedented political pandering was based on a false premise that the Christian right put George Bush in the White House for a second term; that this myth stemmed from early exit polls in the 2004 election, where some pollsters included "moral values" as one of the reasons Bush was re-elected—what voter would ever have denied *that*?—when actually it was because of a combination of John Kerry's personality problem, Osama bin Laden's favorable review of *Farhenheit 911* and the historical fact that American presidents have never been changed in the midstream of a war.

The interference of legislators in a private medical situation boils down to a matter of taxation without representation, as indicated by an ABC poll—conducted by telephone while members of Congress and the president were grandstanding their asses off in a display of bipartisan hypocrisy—a poll which found that 63 percent of their constituents supported the removal of Schiavo's feeding tube. The poll also found that 58 percent of *Republicans* believed that such intervention was inappropriate, and 61 percent supported removal.

Nonetheless, according to satirist Barry Crimmins, Republican mothers now admonish their children, "If you don't feed the vegetable, you don't get any dessert."

And Don Novello alerted me: "I hear there are a lot of feeding tubes on eBay now they say are Terri Schiavo's, so collectors are being told to watch out for fakes. If I was in charge of realilty TV, *I'd buy them all* and put them in a box at the end of a football field and have Michael Jackson and Barry Bonds race—having to use *each other's crutches*—from the other end, grab as many as they can with one hand, like reaching in a jar for pennies on *Super Circus*, and see who gets back first with the most, without complaining."

THE END OF JOURNALISM

A media watchdog group, the Washington-based Project for Excellence in Journalism, affiliated with Columbia University, has just released its annual report on the news business, concluding that journalists should "document the reporting process more openly so that audiences can decide for themselves whether to trust it."

Well, here's a case in point.

United Press International dispatched a story last week about a former U.S. Marine who participated in capturing ousted Iraqi President Saddam Hussein and said that the public version of his capture was fabricated. UPI stated:

"Ex-Sgt. Nadim Abou Rabeh, of Lebanese descent, was quoted in the Saudi daily *al-Medina* as saying Saddam was actually captured Friday, Dec. 12, 2003, and not the day after, as announced by the U.S. Army. 'I was among the 20-man unit, including eight of Arab descent, who searched for Saddam for three days in the area of Dour near Tikrit, and we found him in a modest home in a small village and not in a hole as announced,' Abou Rabeh said. 'We captured him after fierce reisistance during which a Marine of Sudanese origin was killed. . . . Later on, a military production team fabricated the film of Saddam's capture in a hole, which was in fact a deserted well,' Abou Rabeh said."

This story definitely had the ring of falsehood. Could it possibly have been a fabrication *about* a fabrication? I contacted Pam Hess, the UPI Pentagon correspondent.

"My editor and I have been doing our damnedest to kill the story," she told me. "It is actually a clean pick up from the Saudi press but obviously flawed. It came from our Lebanon desk, which translated and ran the story—standard procedures for a wire. However, this was obviously a huge story if true, and very controversial, and should have been run through me first, which it was not.

"So, the story came from UPI—but I don't recommend picking it up. Obviously fabricated. The Marines don't have records of the original source who makes the claims. I have recently heard from some guy who says the fact that the dates (the fruit) were yellow in the background suggest that Saddam was captured and filmed earlier than December—but I'm not sure that rises to the level of reportable."

The story had already been reported by various local media and Internet listservs. Harry Shearer read it on his syndicated radio program, *Le Show*. When I informed him of its fictional nature, he thanked me for the heads-up and added, "Interesting that they'll run it on their wire before checking it."

Especially since it's "obviously fabricated."

The most significant aspect of this hoax is that, in the wake of an increasing incredibility of real news, there is an increasing credibility of fake news.

KARL ROVE LOVES JEFF GANNON

"Military men are just dumb stupid animals to be used as pawns in foreign policy."—Henry Kissinger

Although *The Daily Show* is my favorite daily show, I'm occasionally disappointed in Jon Stewart as an interviewer. When former Secretary of State Henry Kissinger was a guest, Stewart obsequiously lobbed softball questions at him. More recently, when former press secretary Ari Fleischer was a guest, Stewart didn't ask him anything about Jeff Gannon, the $200-an-hour gay prostitute–*cum*–Bush administration propagandist in the guise of a journalist, sitting in the fourth row at White House press conferences and asking ass-kissing questions.

When that same subject came up on HBO's *Real Time*, Bill Maher speculated that Gannon must have been getting it on with somebody in the White House. Then Robin Williams filled in the blanks with an implication that this somebody in the White House was actually Karl Rove. And Walter Storch, editor of the *Barnes Review News*, reported that "Karl Rove was seen by one of my people entering a private homosexual orgy at a five-star Washington hotel over the Mid-Atlantic Leather weekend last year [2004]."

Stand-up comic Barry Crimmins envisions Gannon at a presidential press conference, wearing pink panties with a dog collar on his neck, and asking, "Who do you have to blow to get a seat in the front row?"

Crimmins, a political satirist and activist, has gone from writing for Dennis Miller to writing for Air America Radio. Now, about Miller, he says, "Listening to his act is no longer something we look forward to; it is more like getting stuck in the back seat of your pop's station wagon while he lectures you on 'Americanism' through 30 miles of heavy traffic. . . . He has carved a place for himself on the Mount Rushmore of wrong-headedness, and there he will stay for years to come, a glowering, reactionary oaf for the ages."

As a performer, Crimmins told me, "I've felt pain as I've watched hacks succeed in places where I was not welcome, but what the hell? Why should I expect them to allow me to stand on their soapbox to announce that their suds are polluting the river?"

In 1988, Crimmins was at CNN's New York studio to contribute commentary on the presidential campaign. He was chatting with CNN anchor Norma Quarles in the Green Room. "Suddenly she looked right past me and began sucking up to someone at a clip that was fantastic even for a corporate news anchor." It was Henry Kissinger. Crimmins refused to shake hands with him. Later, Quarles asked him why. "Because," he replied, "I have a strict policy of never shaking hands with war criminals." The title of his new book—published, as is this book, by Seven Stories Press—is *Never Shake Hands With a War Criminal*.

FAST FOOD IN THE FAST LANE

According to *Advertising Age*, McDonald's has offered to pay popular hip-hop performers to infiltrate the fast-food chain's Big Mac into their lyrics. They will not receive an advance on royalties, but rather they'll be paid $5 every time such a song is played. Although the company will have final say over the appropriateness of lyrics, the singers will retain artistic control over how they're incorporated into the track.

Spokesperson Walt Riker explained that this concept is in line with McDonald's 2003 global marketing campaign aimed at 18-to-34-year-olds, which launched the *I'm lovin' it* slogan. "Each McDonald's market," he said, "has the freedom within the *I'm lovin' it* framework to design programs that best resonate with customers." Already, Kanye West and Busta Rhymes have agreed to promote the Big Mac by mentioning it in their rhymes.

Ever since MC Hammer did it for KFC's popcorn chicken campaign in the early '90s, this radio version of product placement has continued to ooze its way into rap music. The BBC reports that "A whole string of products has enjoyed huge success in the United States after rappers started dropping brand names into songs—although not for marketing purposes but bling boasting. Among the happy beneficiaries were brands like Courvoisier, Gucci, Dom Perignon, Bentley and Porsche. Artists who have 'referenced' well-known products include Jay-Z, 50 Cent and Snoop Dogg."

Thus, only ten airplays of a song including a brand name plug for the two-all-beef-patty burger would net $50 for 50 Cent. The implications of this whole practice are, er um, just delicious. Price wars, for example. What's to prevent Burger King from upping the payment to $7 per play? Would McDonald's then make a counter-offer of $10?

Or how about candidates running for political office who are desperately trying to reach that desirable demographic? I can hear it now, stuck into the middle of a rap: "Hillary Clinton was married to the first Negro president I mean this is what they used to call ol' Slick Willy with his little slick willy bein' the answer to the question 'Wassup?' and you know for damn sure that's who we wanna see in the Black House is Hillary 'cause she's a real nigger lover you know what I mean dawg?"

In recent years, an alliance of hip-hop and the porn industry has been developing, and therein lies another possibility. Can't you envision a computer screen with Snoop performing anal sex on a voluptuous blonde—a common theme in the world of Internet pornography—and, accompanied by a heavy drumbeat, he is rhythmically chanting, "Ooh ooh ooh ain't ya glad I mixed some Preparation H with the Astroglide so who's your product-placement daddy *now*?"

But please, gentlemen, try not to come on the keyboard.

JOHNNIE COCHRAN MEETS DR. HIP

Tragedy and absurdity were two sides of the same coin, from O. J. Simpson's "suicide" note with a smiley face in the O of his signature, to the woman who pinched lawyer Robert Shapiro's ass because "I wanted to be part of history," to Simpson walking into the courtroom humming the melody of "Touch Me" from the Broadway hit *Cats* and explaining to reporters that he was thinking about his children.

Of course, I'm reminded of that criminal trial because of Johnnie Cochran's death. I met him once. Shortly before Simpson's civil trial began in 1997, Cochran was the guest of honor and luncheon speaker at a national convention of criminal defense attorneys held in a huge banquet hall at a hotel in Santa Monica. No media were allowed.

One of the attendees was Dr. Eugene Schoenfeld, also known as Dr. Hip from his days as a syndicated columnist for the underground press. He now testifies occasionally as an expert witness, and was at this event for that reason. Nancy and I were his guests.

Cochran's speech reassured the enthusiastic audience: "In the Simpson matter, we just did what *you* do every *day*"—that is, defend their clients by any means necessary and chalk up a bunch of billable hours in the process—and he received a standing ovation.

In the afterglow of his speech, colleagues came up to Cochran to shake his hand and get in a little banter. One well-wisher shared this joke: "If Chris Darden spent as much time trying to nail O. J. Simpson as he did trying to nail Marcia Clark, he might've won the case." The other defense attorneys all had a good laugh at that one.

Schoenfeld joined the line of lawyers waiting to have photos taken of themselves standing alongside Cochran. When it was Schoenfeld's turn, Nancy focused her camera. For this particular occasion, Schoenfeld had stashed a hand printed card underneath the standard, plastic encased ID lapel card. As in the previous poses, Cochran and Schoenfeld put their arms around each other though they were looking, not at each other, but straight ahead and smiling at the camera.

Thus, Cochran didn't notice how, just before Nancy snapped their picture, Schoenfeld subtly managed to pull away the ID card and reveal the hand printed card, which declared, in large printed letters, "O. J. DID IT!" I published that photo on the front cover of *The Realist* that spring. It was the result of a good, old-fashioned guerrilla action.

ACQUITTING WATERMELON

Ever since I was three years old, I wanted to be inducted into the Countercultural Hall of Fame. It finally happened, at the Cannabis Cup in Amsterdam. I joined such luminaries as Bob Marley, Louis Armstrong, Mezz Mezzrow, Jack Kerouac, Neal Cassady, Allen Ginsberg, William Burroughs and Ina May Gaskin, founder of the modern midwife movement.

The previous year, the emcee of this event was San Francisco stand-up comic

Ngaio Bealum, whose parents were both in the Black Panther Party. "You know," he said, "when we were kids, we didn't have bongs. We just had to fill our mouths with water and suck real slowly." He described smoking pot while drinking coffee as "the poor man's speedball."

Ths time, the emcee was stand-up comic Watermelon, who lives in Vancouver, where she sells marijuana-laced gingersnap cookies at a nude beach. She describes herself as "the only nudist, pot-dealing comedienne in the world." She presented me with a silver cup, a framed plaque—and a three-foot-long bud of marijuana.

"That's for you to tickle your wife with," she said.

"Thank you. Y'know, Watermelon, you have very nice pits. Somebody had to say that."

"And I've got a brain that just won't quit, Paul."

"Well, let's see, this cup will be great for keeping my stash in. This plaque will be great for rolling joints on. And this big giant bud—'It's a French tickler,' I'll say, and I'm sure that will get me through Customs without any problem."

Watermelon has just been acquitted of all charges relating to her arrest for selling gingersnap cookies laced with cannabis resin at, yes, Wreck Beach, because, it was explained, "It is no longer in the public interest to continue with the prosecution." The judge admitted having "reasonable doubt," due to the unquantifiable traces of cannabis in the cookies.

Watermelon's attorney had argued that resin wasn't found in the cookies when examined by forensic experts—just cannabinoids—and she wasn't charged with possession of cannabinoids. He said that she regards the beach as her church, adding that now "she'll be able to attend her church again."

"And I thought my cookies tasted good," Watermelon told me, "but victory tastes sweeter."

She plans to focus on extending her cookie brand and newfound legal expertise to the medical marijuana market for patients who'd rather ingest than smoke.

Meanwhile, in an article for *Razor* magazine, Martin Lee writes, "No American has ever been granted Canadian refugee status because of the war on drugs, but the times they may be changing."

ORAL SEX ON THE RISE

"I think the stereotypes don't exist as much any more—girls and boys *both* see oral sex as not being a big deal," says Bonnie Halpern-Felsher, head of a study at two California schools which concludes that about one in five ninth-graders (average age 14-1/2) have practiced oral sex, and almost one-third say they intend to try it during the next six months. Could this be why a state report shows that teen birth rates continue to decline across California?

Ironically, the April issue of the *Journal of Adolescent Health* cites a study of 12,000 youngsters indicating that teens who pledge virginity until marriage are more likely to have oral and anal sex than other teens who have not had vaginal intercourse. The pledging group was also less likely to use condoms during their first sexual experience or to get tested for sexually transmitted diseases.

In one high school, where free condoms are available for students, there is a sign proclaiming that "The Peppermint Condoms Are For Oral Sex Only." Yet there is a certain twisted sense of continuity. We used to practice oral sex as a way of preventing pregnancy. Young people today mistakenly do it as a means of preventing AIDS.

Oral sex is so much in the air these days, it's hard to remember what a tremendous taboo it once was. But in the wake of blow jobs in the White House, kids began embarrassing their parents by asking, "What's oral sex?" Biblical scholars got busy checking to see where God said that oral sex is not adultery.

An entire episode of *Seinfeld* was devoted to oral sex. Moreover, an entire episode of *Curb Your Enthusiasm* was concerned with *Seinfeld* creator Larry David having a pubic hair stuck in his throat as a result of performing oral sex on his wife. And incredible hype from the distributor of *Inside Deep Throat*, General Electric's NBC Universal, claims that *Deep Throat* is the most profitable picture ever made, falsifying its gross as $600 million. That's more than *Star Wars*, which has grossed "only" $461 million.

Surprisingly, oral sex was missing from a proposed amendment on sexual misconduct in the Student Council Code at the University of Oregon. In an effort to prevent date rape, a motion was presented to the University Senate, defining rape as "an offense committed by a student who engages in penetration of another person, and who does not obtain explicit consent." Penetration means "any degee of insertion, however slight, of the penis or any material object into the vagina or anus."

Hey, what about somebody's *mouth*? Forcible fellatio is rape.

THE UPSIDE OF OUTRAGE

Even while you're laughing at Lewis Black ranting and raving about cultural and political insanities, his physical fury fuels his comedy so blatantly that you worry he's going to burst a blood vessel any second. When I asked him over lunch how he originally adopted that angry persona, he responded in a very calm manner.

"I was working one night with Dan Ballard, a very funny and very huge albino comic from Michigan," he recalled. "After I came off stage, he grabbed me and said, 'Listen to me, I am on stage screaming like an idiot and I am not even angry, and you are angry and you're not yelling, so when you go back on stage I want you to start yelling.' So I did, and my persona was born."

In his new book, *Nothing's Sacred*, Black writes about a heckler who "felt I was being too hard on Vice President Cheney. He informed me in no uncertain terms that the vice president was serving his country, and asked what was I doing for my country. I paused and said, 'I do this. This is what I do.'"

Recently, though, he performed at the annual Radio and Television Correspondents Dinner, and sat next to Dick Cheney. A situation like that can make any comedian uncomfortable, except maybe for Don Rickles.

"It truly was hell preparing for the event," Black told me, "like taking a comic's SAT test. President Bush was supposed to be seated to my right while I performed, but divine intervention from the pope saved me from that, so I was now staring at Vice President Cheney—which was bizarre, to say the least. It is an out of body experience. And I am supposed to make him laugh, which I actually did, which also freaked me out, as it made me wonder what was wrong with my comedy. He went on before me, which means that I can now put on my resumé that the vice president opened for me. And he was funny. Then he got serious. I felt sick for a week before this event, because this is one of the most uptight group of folks you could ever perform for.

"It worked out fine, as I had destroyed my usual act, in the name of entertainment. As long as you take the gig, you should be good at it, and I feel that nothing would have been accomplished if I had pissed all over them. I didn't want to spend the next week talking to reporters about it. I stopped and talked to the vice president as I left the dais. One of his closest friends is the brother of a close friend of mine who passed away a number of years ago. I asked him to please say hi to his friend for me—I hadn't seen him in quite some time. So basically I asked the vice president to be my messenger boy, and hopefully it would keep him out of trouble for a few minutes."

But that's what Cheney *does*.

PRIDE AND PARANOIA

In connection with the 10th anniversary of thebombing of the Murrah Federal Building in Oklahoma City, I've managed to obtain an exclusive prison interview with Terry Nichols.

Q. What are your thoughts today about that horrific act of domestic terrorism in which you participated?

A. Oh, I'd say, the irony of how we got caught.

Q. What do you mean?

A. Well, think about the odds. Timothy McVeigh was against the United States government. He didn't want to have anything to do with this government. He didn't even want to have a driver's license. He didn't want to have a license plate on his car. But the reason he got *caught* was because some traffic cop happened to notice that the license plate was *missing* from his car.

Q. And what about you?

A. Well, just like Tim, I hated the federal government. I refused to pay taxes. And yet the reason *I* got caught was because they found a six-months-old receipt for a couple of tons of fertilizer. I can't explain rationally why I ever *saved* that receipt. I mean I wasn't gonna pay my taxes. And what would I do if the bombing failed? Go back to the store where I bought it, show my receipt and say, "I'm sorry, but your fertilizer didn't work. I'd like to get a refund, please?"

Q. I understand that you believe there was a certain relationship between the bombing and the O.J. Simpson murders.

A. Yes, there was some guy, it was his job, his mission in life, to determine that the disembodied leg which was found in the rubble of the Federal Building did not belong to a white man but to a black woman, and furthermore, just like the glove that was planted in the Simpson case, that leg was planted in the rubble by Detective Mark Furhman.

Q. Aha! But whatever the defense and the prosecution and the judge did in that trial, there was also the media fallout. I have a friend who has two young daughters, and they said to him, "Daddy, we have a question to ask you. If you ever killed Mommy—and we're not saying you would ever do a thing like that—but if you ever killed Mommy and we asked you if you did it, would you tell us the truth?"

A. You know, if a character on a TV sitcom ever said that line, there would be a laugh track right after it.

Q. I suppose so. One more question. I understand that you also believe that there was a certain relationship between the Oklahoma bombing and the murder of Laci Peterson and her unborn baby.

A. Oh, definitely. This never came out in my trial, but it was Scott Peterson who sold me those two tons of fertilizer.

DUELING MEMORIES

At Wordstock, the first annual Portland (Oregon) Book Festival, I was invited to open for Norman Mailer and then introduce him.

"The thing I most admire about Mailer," I said, "is a combination of his courage as a writer and how much he respects the craft. He writes in longhand with a number two pencil, he told me once, because it puts him in more direct contact with the paper that he's writing on, and I felt so guilty because I was still using a typewriter at the time. You remember typewriters. In fact, I have a niece who saw a manual typewriter, and she said, 'What's that for?' I explained, and she said, 'Well, where do you plug it in?' 'You don't have to plug it in, you just push the keys.' And she said, 'That's awesome!'

"Anyway, one aspect of Norman Mailer's craft is that he chooses his words very carefully. Or, as he would say, 'One chooses one's words very carefully.' The thing that I recall, the words that he chose most carefully, of all the books he's written, was something that he said when I asked him how he felt about circumcision. He thought for a moment, then he chose his words carefully and, with a twinkle in his eye—one of his main characteristics—he said, 'Well, I believe that if Jews didn't have circumcision, they would punch their babies in the nose and break them. . . .'"

When Mailer came on stage, walking with the aid of two canes because of a severe arthritic condition, he received a standing ovation. He eased himself on to a high chair behind the podium.

"Gee, Paul, I didn't know how to start tonight," he said, "but maybe you got me going. Now, if I ever made that remark, that the reason Jews get circumcised is to keep them from breaking their babies' noses, all I can say is that I must have been down in the lower depths of a very bad marijuana trip. But I think, even at my worst, I couldn't really have said that. Paul is a master of hyperbole. He loves hyperbole, as for example when Lyndon Johnson attacked the wound in JFK's head.

"At any rate, if I did say it, I would forgive myself now for having said it, because circumcision happens to be something that every Jewish male thinks about every day of his life. It makes us obsessive for a very simple reason. We don't know if it's an asset or a liability. And I'm not speaking of it lightly. I'm speaking of psychic castration that may make us smarter or it may not. We worry about things like that. So I will say categorically, that if I ever made that remark, I was out of my head, and to the best of my marijuana memory, I never made it. I want to thank you, Paul, for making that up and giving me a beginning tonight, and for warming up this audience. . . ."

CONFESSIONS OF A RACIST

[This was a blog, published on HuffingtonPost.com.]

Oh, sure, *Crash* is intertwined with more coincidences than an entire season's episodes of *Seinfeld*, and, yeah, maybe there's an unrelenting amalgam of racial conflicts, but for me, seeing that movie certainly served to trigger an exploration of my own evolution as a prejudiced Caucasian-American heterosexual male, privileged at birth. At the age of four, I was so innocent that, riding in the subway with my pregnant mother, on the way to my violin lesson, I pointed to a colored baby and said, "See, that's the kind I want." I didn't understand why my mother was embarrased and shushed me.

By 1950, though, when my first girlfriend told me that she had dated a Negro, I blurted out, "Did you kiss him on the lips?" I was even more stunned than she was. Hearing myself say that was a shocking wake-up call. It would be necessary to unbrainwash myself from all the nuances of bigotry that I had so thoroughly and unconsciously absorbed by cultural osmosis. I became involved in the civil rights movement and later published anti-racist material in *The Realist*.

In 1961, Dick Gregory requested that I interview him. It turned out that we had the same favorite poem, Rudyard Kipling's *If*—both of us kept a copy in our wallets. He told me how he first knew he was black at the age of five, when white people would give him a nickel to rub his nappy hair for good luck, and I told him how I felt like a freak at the age of six, when I was a child prodigy and became the youngest concert artist in any field to perform at Carnegie Hall, and white people would rub my wavy hair—for free. Gregory and I became close friends and fellow demonstrators. He told me that I was the first white man he'd ever invited to his home to meet his family. After dinner, I watched television with his kids and laughed with them at the Clairol commercial that spouted, "If I have only one life to live, let me live it as a blonde!"

In 1971, I had a radio talk show at a station where the ratio of whites and blacks was about even. There was a party at the home of a staffer, where a bunch of us—same ratio—were getting stoned in the kitchen, and becoming slightly hysterical as we took turns parodying racial stereotypes. A black acquaintance patted me on the shoulder and, not realizing that he had just entered, I continued in the established mode and said what was intended as a contribution to that running gag, "Oh, excuse me, I forget your name, you all look alike." It was as if I had punched him in the solar plexus. "Yes," he hissed, "we all do look alike." Now, 34 years later, I still have a twinge of shame that my carelessness allowed me to hurt him like that.

Just a few days ago, I was watching the news when the bell rang. My wife Nancy went to the door. I could hear a salesman's voice. He wanted to sell us window-washing equipment, but this wasn't a good time for us. Instead of leaving his card, he increased the pressure. I called out, "She said not now!" He continued attempting to persuade her. I shouted, "Please leave!" On a visceral level, I felt bad, but when I looked out the window and saw an African-American walking away, I felt *way* worse. Equality was my original goal, but I seem to have become a reverse racist in the process.

THE RUMPLEFORESKIN AWARDS
FOR 2004

The Chutzpah Above and Beyond the Call of Duty Award—to Mark Geragos, attorney for Scott Peterson, for seeking donations to continue the investigation into the murders of Peterson's pregnant wife to help "free the man we know is innocent."

The Best Legal Argument Award—to Aaron McKinney, co-murderer of Matthew Shepherd, denying that they killed him because he was gay: "I would say it wasn't a hate crime. All I wanted to do was beat him up and rob him."

The Influencing the Jury Pool Award—to *Mad* magazine for its cover showing Michael Jackson with his arm around Alfred E. Neuman, who, despite his "What, me worry?" philosophy, is looking frightened. Very frightened.

The Most Presidential Statement Award—to George W. Bush, who, while visiting wounded troops at Walter Reed Army Medical Center in Washington and expressing condolences to relatives of service members killed in Mosul, said, "Today, we had a rocket attack that took a lot of lives. Any time of the year is a time of sorrow and sadness when we lose a loss of life."

The Reporters Simply Doing Their Job Award—to syndicated columnists Russell Mokhiber and Robert Weissman, who asked Scott McLellan, the president's press secretary: "Scott, on the Middle East—many evangelical Christians in the United States are supporting right-wing Jews in Israel who want to rebuild the temple on the Temple Mount in Jerusalem. They [evangelical Christians] believe this is a prerequisite for Christ's return to earth. They believe that when Christ returns to earth—they call this The Rapture—he will take back with him the true believers. And the rest—the non-believers, Jews, Muslims—will be left behind to face a violent death here on earth. As a born again Christian, does the president support efforts to rebuild the temple on the Temple Mount?" McLellan ended the press conference right there, and they didn't get a chance to ask their follow-up, "Does the president believe in The Rapture and does he believe that during The Rapture he will be snatched up and taken by Christ to Heaven, or will he be 'left behind' to face a violent death here on earth?"

The Abstinence Makes the Heart Grow Fonder Award—to anybody even remotely connected with federally funded programs that present untrue information to students, such as the textbook which states that touching another person's genitals "can result in pregnancy" and that exposure to sweat and tears is a risk factor for HIV transmission.

The Best Reason for Resigning Award—this one is a tie: to Colin Powell, who wanted to spend more time with his conscience; and to Bernard Kerik, who wanted to spend more time with his nanny.

The Conspiratorial Freudian Slip Award—to Donald Rumsfeld, who said on Christmas Eve at Camp Victory in Baghdad: "And I think all of us have a sense if we imagine the kind of world we would face if the people who bombed the mess hall in Mosul, or the people who did the bombing in Spain, or the people who attacked the United States in New York, *shot down the plane over Pennsylvania* and attacked the Pentagon, the people who cut off people's heads on television to intimidate, to frighten—indeed the word 'terrorized' is just that. Its purpose is to terrorize, to alter behavior, to make people be something other than that which they want to be."

The Recycling for the Environment Award—to Nicole Kidman, for passing on her fake nose in *The Hours* to Jim Carrey to use as his fake nose in *Lemony Snicket.*

The Totally Erasing the Previously Merely Blurred Line Between Satire and Reality Award—to the editors of the online *Ironic Times*, for this headline and subhead: "Pfizer: Celebrex Doubles Risk of Heart Attack—but still an effective treatment for arthritis"—which is essentially what was stated by Pfizer CEO Hank McKinnell.

The Best Perspective Restorer Award—to *Yahoo! News: Entertainment*—*AP Gossip/Celebrity*: "Czech supermodel Petra Nemcova, who appeared on the cover of 2003 *Sports Illustrated* swimsuit issue, was injured . . . in the Asian tsunami disaster."

The Minimalist Approach to the Cultural Divide Award—to Bill Donahue, head of the Catholic League, for providing middle America's new mantra: "Hollywood Loves Anal Sex."

The Maintaining High Standards Award—to the Estate of Johnny Cash, for refusing to allow a hemorrhoid commercial to use Cash's song, "Ring of Fire."

Finally, *The Edible Miracles Award*—to the Virgin Mary, who appeared in Times Square on New Year's Eve, and on her chest was the distinct image of a grilled cheese sandwich.

May the year 2005 prove to be better than a catastrophic success for you and all your loved ones. And be sure to get vaccinated against Mad Tofu Disease.

THE DEVIL IN THE DESERT

During the four years and ten weeks that Nancy and I have lived in Desert Hot Springs, we've observed the evolution of a small town into a burgeoning city. One of the early signs was the opening of a Thai restaurant. So many customers showed up on the first night that they ran out of food. The latest sign is that the rumor of a Starbucks being on the way has turned out to be true.

In our neighborhood, the city has just put in a sewer system and paved the roads. On the main street, Palm Drive, traffic lights have replaced the honor system at a couple of intersections. A UPS branch recently opened. A medical center is on the cusp of pure fantasy and planning stage. And, to quote the front-page headline in the current issue of a gung-ho conservative, bi-weekly tabloid, the *Valley Breeze*, "Desert Hot Springs Police Add New Taser X-26 Weapon to its Arsenol [sic]."

The population was 7,000 when Nancy first visited here in 1978. Now it's 20,000. There are 40 hotels and spas that pump the odorless, healing mineral water out of the ground at 120 to 180 degrees. And last year, the cold water, which is filtered through sand several hundred feet below the hot water aquifer, won the Gold Medal for Best Tasting Muncipal Water at the Berkeley Springs International Water Tasting competition. We no longer buy bottled water.

Our move from Venice Beach to Desert Hot Springs—from the motion of the ocean to the magnificence of the mountains—was prompted by the fact that the rent in Venice kept going up exponentially, a 7 percent increase every year for 16 years. Then we discovered that in Desert Hot Springs, anybody could get a mortgage if they had a pulse. We had never owned a house before. Now we were ecstatic, owning our own home and a garage—even the car had its own room—yet we were simultaneously aware of the preposterousness of "owning" land.

We'd been coming here occasionally on weekends since 1985, so we knew about the intense heat, but we've learned to appreciate air-conditioning. We loved the isolation—nobody drives to Desert Hot Springs by accident—and the sparse traffic. There was only one movie theater here, and that building is now a church, but there are art houses as well as cineplexes in the more ostentatious cities, Palm Springs and Palm Desert, and on the way we pass streets named after such celebrities as Frank Sinatra, Dinah Shore, Bob Hope, Sonny Bono, Gerald Ford and, most recently, Kirk Douglas.

"You don't have to be dead to have a street named after you," Nancy said, "but it helps."

We made the move shortly after I published the final issue of *The Realist*. My main obsession these days is working on a novel. Writing fiction enables one to have imaginary friends without being considered crazy. We were fortunate to have *real* friends who had already moved here. We met Lane and Carol Sarasohn in 1987, when Lane, Carol and I were writers, and Nancy shot mini-documentaries, for a short-lived series on Fox TV, the *Wilton North Report*. Now, with his two co-editors in Los Angeles, Matt Neuman and Larry Arnstein, Lane produces *Ironic Times*, a weekly online satirical publication, from his home in the desert.

One afternoon, as Lane was about to climb into the hot tub with Carol, he suddenly felt guilty about not having a regular job. He got dressed and went for an interview with the owner of the Desert Hot Springs Spa Hotel and the Miracle Springs Hotel, Mike Bickford, known by his employees as Mr. B. Within a few months, Lane became his chief assistant and troubleshooter.

Every month, I go with him to the Mayor's Breakfast. After reciting the Pledge of Allegiance, everybody stands up, one by one, and introduces themselves. Here a chiropractor, there a realtor. My favorite is an undertaker who says the same thing each time: "I'll be the last one in town to let you down."

Lane later became General Manager of both hotels and is now serving his second term as president of the Chamber of Commerce, but before all that, he gave my first album, *We Have Ways of Making You Laugh*, to the hotel's event organizer, and she arranged for me to perform at the Desert Hot Springs Chamber of Commerce officers and board of directors installation dinner.

According to the alternative paper, the *Desert Post Weekly* (which, strangely enough, is published by the mainstream daily, the *Desert Sun*), "In the extraordinary case of Desert Hot Springs, there is a convergence of five energy vortexes meeting in one place. In general, people are drawn to energy vortexes and power spots in search of enlightenment and inner peace; they are attracted by the invisible force and its therapeutic effects."

The paradox of my own peculiar spiritual path is that I'm an unbeliever who engages in constant dialogue with the deity I don't believe in. As a stand-up comic, I always say, "Please, God, help me do a good show," and then I always hear the voice of God boom out, "Shut up, you superstitious fool!"

Desert Hot Springs had changed its official slogan from "People, Pride and Progress"—no, it wasn't a multiple choice question—to "Clearly Above the Rest," and so it came to pass that the theme of the installation dinner would be Heaven. The waiters and waitresses would be dressed as angels. The stage would be overlain with a cottony white cloud, enhanced by a fog machine. There would be a blond angel playing the harp.

At 7 p.m., the salad would be served. At precisely 7:15, a clatter of pots and pans would be heard, and then I would be thrown out of the kitchen, directly into that heavenly scene. Oh, yes, and I would be dressed as the devil, who had been kicked *out* of heaven. (The devil is not merely a metaphor. A recent poll indicates that one out of every four Americans believes in the existence of the devil. Literally.)

I had rented a devil's costume—red pants, shirt, bowtie, jacket, cape, tail and horns, with a golden three-prong pitchfork—all of which I donned in a bathroom for the staffers behind the banquet hall at Miracle Springs. I looked in the mirror, pulled my hair into a point on my forehead and said—to the image of Satan—"Please, God, help me do a good show." I may have been the personification of evil, but for an instant it felt like God and the devil were in perfect harmony, until I heard the voice of God boom out, "You must be kidding!"

Then, while pacing nervously in the corridor, I overheard a woman say to her companion, "Right now, I would sell my soul for a massage." I surrendered to the impulse, walked behind her, tapped her on the shoulder and said, "Just sign right here."

I had never played a character before, but now I was really getting into the role. I proceeded to conduct a one-devil roast of various local leaders in the audience whose eternal souls I had previously purchased, revealing how I kept my part of each deal. I admitted my function in getting the president of the Chamber of Commerce re-elected and confessed that I had secured a green card for the police chief's undocumented Mexican nanny.

A court decision had required the city to pay $3 million plus legal fees to real-estate developers who unsuccessfully attempted a low-income housing project, but I disclosed that, in order to raise the money, I had set up a meth lab for the mayor. Actually, in order to keep from going broke by paying the judgment, the city would later declare bankruptcy. However, the new slogan would *not* be changed to "Clearly Above the Credit Limit."

While living in Desert Hot Springs, I've had two collectiions published, without leaving home. Also, two comedy albums have been released, though to prepare for those I've gone on tour, performing in Los Angeles, San Francisco, Portland, Seattle and New York. (Palm Springs has the only airport in the country with a putting green, but it's now closed for security reasons because golf clubs can be used as weapons.) The protagonist in my novel is a controversial comic, and in those segments where he's onstage, *he* performs what *I've* developed onstage. I'm just schizophrenic enough to resent this nonexistent comedian for stealing my material.

Nancy advised me not to mention how much I missed living in Venice, but in the very process of writing about Desert Hot Springs, I realize that I've somehow become attached to living here. I remember sitting in the passenger seat of a car being driven by a photographer for *111* magazine, named after the highway which runs through all the desert cities except Desert Hot Springs. I had rented that devil's costume again and I was wearing it for a photo shoot. At a red light, a van from a Christian church pulled up alongside us, and I waved at the driver. The light turned green, and we continued on our way. The church van caught up to us, and now the driver held up a Bible, while the kids in the back of the van were laughing and waving to me. It was a unique and precious moment, worthy of being preserved in amber for posterity.

BLOWING DEADLINES WITH HUNTER THOMPSON

High Times founder Tom Forcade and gonzo journalist Hunter Thompson were both dedicated dopers and enthusiastic adventurers. One time, Forcade phoned me on behalf of Thompson to invite me on board a rented yacht from which he wanted to cover the America's Cup yacht race in Rhode Island. I had to turn down the invitation because I was in the middle of preparing an issue of *The Realist*.

Forcade called again, and said, "Hunter is really pissed."

"Well, tell him just because he doesn't believe in deadlines, I still do."

I first met Hunter in 1965 on the Berkeley campus at a Vietnam Day Teach-In which I emceed. When his first book, *Hells Angels*, was published in 1967, I assigned him to write a behind-the-scenes article about his promotional tour. He was having financial problems, so I paid him $200 in advance. Later, I had to extend his deadline, and I offered to send him some LSD if it would help.

"Good," he wrote back. "I've blown every deadline I've had for the past two months. All at once I got evicted, my wife went into a lingering two-month miscarriage and my lawyer came out from San Francisco and flipped out so badly that two sheriff's deputies took him one Saturday night 200 miles across mountains to the state loony bin. . . . As for acid, thanks but I'm suddenly OK."

Soon after, another letter arrived, asking, "Can I get any leeway on the July 1 delivery date? . . . In the meantime, you can send me some acid to help me level out. And I'll send you a dozen just-born marijuana weeds. You can plant them in Central Park."

As it turned out, he bungled his book tour by appearing as either a blathering drunk or an insane mumbler. He walked off his first TV show when the interviewer said, "Tell me, Hunter, what do you think of the Hells Angels?" Who could blame him?

But at least he was honorable with me. In October, he wrote, "There's no avoiding the fact that I blew this one completely. I'm sending you $200 of the $1,900 I now show as book-profit on the hardcover edition. . . . With [Lyndon] Johnson as president, I feel on the verge of a serious freakout but if I ever get over that hump I'll write a good article for you. In the meantime, we're at least even on the money. This check is good. I've sworn off money articles a/o December, so maybe I'll level it out then. If not, I might run for the Senate or send off for a Carcano [the rifle ostensibly used to kill President Kennedy]."

Instead, 38 years later, Hunter pointed a handgun at himself.

San Francisco Chronicle editor Phil Bronstein had wanted him to cover the O.J. Simpson trial for the *San Francisco Examiner* which he then edited. He told me, "I thought Hunter would be the perfect person to write about the trial." They met at a waterfront restaurant. "Hunter's face was all banged up," Bronstein recalled. "He claimed he had gone night-diving and scraped his face on a rock. The waiter had some glandular problem, causing his eyes to bug out, but Hunter accused him of staring. Then he started telling me about these rumors he heard from friends in the L.A. coroner's office about nasty activities with dead bodies, including the infamous bodies involved in the Simpson case. Teeth marks on the butt and things like that. He said that he would cover the trial if we put him up at the Chateau Marmont in a suite with three satellite dishes, four fax machines and several assistants."

That particular assigment was withdrawn because Hunter was such a flaky prima donna.

When Lee Quarnstrom was executive editor at *Hustler*, he wanted to interview Thompson. "Hunter wanted $5,000 for the interview," he told me. "He said, 'Get Larry Flynt to kick in some of his money.' I said, 'Well, we don't pay for Q&As.' So he called me back and he said, 'OK, I'll do the interview for nothing, if *Hustler* will fly us both to Bora Bora and you can conduct the interview on a veranda as we sip mai-tais and watch the sun set into the Pacific.'"

And Art Kunkin, publisher of the *L.A. Free Press*, told me, "Hunter wanted me to put him up at the Chateau Marmont, and I wouldn't do it, and he threatened to kill me. He was pissed at me for not having the kind of budget to do that."

In 1970, I assigned three stoners who were running for sheriff—Stew Albert in Berkeley; George Kimball in Lawrence, Kansas; and Hunter Thompson in Aspen, Colorado—to write about their experiences and observations during those election campaigns. Albert and Kimball came through, but I kept hearing nothing from Thompson. I sent him a follow-up note, and he finally replied: "Yeah, your letter got thru & found me in the middle of writing almost exactly the piece you asked for—but I've already agreed to give it to *Rolling Stone*. [Jann] Wenner asked about a month ago. . . ."

As a writer, I could understand. As an editor, I was frustrated. Like other editors, though, I was willing to tolerate Hunter's irresponsbility in the hope of presenting his talent.

Several years ago, at a memorial for Allen Ginsberg, Hunter was supposed to make an appearance but he didn't show up; Johnny Depp, who played him in the movie version of *Fear and Loathing in Las Vegas*, did. I told the audience I was disappointed because I was hoping to present Depp, Thompson and Bill Murray (who played him in *Where the Buffalo Roam*) all together, and then I would say, "Will the real Hunter Thompson please fall down."

POSTSCRIPT: THE MEDIA MORTUARY

There are, of course, conspiracy theories that Hunter Thompson was actually murdered, just as there had been about another friend who also committed suicide, Abbie Hoffman. A week after Abbie's death, the autopsy report was released, and his picture was on the left side of the front page of the *Los Angeles Herald-Examiner*. On the right side was a photo of Lucille Ball, who was about to undergo serious surgery.

That evening, I had dinner at a Hollywood restaurant with Steve Allen. CNN's entertainment reporter had made an appointment to meet Steve at the restaurant, and he interviewed him outside—*twice*—once for if Lucille Ball survived the operation, and once for if she didn't. Although I could understand the practicality of such foresight, I was somehow offended by it.

Sure enough, the next day, there was Steve Allen on CNN, standing outside the restaurant and saying, "We all hope Lucy will pull through. There have been many success stories in the history of television, and yet the affection that millions of Americans hold for Lucille Ball is unique." A week later she died, and sure enough, there was Steve Allen on CNN again, standing outside the restaurant and saying, "Lucy will be greatly missed. There have been many success stories. . . ." Then George Burns came on and said, "I had a lot of fun with Lucy," but I couldn't tell whether he had taped that before or after she was dead.

I learned of Hunter's death when a reporter for Associated Press phoned to ask what my reaction was. As he would write: "'I'm stunned,' said Krassner, who was nearly speechless for several minutes after hearing the news. 'It's hard to believe I'm referring to him in the past tense.'"

Bear in mind that this was on a Sunday evening in the middle of a three-day Presidents Day holiday weekend. I don't know who else or how many others that reporter called before or after me, but apparently I was the only one who happened to be accessible at the time. As a result, after the AP report was dispatched, I was deluged with interview requests from print, radio and TV corre-spondents. Each time I found myself uttering some new observation, if only to keep myself from getting jaded.

During one call, I said, "Hunter was larger than life, sort of like a Macy's Thanksgiving Day Parade float." On the next call, I added, "Except that it was filled with nitrous oxide."

Among the interviews was NPR's *All Things Considered*. After it was broad-cast, I learned that I was considered "big enough now" to merit the preparation of an advance obituary for NPR. I don't take it personally. This is a purely prag-matic process. I'll be right up there with Charlie Manson, who is certainly a high achiever in his own field of endeavor. My personal definition of success is sim-ply trying to do the appropriate thing every moment. As Ken Kesey once told me, "My energy is what I do. My image is what other people think I do."

My friend, radio journalist Jon Kalish, was given the assignment to put me "in the can." He is allowing me the rare opportunity of fact-checking my own obit-uary. I asked him if it would be possible to include my Web site.

GEEZERSTOCK

When I was a kid—this was before television—the radio was my best friend. Lionel Barrymore—brother of fellow actors John and Ethel, granduncle of Drew—was confined to a wheelchair and played the crippled Dr. Gillespie in the original *Dr. Kildare* movies. He also had a radio program where he would spout maxims and dispense homilies. In his authoritative, quavering voice, he once said, "Happiness is not a station you'll arrive at, it's the train you're travel-ing on." That single sentence immediately became my entire philosophy of life.

A few decades later, I would read in *Hollywood Is Four-Letter Town* by James Bacon: "Lionel Barrymore once told me, as he sat in his wheelchair crippled with arthritis, that he would have killed himself long ago if it hadn't been for [film producer] Louis B. Mayer: 'L.B. gets me $400 worth of cocaine a day to ease my pain. I don't know where he gets it. And I don't care. But I bless him every time it puts me to sleep.'" So happiness wasn't a radio station you'd arrive at, it was the wheelchair you were traveling on, and for Lionel Barrymore it must have been an express trip all the way.

I remember publishing *The Realist* (when *People* labeled me "father of the underground press," I immediately demanded a paternity test). I remember celebrating the Summer of Love in 1967. I remember naming and co-founding the Yippies (Youth International Party) and going to the Democratic National Convention in Chicago in 1968 to protest the Vietnam war. I remember the Woodstock Festival in 1969—the music, the mud, the sense of community, the bare breasts, the warning not to ingest the brown acid.

Suddenly I'm 72 years old. I must have been in deep denial since years before I had automatically been accepted into the league of senior citizens, except in Portland, Oregon, where they refer to us as "honored" citizens. Whatever title gets me on the bus and into the movies cheaper is fine with me.

I've noticed that the network news shows seem to be aimed at middle-aged and elderly viewers. They are all sponsored by prescription drugs promising to prevent erectile dysfunction. The Viagra commercial—with background music by Queen singing "We Are the Champions"—features men dancing in the streets, ecstatic at the prospect of asking their doctors if a free sample is right for them. Personally, I don't have any problem getting a hard-on, but I've begun to worry that it's really rigor mortis settng in, on the installment plan.

Although any part of my body can attack me without warning, for no reason at all (okay, maybe revenge), I'm in pretty good shape for my age, except for an awkward, twisted gait due to a police beating—in 1979, while covering the trial of ex-cop Dan White for the murder of San Francisco Mayor George Moscone and Supervisor Harvey Milk—when I got caught in the post-verdict riot, and my injuries were exacerbated by hereditary arthritis. I went to a New Age healer who wondered if a brace might help. She placed one hand on my hip and with the other she held the hand of her receptionist.

"Yes," uttered the receptionist.

"Yes," repeated the New Age healer.

"I don't mean to be rude," I interjected, "but would you mind if I look for a second opinion . . . maybe from another receptionist?"

My friends have grown older, and the musicians we listened to in the sixties have grown older along with us. I imagine myself emceeing the Geezerstock Festival, standing on an outdoor stage, looking out at a vast audience of grey-haired hippies with paunches and granny glasses, as I speak in a slow, shaky voice.

"Are you having fun? . . . I can't hear you! . . . No, I mean I *really can't* hear you! . . . I have an announcement. The Port-o-Potties that are painted green should be used only by those who have to pee at least once an hour. The Port-o-Potties that are painted red should be used only by those who have to pee less than once an hour. . . . It's now my pleasure to introduce the Rolling Stones. They've been very busy, gathering moss. Here comes Mick Jagger with the aid of a walker. And Keith Richards is being carried out on a gurney. . . . Oh, wait, I've just been handed another announcement: Warning—do *not* take the brown antacid. . . ."

Two years ago, I wrote a piece for the AARP magazine, *Modern Maturity*. When my subscription copy arrived—the issue that my article was supposed to be in—it wasn't in there. I checked with an editor, who asked how old I was. I told her that I was 70, but I didn't understand what difference that made. She explained that there were three editions: one for readers 50 and over, one for readers 60 and over, and one for readers 70 and older. I was too old to read my own article.

My dentist, in his early 50s, had a copy in his waiting room. I felt like I was cheating as I leafed through the pages, but it did include my article. There was a time when I was considered too young to read certain things, and now I'm considered too old to read certain things. Apparently something must've happened to me in between. Like, say, my life? But, as Lionel Barrymore once said on the radio, "When you stop growing old, you're dead."

I still write columns and articles, I still perform stand-up satire—my 6th album has been released—and I'm finally working on my long awaited (by me) first novel, about a contemporary comedian inspired by my friendship and association with Lenny Bruce. I keep wondering what he would be saying in these insane times.

In 1964, Lenny was unable to get work because he had been arrested so many times that night clubs were afraid they'd lose their liquor licenses. Lenny's work was his life, so, with his permission, I wrote an obituary—this was two years before he actually died—and that became the excuse when, without my permission, a short-lived magazine, *Cheetah*, published a fake obituary of me. Associated Press called, and I explained that it was a hoax.

"Are you sure?"

"Of course," I replied. "I'd tell you if I was dead."

On WBAI radio in New York, Bob Fass was taking phone calls on his midnight free-form show, *Radio Unnameable*. Listeners were discussing whether that obit was legit. Then someone called and said, "You know, I didn't even know that Paul Krassner was alive until I heard that he was dead."

And, at that precise moment, my sense of false humility was finally restored.

ABOUT THE AUTHOR

PAUL KRASSNER is the only person in the world ever to win awards from both *Playboy* (for satire) and the Feminist Party Media Workshop (for journalism). He has been inducted into the Counterculture Hall of Fame at the Cannabis Cup in Amsterdam, has received an ACLU Uppie (Upton Sinclair) Award for dedication to freedom of expression, and has been described by the FBI as "a raving, unconfined nut." Krassner takes none of this personally.

OTHER BOOKS BY PAUL KRASSNER

How a Satirical Editor Became a Yippie Conspirator in Ten Easy Years

Tales of Tongue Fu

Best of The Realist [Editor]

Confessions of a Raving, Unconfined Nut: Misadventures in the Counter-Culture

The Winner of the Slow Bicycle Race: The Satirical Writings of Paul Krassner

Impolite Interviews

Sex, Drugs and the Twinkie Murders: 40 Years of Countercultural Journalism

Pot Stories For the Soul [Editor]

Psychedelic Trips For the Mind [Editor]

Magic Mushrooms and Other Highs: From Toad Slime to Ecstasy [Editor]

Murder At the Conspiracy Convention and Other American Absurdities